1995 - Merr Xma
Mike

Love
mum
xxx

IN THE CREASE

IN THE CREASE

*Goaltenders Look
at Life in the NHL*

DICK IRVIN

M&S

Canadian Cataloguing in Publication Data
Irvin, Dick, 1932–
In the crease: goaltenders look at life in the NHL

Includes index.
ISBN 0-7710-4361-9

1. Hockey goalkeepers – Anecdotes.
2. Hockey – Canada – History.
3. National Hockey League – Anecdotes. 1. Title.

GV848.5.A118 1995   796.962'092'2   C95-931885-2

The publishers acknowledge the support of the Canada Council
and the Ontario Arts Council for their publishing program.

Typesetting by M&S, Toronto
Printed and bound in Canada on acid-free paper.

McClelland & Stewart Inc.
The Canadian Publishers
481 University Avenue
Toronto, Ontario
M5G 2E9

1 2 3 4 5   99 98 97 96 95

Contents

"In hockey, without a good goaltender you're dead."
— DON CHERRY

Preface

On November 16, 1926, the New York Rangers played their first game in the National Hockey League in Madison Square Garden against the Montreal Maroons. The *New York Sun* assigned a writer who had never seen a hockey game to cover the opening night. It was a rough game with plenty of penalties. In his column the next day this anonymous scribe wrote: "The new game in town resembles a cross between a tong war and the latest prison riots." His last line was: "The goal nets were guarded by two young men whose parents obviously never gave them any good advice."

The two young men were Clint Benedict of Montreal and the Rangers' Hal Winkler, who shut out the Maroons, 1–0. Had that reporter seen Montreal play New York about seventy years later, the two young men guarding the goal nets would have been Patrick Roy and Mike Richter, and he likely would have had the same opinion about parental solicitude. Hockey goaltenders have always been considered different mainly because, like the man from the *New York Sun*, the rest of us have never quite been able to understand why they do what they do.

This is a book about goaltenders written mainly in the words of men who have played that precarious position in the National Hockey League, past and present. As I interviewed them I came to realize there is no deep secret to explain why they first put on goaltending equipment. They did it simply because they wanted to do it. For many, the earliest hockey memory is putting up their hand when their first coach asked a roomful of five- or six- or seven-year-olds, "Who wants to play goal?" Seven-year-old Rick Wamsley pleaded with his coach, "Can I play goal, Mr. Barker? Please, Mr. Barker, let me play goal!" Ron Hextall told me he can't remember exactly when he first wanted to be a goalie so he takes his mother's word for it that he was two years old.

In 1977 the American journalist George Plimpton attended the Boston Bruins' training camp and played five minutes as their goaltender in an exhibition game against the Philadelphia Flyers. In his book *Open Net* Plimpton described the position as the least glamorous in sports, and wrote that a goaltender "resembles a bottle-shaped structure, stuffed stiff as a strawman, and about as graceful. He remains so throughout the game, unlike a baseball catcher who has the chance to go up to bat on occasion, discard the accoutrements of his trade – the chest protector, shinguards, and so forth – and at least for a while resemble his fellow players."

Glenn Hall, who played 60,378 more minutes against NHL opposition than Plimpton, once described a night in the goal crease as "sixty minutes of hell." But as long as hockey has been played young men have bundled themselves up in the goaltender's gear, trundled out onto the ice, and endured their sixty minutes.

In this book you will read memories and anecdotes told to me by goaltenders whose careers span the last forty-five years. I interviewed seven greats who have been elected to the Hockey Hall of Fame. I chatted with high-profile players of today such as Mike Vernon, Sean Burke, Patrick Roy, Mike Richter, and Bill Ranford. I also talked with men named Meloche and Maniago, Myre and Millen, Wolfe and Weeks, who played hundreds of games, faced thousands of shots, yet received little attention when they quietly ended their careers. They reminisced with me about how it began, of the people and places, highs and lows, traumas and trades, the laughter and the sad times that are all part of life in the goal crease in the National Hockey League. Not one led me to believe he didn't love almost every minute he has spent tending goal.

And not one complained to me about the advice his parents never gave him.

A Look Back

I first learned goaltenders might be a strange breed when my father told me a story about Red McCusker. They were teammates on the Regina Caps of the Western Canada Hockey League in the early 1920s. McCusker was the goalie. During a game in Regina the goal judge signalled a goal against the Caps, a call that was disputed by their hot-headed goalie, who insisted the puck had never crossed the line. The final score was 1–1.

After the game McCusker was still fuming. As he was changing out of his equipment the door to the Caps' dressing room opened and McCusker saw the goal judge standing in the hallway. The goalie immediately saw red and, despite the fact that he was clad only in his long underwear, dashed out of the room and charged the goal judge, who took flight, and the chase was on. The goal judge fled through the lobby and out the door with McCusker in pursuit, the rear flap in his longjohns waving in the winter wind and his bare feet slipping and sliding on the frozen street. McCusker finally gave up, but the goal judge obviously got the message.

When the Caps played in Saskatoon, McCusker wore a tin helmet to protect him from the barrage of eggs, vegetables, and chewing-tobacco spit directed at him by fans standing on the catwalk located almost directly above the net. I'm sure McCusker was neither the first nor the last goalie to get this kind of treatment. Gump Worsley claims that in his long career items thrown at him included beer, soup cans, a dead rabbit, an octopus (also dead), folding chairs, and a cheese sandwich wrapped in brown paper. He was KO'd one night when a hard-boiled egg scored a direct hit on his brushcut.

The first goaltender to have his name inscribed on the Stanley Cup was Tom Paton, a member of the 1893 Montreal Amateur Athletic Association team. But Paton, Herbert Collins, Robert Jones, and other early Cup-winning goalies are long forgotten. So is Harry "Happy" Holmes, who won four Stanley Cups with four different teams between 1914 and 1925.

There were many colourful characters who became legends during hockey's early days, including Fred "Cyclone" Taylor, "One-Eyed" Frank McGee, and Edouard "Newsy" Lalonde, all forwards. The first goalie to attain legendary status, and earn a memorable nickname, was Georges Vezina, the "Chicoutimi Cucumber," so named because he came from Chicoutimi, Quebec, and stayed cool no matter how hot the action around his goal crease. Vezina played for the Montreal Canadiens from 1910 until 1925. When he joined the team it was a member of the National Hockey Association, the forerunner to the National Hockey League. With Vezina in goal the Canadiens won the NHA championship twice, the NHL regular-season championship three times, and the Stanley Cup twice. A lasting part of his legend is the claim that he stopped 78 of 79 shots in a playoff game against Ottawa. That was long before they kept official records of shots on goal, but apparently someone was counting them that night. Perhaps it was one of his twenty-two children.

On November 28, 1925, the Canadiens opened a new season against the Pittsburgh Pirates at the Mount Royal Arena, in Montreal. When he reached the dressing room after the first period Vezina collapsed. He revived and started the second period but collapsed again and was carried off the ice, bleeding profusely from the mouth. Vezina was taken to hospital where he was diagnosed with tuberculosis. He died four months later in his Chicoutimi home at the age of thirty-nine.

Vezina's name is remembered partly because a year after his death the NHL established a trophy in his honour. For the next fifty-six years the Vezina Trophy was won by the goaltender or goaltenders of the team that allowed the fewest goals in a season. Then in 1982 the league created the Jennings Trophy for fewest goals against. The Vezina Trophy is now awarded to the goaltender voted the season's most outstanding by the league's general managers.

Eight years after Georges Vezina died, tragedy would strike another great goaltender, Charlie Gardiner, while he too was still playing the game. Gardiner grew up in Winnipeg but was born in Scotland. In the late 1920s and early '30s he was a Vezina Trophy winner and an All-Star with the Chicago Blackhawks. He was one of the first goaltenders to leave the immediate confines of his crease to make saves and handle the puck, a style which earned him the nickname "The Wandering Scot."

In 1934 Charlie Gardiner was the star of the playoffs

when the Blackhawks won their first Stanley Cup. During those playoffs it was obvious to his teammates that their goaltender was not well. In the final game against Detroit he shut out the Red Wings, 1–0, in double overtime. Shortly after the game he was admitted to hospital, where he underwent brain surgery. The operation was not successful and Charlie Gardiner, then hockey's best goaltender, died two months after earning the Stanley Cup-winning shutout. He was twenty-nine.

There are two goaltending records that will never be broken. One is Glenn Hall's feat of playing 502 consecutive games. The other is the 22 shutouts in one season recorded by George Hainsworth, who succeeded Vezina in goal for the Canadiens. Hainsworth may not have replaced the Chicoutimi Cucumber in the hearts of fans in Montreal, but he certainly did the job in the net, winning the Vezina Trophy in each of its first three years. In those days NHL teams played a 44-game schedule. In his first season in Montreal, Hainsworth allowed 67 goals and had 14 shutouts. The next year he allowed 48 goals and had 13 shutouts. Then, in 1928–29, he allowed just 43 goals and had the amazing total of 22 shutouts. But was it amazing?

Five games were played on opening night in 1928–29. Hainsworth didn't get a shutout (the Canadiens defeated the Montreal Maroons 3–1) but five goaltenders did. The other scores that night were 1–0, 2–0, 2–0, and 0–0. That's how the scoreboards almost always looked throughout that season, so either the goalies were unbelievably great, or the forwards were unbelievably lousy. Take your pick. The Chicago Blackhawks were shut out 20 times. (My father played for Chicago that year. He finished the season with 6 goals and 1 assist, which made him the third-highest point scorer on the team. Then he retired. I can see why.)

Forty-three games were played before a team scored as many as five goals in one game. When the season ended one team had scored six or more goals only three times. Hainsworth had his 22 shutouts, but there were two goalies with 11, two with 12, and two more with 13. There were 90 shutouts in the regular season and seven more in the play-offs. Exciting hockey? Maybe once in a while, but surely not too often.

Prior to the 1928–29 season the NHL had altered some rules to help open up the game. Before then, for example, forward passing in the attacking zone had been prohibited. In 1928–29, teams were permitted no more than twelve players plus the goaltender in uniform. There had to be a fatigue factor. And back then they didn't resurface the ice between periods, they just scraped away the snow. There must have been nights when the skaters were ankle-deep in ruts by the third period. You wonder how many shots on goal there were on most nights.

Hainsworth and the Canadiens had the season's best record, but Roy "Shrimp" Worters, the goalie for the New York Americans, won the Hart Trophy as MVP. Worters played 38 games and had 13 shutouts. Toronto's Ace Bailey led the league in scoring with 32 points, so how could they have given it to a forward?

The Canadiens won the Stanley Cup in 1930 and 1931 with Hainsworth in goal. Two years later they traded him to Toronto for Lorne Chabot, a goaltender who seems to have been underrated by hockey historians. Chabot had an interesting career. He was the losing goaltender in the longest game ever played and the winner in the second longest. He replaced Charlie Gardiner in Chicago and promptly won the Vezina Trophy.

Chabot was in goal for the New York Rangers in the

second game of the 1928 Stanley Cup finals against the Montreal Maroons when a shot by Nels Stewart struck him in the eye and knocked him out of action. In a move that has become famous in the lore of the game, the Rangers' coach, forty-four-year-old Lester Patrick, donned the pads and New York won in overtime. Chabot was back in goal the next game and the Rangers went on to win their first Stanley Cup. Four years later Chabot was Toronto's goalie when the Maple Leafs won their first Stanley Cup. Naturally, he was tough. When someone asked him why he always shaved just before a game, Chabot replied, "Because I stitch better when my skin is smooth."

When George Hainsworth reached the end of the line after three seasons in Toronto, he was replaced by a bouncy twenty-two-year-old from Brandon, Manitoba, Walter "Turk" Broda. (Brandon would also be the home town of future NHL goalies Ron Hextall and Glen Hanlon.) A colourful character, Broda played on five Stanley Cup-winning teams in Toronto in a fifteen-year career that was interrupted by two years' army service in the Second World War. He was a terrific performer in the playoffs. Broda used to modestly shrug that compliment off by saying he was too dumb to realize how important the playoffs were.

A scrapbook in my basement contains a page from a 1937 Toronto Maple Leafs game program. Sportswriter George Fairfield contributed to this particular program a lengthy poem, "Tall Tales from the Dressing Room." One verse goes like this:

Turk Broda grinned, unfixed a pad and kicked it from his
    leg,
Then talked about a shot he stopped one night in
    Winnipeg:

"That shot," said he, "was moving! I can almost feel it yet;
For it bent me in the middle and it hurled me through
   the net,
Through the back-boards and the people; and I scrambled
   to my feet
To discover I was standing on the sidewalk in the street!
But I sold the puck to someone (that was clever don't you
   think?)
For a dime to buy a ticket to get back inside the rink!"

A couple of years after Broda arrived in Toronto, another future Hall of Famer, Frank Brimsek, became an instant hero in Boston. Cecil "Tiny" Thompson had been a popular goalie in Beantown for ten years, but the Bruins' boss, Art Ross, was thinking Thompson's best days were behind him. Thompson was recovering from an eye injury when the 1938–39 season began and he was replaced by Brimsek, an American from Eveleth, Minnesota, who had been playing for the Bruins' farm team in Providence. The Bruins won both games and Brimsek allowed only three goals. A few weeks later Ross sold Thompson to Detroit in a move that was vehemently criticized in Boston, but not for long. In Brimsek's first game as Thompson's permanent replacement the Bruins lost, 2–0, in Montreal. Then Brimsek racked up three straight shutouts, the streak lasting 231 minutes, 54 seconds, breaking a Bruins record that had been held by Thompson. The streak ended at the Boston Garden during a 3–2 win over the Canadiens. Brimsek then promptly registered three more consecutive shutouts, giving him six in his first seven games as a regular in the NHL. He finished the season with 10 shutouts in 41 games, won the Calder Trophy as the top rookie, the Vezina Trophy as the top goaltender, was named to the First All-Star Team, and the Bruins won the Stanley Cup. By the time Brimsek's breathtaking first season was over they were calling him "Mr. Zero," a nickname that stuck with him throughout his ten-year career. Rocket Richard says Frank Brimsek was the best goalie he ever faced.

Goaltenders often suffer from bad nerves. Wilf Cude played over 300 games in the NHL during the 1930s, most of them for the Montreal Canadiens. An excitable type, Cude's nerves finally drove him out of the crease. The night after a particularly tense game Cude's wife served him a steak for dinner. Cude looked at the big piece of medium-rare for a few moments, then picked it up and hurled it at the dining-room wall. The steak stuck and Cude said, "If that thing comes down, I'm quitting." The steak came down. Cude quit.

During the war years a goaltender from Calgary, Frank McCool, played for the Toronto Maple Leafs. His nickname was "Ulcers" for a very simple reason: he had ulcers. McCool had a brief but shining moment in the NHL sun. He was voted rookie of the year in 1945 and then, after starring in a first-round playoff upset of the league-champion Canadiens, faced Detroit in the Stanley Cup finals. In the first three games McCool shut out the Red Wings, 1–0, 2–0, 1–0. Detroit won the next three. With the score 1–1 in the second period of the deciding seventh game, McCool skated off the ice and into the dressing room, where his coach, Hap Day, found him drinking a mixture of milk and stomach powder. McCool told Day that his ulcers had got the best of him and he couldn't keep playing. Day said, "You have to play, Frank. We don't have anybody else." So McCool went back and spent the rest of the game alternately stopping shots and bending over double. Toronto won the game, and the Cup, 2–1, on a goal by Babe Pratt. McCool played the first 22 games of the following season, until Turk Broda returned from his army duty. Ulcers quit goaltending, went home to Calgary, and became a sportswriter.

While Turk Broda and Frank Brimsek were in the armed forces in the mid–1940s, Bill Durnan arrived in the NHL as a twenty-eight-year-old rookie for the Montreal Canadiens. Durnan had been an outstanding amateur goaltender (and the best softball pitcher in Canada) during the late 1930s and early '40s. After backstopping the Kirkland Lake Blue Devils to an Allan Cup championship in senior hockey in 1940, Durnan moved to Montreal to play for another senior team, the Montreal Royals. That same year my father became coach of the Canadiens, then a floundering franchise. The most frustrating of the many frustrating experiences he endured during his first three years in Montreal was watching Durnan play his home games for the Royals right in the Forum. It was obvious the amateur team had a much better goaltender than the professional team that played in the same building.

Durnan had been soured on turning pro because the Toronto Maple Leafs had cancelled an agreement to give him a tryout after he suffered a knee injury while wrestling with some buddies on the beach when he was twenty years old. After that he said he wanted no part of the NHL. So, try as they might, the Canadiens couldn't convince Durnan to leave his job in the accounting department at Canadian Car and Foundry. His boss there was Len Peto, who was also on the Canadiens' board of directors. Peto thought Durnan was a good accountant, but he too tried to convince him to make hockey his full-time job. Finally, on the first day of the 1943–44 season, Bill Durnan signed a $4,200 contract with the Montreal Canadiens. The rest is history, as the saying goes.

Durnan played seven years and won the Vezina Trophy six

times. The Canadiens finished in first place each of his first four seasons, and won the Stanley Cup his first year and again in 1946.

Durnan was ambidextrous: he could catch the puck with either hand. He would hold his stick in both hands when the other team was heading his way, then switch it to one hand or the other, depending on which side the play was coming from. Doug Bentley, a star forward for the Chicago Blackhawks in that era, said Durnan was the toughest goalie to score on: "Every time I looked up to take a shot at him all I could see was a big mitt between me and the net."

A few years after Durnan retired, *Hockey Night in Canada* made a film with him in the Canadiens' dressing room. Leaning on a goal stick Ken Dryden fashion, Durnan had this to say:

The fellows that have handled sticks like this, and the fellows handling them now, have a real tough job. They've got 13,000 bosses in the rink every night. They are blamed for some of their teammates' mistakes, and they are blamed for their own.

I like to remember the night the Montreal fans gave me a car. But I also remember the night those same fans booed me and caused me to have a very restless night at home.

I think you will agree that nerves have a great deal to do with goaltending. But my nerves didn't go on me when I quit. Actually, I was thirty-five years of age and I think that was time enough for anybody to give in.

My father, who was Durnan's only coach in the NHL, might have been surprised to hear him say that. Durnan quit during the 1950 playoffs following a season in which he had won his sixth Vezina Trophy and earned his sixth First All-Star Team selection. Montreal played New York in the first round and lost the first three games. The day after the third game, depressed and tearful, Durnan told his coach he was quitting then and there. Durnan said he was losing sleep thinking about the goals that had beaten him. Although he always maintained he hadn't suffered some form of nervous breakdown, not many people, including his coach, believed him. He never played another game. He's still considered one of the best, but had Bill Durnan's career started earlier he might have earned the nod as the greatest of them all.

The next Hall of Fame goaltender to play for the Montreal Canadiens was Jacques Plante. Not only was Plante one of hockey's greatest goalies, he was also one of hockey's most memorable characters. When I first saw Plante he was wearing a tuque while tending goal for the Montreal Royals senior team in 1951. He had knitted it himself, as he had his socks, sweaters, and underwear. He was also coming out of his goal a lot at a time when goaltenders stayed home. Plante seemed to love living dangerously: handling the puck behind the net, passing it across and up the ice, and directing traffic by shouting a variety of instructions to his fellow Royals. You couldn't help but notice him. In fact, there were games when you hardly noticed anybody else.

When the Canadiens promoted Plante to the big club they made him get rid of his tuque but let him keep his revolutionary style of play. We take wandering, puck-handling goaltenders for granted today, but back then Plante was unique. He was the pacemaker for the Ed Giacomins and Ron Hextalls who followed him. And of course Plante gets the credit for the mask, another aspect of goaltending we take for granted now. Many retired goalies talked to me about Plante's foresight in wearing and promoting the mask. I don't think the current crop appreciates his contribution in the same way, but they should.

Plante wasn't the first goaltender in the NHL to wear a mask. Clint Benedict of the Montreal Maroons wore a crude-looking contraption in 1930 after a shot by Howie Morenz sliced open his forehead, putting him out of action for several weeks. He was injured again when the mask was jammed against his nose in a goal-mouth scramble. Benedict had been around for many years and at that moment he decided enough was enough. He took off the mask and, after the game, he retired.

Jacques Plante had wanted to wear a mask in a game long before he finally did but his coach, Toe Blake, was convinced a mask hampered a goalie's vision. Besides, nobody else had one. Blake allowed Plante to wear one in practice but not in a game. On a Sunday in New York, November 1, 1959, a bare-faced Plante was hit on the left side of his nose by a puck shot by the Rangers' Andy Bathgate. Plante was taken off the ice to be patched up and, as the two-goalie system wasn't in use yet, the game was held up until he came back. One of his teammates, Bob Turner, told me, "Everybody felt sorry for Jacques when they saw how badly he was cut. Heck, he was the happiest guy in the rink when he got hit." So, when a happy Jacques Plante returned to the ice he had seven stitches in his nose and a mask on his face. The profession of goaltending would never be the same.

The first person to talk with Plante about a mask was Bill Burchmore, who worked for Fiberglas Canada. Burchmore, who saw Plante suffer a severe cut on the forehead during a Montreal–Boston playoff game in 1958, eventually interested him in the idea. With help from Dr. Ian Milne, a Canadiens team doctor, and Bill Head, the club physiotherapist, he made a plaster cast of Plante's face at the Montreal General Hospital. Burchmore and Plante then combined on the manufacture of the mask that made hockey history.

Jacques Plante was passionately involved in the design and making of every mask he wore. One of my first assignments for *Hockey Night in Canada* was to interview Plante in the summer of 1970. This was a few months after he had suffered a serious concussion in St. Louis when hit on the forehead by a Phil Esposito deflection of a Fred Stanfield shot during the 1970 Stanley Cup finals. Plante compared the sudden impact on his brain when the shot hit him to that of a car's engine going from zero to 800 miles per hour in one second. He then related how he had redesigned his mask for better protection. With the earnest interviewer nodding as though he understood everything he was told, Plante described the epoxy resins used in the manufacture of his new mask and how it had held up when tested by a machine shooting pucks at 140 miles per hour. He said, "Bobby Hull's shot has been clocked at 118 mph so I think I can wear it in a game and not worry about it."

Plante was a student of the game. My father was his first NHL coach and thought he had the best overall knowledge of hockey of any young player he had met. Plante was also the best interviewee in the game. We joked that all you had to do for a five-minute interview with Plante was ask, "What's new?" and he would take care of the rest.

How sharp was Plante? The great baseball hitter, Ted Williams of the Boston Red Sox, was famous for knowing a ball from a strike almost as soon as the baseball left the pitcher's hand. Some people claimed that if Williams didn't swing at a pitch the umpires automatically called it a ball because his eyes were better than theirs. One day at Fenway Park, Williams took a called third strike, which shocked the fans and his teammates. It probably shocked the umpire, too. Back in the Red Sox dugout, Williams complained that home plate was out of line and kept muttering about it the rest of the game. His teammates rolled their eyes and snickered at what sounded like a lame excuse for striking out. As soon as the game ended, Williams got the groundskeeper to check home plate. Guess what: it was out of line.

A few years later, Jacques Plante was playing in Chicago and was beaten for a couple of early goals. In the dressing room between periods he complained that the net was too high. He said that when he leaned back against the crossbar it hit his back in a different spot than usual. His teammates, too, rolled their eyes and snickered. Before the next period Plante insisted the referee measure the net. Guess what: it was too high. There are many reasons superstars get to be superstars.

Toe Blake thought Plante was the best goalie he had ever seen, but didn't care for him as a person. Plante drove Blake nuts with his theories and weird ways. Their best-remembered confrontation came about because of Plante's asthma. Plante claimed that the worst place for his ailment was the Royal York Hotel where the Canadiens stayed in Toronto. So Blake allowed him to spend the night before a game at the Westbury Hotel. The next day Plante told Blake he didn't think he could play. The furious coach demanded an explanation. "I dreamed all night I was at the Royal York," Plante replied. "I'm still stuffed up."

Plante's career as a professional goaltender spanned twenty-three years, including three years when he was retired. During that time he worked with me as a colour commentator on telecasts of junior hockey games. He also put on the pads again on December 16, 1965, and played in an exhibition game with the Montreal Junior Canadiens, turning in a remarkable performance against the Soviet Red Army team. The Juniors beat the Russians, 2–1, with Plante stopping 25 shots. When the game ended Plante received what might have been the greatest ovation of his career from the capacity crowd in the Montreal Forum. Scotty

Bowman was coaching the juniors and it was Bowman who in June 1968 brought Plante, then thirty-nine, out of retirement and back into the NHL with St. Louis. In his first year back Plante played 37 games, had five shutouts and a 1.96 goals-against average, and shared the Vezina Trophy with Glenn Hall.

Jacques Plante played on six Stanley Cup-winning teams, including the Montreal club that captured five in a row starting in 1956. His name is on the Vezina Trophy a record seven times. Plante won the Hart Trophy as the NHL's most valuable player in 1962, the last goaltender so honoured. He played for five NHL teams and finished his remarkable career in the WHA with the Edmonton Oilers when he was forty-six years old.

Plante moved to Switzerland when he retired, but often returned to North America to coach young goalies for various NHL teams. In the fall of 1985 he was working for the St. Louis Blues when it was discovered he had stomach cancer. Jacques Plante died a few months later, in Switzerland, at the age of fifty-seven. It happened that a team of bantam hockey players from Quebec was playing in a tournament in Switzerland at the time of his death. When his coffin was carried from the church following the funeral mass it passed under an arch of hockey sticks held aloft by the young players from his native province.

The greatest display of goaltending I ever saw took place at the Montreal Forum October 22, 1951, in a game that has long been forgotten by everyone but me. When it was over, the Canadiens had outshot the Detroit Red Wings 48–12. Final score: Detroit 3, Montreal 1. I have watched a lot of goalies stop a lot of shots since then, but I have never forgotten the Detroit goalie's performance that night. It was the first time I had seen him play, and maybe that's why I usually answer Terry Sawchuk when asked to pick the all-time best goalie.

Terry Sawchuk began playing goal in his native Winnipeg when he was ten years old, using a set of pads he inherited from an older brother who had died after developing a heart murmur. Five years later, Terry was at the Detroit Red Wings' training camp. He went from there to the Galt Juniors in the OHA, to Omaha of the United States League, Indianapolis of the American League, and then made the Red Wings in 1950 when he was twenty years old. He won the best-rookie award in every league he played in. In 1952 Detroit won the Stanley Cup in the minimum eight games. Sawchuk allowed just five goals for an average of 0.62. He had a unique style, crouching low to see shots that otherwise might be screened. In his early years he weighed just over 200 pounds, yet he could be up, down, and up again faster than any goalie I've ever seen. He had 65 shutouts in his first six NHL seasons.

After two more Stanley Cups in Detroit in 1954 and 1955 Sawchuk was traded to the Boston Bruins. From then on his story has a darker cast. He had had three operations on a damaged elbow, the last one in 1952 to remove sixty pieces of bone. He had a ruptured appendix, suffered severe chest injuries in a car accident, and was stricken with infectious mononucleosis. A broken right arm didn't heal correctly and was left a few inches shorter than his left arm. He suffered a fractured instep, ruptured disks, punctured lungs, and severed tendons in both hands. He went through a fit of depression during his second year in Boston and quit playing for several weeks. He played thirteen years in the league before he wore a mask, and his face took a beating. In the early 1960s *Life* magazine ran a full-page photo of Sawchuk. Pencilled over his face were lines representing all the stitches he had taken. There were more than two hundred. Journalists who dealt with him usually found him surly, unhappy, and unco-operative. He was troubled by weight losses, planned and unplanned. His Detroit teammate Ted Lindsay agreed with me that at one time Sawchuk might have been the greatest goalie the game had ever seen. "But then somebody convinced him to lose weight," Lindsay said, "and he was never the same after that." At times his weight dropped below 170.

The trade to Boston was the first of many. After two years in Boston, Sawchuk was back in Detroit for seven seasons. Then he was traded to Toronto in 1964, drafted by the Los Angeles Kings when expansion arrived in 1967, then traded back to Detroit a year later. He was with the New York Rangers in 1969–70 for what would be his last season. Sawchuk's last great moment was in 1967 when he and Johnny Bower and the rest of Punch Imlach's "Over the Hill Gang" won the Stanley Cup.

He never lacked confidence in his game. Bob Pulford, who played with Sawchuk in Toronto, recalls one night when the team was leaving the dressing room to start the game. Sawchuk, leading the way, suddenly turned, stood in the doorway, and said, "Just get me one tonight, boys." The Leafs got one. The final score was 1-0.

Danny Gallivan and I broadcast Sawchuk's last game during a New York–Boston playoff series in 1970. In the second game the Bruins scored a couple of quick goals on Ed Giacomin. The Rangers' coach, Emile Francis, pulled Giacomin to stall for time and cool the Bruins down. Sawchuk went in for a few minutes before Giacomin returned. It was the 1,077th time Terry Sawchuk played in an NHL game. No goalie had ever played in that many before, and no goalie ever will again, just as no goalie will ever equal Sawchuk's career record of 103 shutouts.

Shortly after the Bruins eliminated the Rangers in 1970 Sawchuk and a teammate, Ron Stewart, had a scuffle.

Sawchuk suffered severe internal injuries and never recovered. Terry Sawchuk died May 31, 1970, fifty-two days after his last game. He was forty years old.

If the good die young, so do too many goaltenders. Turk Broda passed away at 58, Jacques Plante at 57, Bill Durnan at 56. George Hainsworth was killed in an automobile accident when he was 55. Lorne Chabot died at 46, Terry Sawchuk at 40. George Vezina was 39, Charlie Gardiner, 29.

God Rest Ye, Merry Gentlemen.

2

The Gumper

GUMP WORSLEY

In June 1993 the Hockey Hall of Fame opened its new head-quarters in Toronto. All honoured members were invited to attend and, with our hosts pulling out all the stops, a great time was had by all. At the dinner on the night of the opening ceremonies there were more superstars in the same place at the same time than ever before in hockey history.

The following morning there was a breakfast hosted by the then fairly new commissioner of the National Hockey League, Gary Bettman. At one table were the Irvins, Wilma and Dick, and the Worsleys, Doreen and Lorne. Mr. Bettman spent a lot of time table-hopping, chatting with his guests in a cordial if somewhat stiff fashion. When he reached our table I knew he had no idea who I was, and I wasn't sure if he recognized the Hall of Fame goaltender sitting across from me either. Mr. Bettman said to us, as he had been saying at each of his table stops, "If there is anything we can do, just let us know." Whereupon Mr. Worsley promptly replied, "Yeah, there is. How about getting us our pension money?"

Lorne John Worsley, a.k.a. Gump, is one of hockey's great characters. His nickname belonged to a comic-strip character, Andy Gump, but they'll have to run that one by me again. Andy Gump didn't have a chin. Worsley has one, and there were times during his career when coaches accused him of having at least two.

Worsley tended goal in the NHL for more than two decades. The short, pot-bellied Gumper didn't look at all like a well-conditioned athlete. Perhaps because of the way he looked, and the stories that circulated about his escapades off the ice, fans nursing a beer or three while watching the game could identify with him much more easily than they could an elegant Jean Béliveau, or a flashy Bobby Hull.

The Gumper was a perfect fit with the New York Rangers, a team he was part of for ten years when they never won anything and made people laugh a lot. He joined them for the last 50 games of the 70-game 1952–53 season and was voted rookie of the year. The next season he didn't make the team. Johnny Bower did. Worsley is the only Calder Trophy winner in NHL history to miss the entire season after his winning one. But following a year in the minors with Vancouver, the Gumper was back in New York and Bower was dispatched to Vancouver, and for the next nine years Worsley was the occupant of the Rangers' goal crease, a position he likened to that of a duck in a shooting gallery. When asked which team gave him the most trouble, he always answered, the Rangers.

Gump Worsley never did anything to dispel the notion that he liked living life high off the goal stick. He publicly feuded with one of his coaches in New York, Phil Watson. When Watson told the press Worsley was playing poorly because of his beer belly, Gump replied, "That's not right. He knows I only drink Scotch."

When Jacques Plante was hit by Andy Bathgate's shot in New York, November 1, 1959, Worsley was in goal at the other end of the ice. One might say the face of goaltending was changed that night, yet Worsley would play almost fifteen more seasons before finally wearing a mask to protect his own.

Worsley and Plante had known and watched each other since their junior-hockey days in the late 1940s. In 1963, the fabulous Plante era ended in Montreal when he was traded to the Rangers, in exchange for Worsley. Gump was, as he put it, finally out of the Rangers' jailhouse. Two seasons later the Canadiens defeated the Chicago Blackhawks 4–0 in the seventh game of a dramatic final playoff series with Worsley getting both the shutout and his first sip of champagne from the Stanley Cup. It happened exactly two weeks short of his thirty-fourth birthday. By the time he left the Canadiens four and a half years later, the Habs had won the Cup three more times.

Gump Worsley played 860 regular-season NHL games, and another 70 in the playoffs. He wore a mask in only six games. He played his last game with the Minnesota North Stars, April 2, 1974, at the age of forty-five. Only three goaltenders, Terry Sawchuk, Glenn Hall, and Tony Esposito, have played in more games. Worsley and Sawchuk are the only goaltenders to have played in twenty-one seasons. Despite those ten years in the Rangers' shooting gallery, Worsley's career goals-against average was a respectable 2.90. He didn't look like an athlete, his style was eccentric, and at times he didn't live the way an athlete is supposed to live, but he was one hell of a goaltender.

GUMP WORSLEY

I started playing goal mainly because of my size. I played outdoor hockey in Point Saint Charles for a man named Phil Walton. He said if I wanted to play in the league I'd have to be a goalie because I was too small to play anywhere else. I was four-foot-eleven at the time. I never got much taller, but I got fatter. [Laughs]

I played junior for the Verdun Cyclones. Jacques Plante was the goalie in Quebec. Bernie Geoffrion played for Montreal Concordia and Jean Béliveau was in his first year in Victoriaville. A guy named Bobby Bleau was the goalie for the Junior Royals, who played their games at the Forum, and they won the Memorial Cup. Dickie Moore was on that team. I was supposed to go with them but the Cyclones were a Rangers-sponsored team and the Royals belonged to the Canadiens. The Rangers wouldn't trade me and that's how I ended up with New York. There was no draft in them days.

I went to my first camp with the Rangers in 1949, in Lake Placid. They assigned me to play for the New York Rovers in the Eastern League. That's when I left Montreal for the first time. Charlie Rayner was the Rangers' goalie then, and he turned out to be the only real goalie coach I ever had. He was really good to all the young guys who were there. He told me once, "I'm gonna quit sooner or later and somebody is going to get my job. It might as well be you." He's a great guy, and we're still friends.

I bounced around a bit after I turned pro. I played for the Rovers, New Haven, St. Paul, and Saskatoon. I was young and feeling my oats and we had a pretty good time, if you know what I mean. I never got discouraged. The time guys like me spent in the minor leagues was when we were learning our trade. A lot of guys went to the American Hockey League and never got out of it. Good hockey players, but there were only six teams in the NHL. They'd get called up when somebody got hurt and then go back down again. Not too many stayed after they got called up.

I was playing in Saskatoon in '52–53 when Charlie Rayner got hurt and they called me up. He screwed up his knee and never played again. I played the last fifty games and won rookie of the year. The next year I asked for a $500 raise and ended up in Vancouver. Everybody thinks Johnny Bower beat me out of a job but it had to be the money. The next year, Camille Henry won the rookie award with the Rangers and he asked for a $500 raise. I got news for you: he ended up in Providence for most of the year.

My first game in the NHL was in Detroit. We lost 5–3 and Ted Lindsay scored their first goal. It was a tip-in. Howe took the shot. Bill Cook was our coach and in them days they never told you anything when you started. They just said, "You're it. Go ahead." You never got told about different players' moves or how guys shot the puck. You heard the games on the radio but there was no TV in them days. You never saw those guys before and it was tough.

In all that time I spent with the Rangers there were some long seasons because we were out of it almost from day one. After ten games we knew we weren't gonna make the play-offs and it would be a long winter. But there were other years we were in there fighting for position. It was more enjoyable when you were in the hunt for a playoff spot.

Playing in New York was different than anywhere else. Inside the building the place was jammed all the time and they'd cheer you or boo you or whatever they thought you needed that night. But when you stepped out of the rink and walked one block away nobody knew you. Nobody cared who you were. It's tough to play in an atmosphere like that.

Another reason it was tough to play for the Rangers in those days was the constant turmoil in the front office. In the ten seasons Worsley played in New York the team changed coaches seven times. They enjoyed their best years when Phil Watson was the coach. Watson was a fiery, quick-tempered individual who played thirteen seasons in the NHL, twelve of them with the Rangers. He was with them when they won the Stanley Cup in 1940, an achievement the franchise wouldn't repeat until fifty-four years later.

Watson took over as coach in 1955. In the next three seasons the New Yorkers finished third, fourth, and second. It was the first time since the early 1940s they made the playoffs three years in a row. After his team lost a race to the wire with Toronto for the final playoff spot in 1959, Watson was fired.

Gump Worsley was Watson's goalie in almost every game he coached the Rangers, save for the 1957–58 season when injuries limited him to 37 games. Theirs was an uneasy relationship, to say the least, and their constant bickering was widely publicized. Following one season the two men appeared together on a live television sports program in Montreal and went at each other hammer and tongs. Old-time fans in Montreal still remember that one. Simply put, Phil didn't like Gump, and vice versa.

GUMP WORSLEY

We got along sometimes but we didn't get along most times. With Watson it was always me, me, me, I, I, I, if we won. And then he'd point fingers at everybody when we lost. Once we played in Toronto Saturday and in Detroit Sunday, and we won both games. We got a shutout in Detroit, and that was when they had a powerhouse. We were in the dressing room whooping it up after the game and Watson comes in and says,

"What are you guys so happy about? You were lucky to win tonight, and you were lucky to win last night." It just deflated everybody. Your ego went right down the tube. You'd ask yourself, "Just what does this guy want from us?" We win on the road Saturday and Sunday, beat two tough teams, and he's not happy. He was just a real jerk, to be honest with you. Nobody liked him. I don't even think he liked himself half the time. It's a wonder we played as well as we did during those years.

A lot of people have asked me what it was like to play for Doug Harvey when he came to New York. The Canadiens traded him because he had been one of the guys who tried to form a players' union. He was our playing-coach for one year in New York and, because of the reputation both of us had, people figured it must have been an interesting time, and it was.

I was the oldest guy he had playing for him and when we went on the road he'd want me to go out with him after the game. At first I told him I couldn't do that because he was the coach, and he'd say, "Gumpy, come on with me. I have to have somebody to go out with." Doug always was one of the boys. So I'd go out with him and have a few brews or whatever it was we were having that night. The next day the guys would come up to me and say, "Where were you?" and I'd have to tell them I was with Harvey. They'd go after me, "How come you get to go out with the coach, blah, blah, blah?" I'd tell them it was because he had nobody to go drinkin' with, and then they'd be all over me wondering what he said about the game. I'd tell them he didn't say nothin' about the game, but really he had said a lot of things. He would ramble on about who played good and who played bad, but the next day I couldn't tell any of that to the guys.

Doug was a good coach that year and he played terrific. Won the Norris Trophy again. We made the playoffs and, with a bit more luck, we might have beaten Toronto and made the finals. Then they told him they just wanted him to coach, not play any more, and that's what ruined him. He was always saying to me, "I don't want to coach. I want to play." He stayed with us for one more year, as a player, but the wheels were coming off. They sent him to Baltimore and he drifted around for a few years. St. Louis picked him up for a while but after that everything seemed to fall apart. It was a real shame.

The season Doug Harvey gave up coaching the Rangers, 1962–63, was Gump's last in New York. During the 1963 NHL summer meetings in Montreal the phrase "block-buster trade" was hauled out to describe a deal made between the Rangers and the Montreal Canadiens. Going to New York from Montreal were Donnie Marshall, Phil Goyette, and the legendary Jacques Plante. Plante was still a fine goaltender, but the team's management, especially Toe Blake, had reached the end of their patience with their masked marvel's idiosyncrasies. In return the Habs received forwards Dave Balon, Len Ronson, Leon Rochefort, and goaltender Gump Worsley.

It would be nice to write that Gump became an instant star in the Forum. But Worsley played only eight games for the Canadiens in 1963–64, splitting his time between the injury list and their American League farm team in Quebec City. Gump says the Canadiens told him they'd bring him back from Quebec as soon as he was in shape. "I'm still waiting for that phone call," he says today.

The next season, 1964–65, he was finally a full-time Canadien, sharing goaltending duties with Charlie Hodge and beginning the most successful part of his long career. In the next five seasons Gump was a member of four Stanley Cup-winning teams and shared the Vezina Trophy twice, with Hodge in 1966, and Rogie Vachon in 1968. He loved playing for the Habs' storied coach, Toe Blake. Claude Ruel, Blake's successor, was another story.

The 1960s was a period of change for the men in the goal crease. There were breakthroughs in equipment designed to make their life a bit easier, and the arrival of the curved stick in the hands of players like Bobby Hull and Stan Mikita to make their life harder. Most teams were moving into the era of the two-goalie system. Old pros like Worsley had to adjust.

GUMP WORSLEY

Television put the two-goaltender system in. They say no, but it was them. When we got cut it would take fifteen or twenty minutes or half an hour to get stitched up. They'd hold up the game for us. You guys on TV had to find all kinds of things to talk about to fill in, plus the game would run over into the next program. They always said it wasn't them, but they wanted to speed up the game.

When you've got two goalies you've got a problem if there's a young guy involved. If you have two veterans you're all right because they know they can play only a certain number of games. Like Cesare Maniago and me in Minnesota, we had no problem. We roomed together, hung around together, everything. They'd say to one of us, "You're playing tonight," and it was okay with the other guy. But these young guys, they all want to be the hero.

The equipment today is really something, a big difference. I did an ad the other day for Zellers and they gave us equipment to wear on the ice. I couldn't move. I was like a robot. No wonder they just stand there and let the puck hit them. They can't get hurt.

I've still got the shoulder pads I wore from junior right

through my whole career. Sawchuk did that, too. He wore the same ones his whole life. When I came to the Canadiens I put my equipment down on the floor in the dressing room and I guess it didn't look like much compared to what Plante had been wearing. Blake went by and said, "Where's the rest of your equipment?" I said, "That's all there is," and he said, "You're nuts."

When the curved stick came in the people sitting behind me in the fifteenth row had more trouble than I did because the guy shooting it had no real idea where the puck was going. That was the biggest worry for a goaltender. You didn't know if it was going to be coming at you along the ice, up in the air, or wherever, especially when they first came in because there was no measurement rule. They could be curved two or three or four inches. Then they put in the rule. But the players all cheated, and they still do. Look at Marty McSorley. Likely cost his team the [1993] Stanley Cup. His team's a couple of minutes away from going up 2–0 in the finals and he's caught with an illegal stick. It was hard to believe.

A lot of things changed for us when I got traded to the Canadiens. For one thing, I didn't have to play against them anymore. I didn't have to face Béliveau and the rest. It was a shock because I went from getting 40 shots a game to 20. It was a big difference standing there doing nothing for five minutes at a time.

And living in Montreal full time was a big difference. Walking down the street, people knew who you were. When I was with the Rangers everybody around Montreal was happy with me because the Canadiens were always beating us. Now I'm with the Canadiens and Doreen goes to a shopping centre and strangers say to her, "Your husband's a lousy goalie."

My kids would hear it in school. Other kids would say, "You're father's no good." You won't believe this one. One of the teachers in the school said to one of my kids, "You want to pass French? Then get me two tickets to a game at the Forum." I went to the school about that guy.

My first Stanley Cup, 1965, was quite a thrill, one of the biggest. I'd waited a long time. We were playing Chicago and both Charlie and I had played, but I hurt my knee and they told me I wasn't going to be able to play in the seventh game at the Forum. Before the game I was sitting in the coffee shop with Doreen and Toe's wife when one of our trainers, Red Aubut, came looking for me and said, "You're going to play tonight." I said, "Yeah, sure I am." He said, "No joke. Toe told me to find you and tell you that you're playing." So I dropped my coffee and went in and shut them out, 4–0. Big Jean scored the first one after just fourteen seconds, boom, just like that, to take the pressure off. It was 4–0 after the first period.

Toe was super to play for. Just great. He never bothered me except one night in Detroit when he pulled me. First time in my life I ever got yanked during a game. I was having a tough night and we got beat 6–3 in the end. When he pulled me out of the net and I got to the bench I was so mad I threw my stick. My glove came off at the same time and it hit the glass behind the bench and then hit Blake on the back of the head and knocked his hat off.

I was cursing and swearing the rest of the night on the bench and in the dressing room, and I still was when we got on the train to go back to Montreal. We were just leaving the station when Béliveau told me Toe wanted to see me in his compartment. So I went in and all he said to me was, "I'm glad you were mad when I pulled you. Now, go to bed."

The next morning I was sitting with Jean-Guy Talbot having breakfast and all of a sudden a newspaper flies on the table in front of me and there's an action picture of me from the game the night before. Toe is standing there and he says,

"You weren't mad when they took that picture," and he walked away. That's the last I ever heard of it.

He was like that. If he had something to say to you he'd call you into his compartment or his office where nobody else was around. He'd come into the dressing room between periods and say, "Some guys aren't playing tonight. What's wrong with those guys?" He'd never say anyone's name, but you knew. Me, Béliveau, Provost, Henri, we could always tell who it was and our heads would drop as he was talking.

But he never talked to me about goaltending. I'd start to ask him about something that happened to me in a game, a goal that I thought I should have stopped or something, and he'd just turn away and say, "Don't ask me. I know nothing about it."

The only ones we could talk to were the other goalies. Like me and Charlie in Montreal, or with Cesare in Minnesota. I'd go into the room between periods or after a game and I'd say, "Charlie, what the hell happened on that first goal? I missed it by a foot." And he'd say, "You were out too much to the left," or, "instead of coming out straight at him you veered to the left." You did that because goalkeepers look at goalkeepers in a totally different way than a coach or a forward or anybody else.

Things changed for me when Toe retired and they brought in Claude Ruel. We won the Cup his first year, 1969, but the team didn't even make the playoffs in his second year, but by then I was long gone. I never liked to practise. Everybody knew it. Blake knew it. But Ruel tried to make me into a practice goalkeeper. There was no way, and we got into it pretty hot and heavy. I had a nervous breakdown, or I almost did.

I even went to a shrink. The shrink told me to change occupations. When I told that to Sam Pollock [the general manager] he jumped about this high. But finally I said, "That's enough." I phoned Doreen from the Forum and told her I was coming home. Then I went to see Pollock and told him I was quitting. He said, "Nobody ever quits the Montreal Canadiens," and I said, "Well, I just did." And I went home.

When Gump proved to Sam Pollock that someone could indeed quit the Montreal Canadiens, he was forty years old and thought he had played his last game. As things turned out, he would play a few more games that season, and four more years, as a member of the Minnesota North Stars.

He had changed teams again, but one thing that didn't change was his fear of flying. Gump could be calm and cool in the goal crease, but in a plane he was a basket case. I took my first trip on a Montreal Canadiens' charter flight in 1968 as a member of the Hockey Night in Canada *crew covering their quarter-final playoff series against the Boston Bruins. I was keyed up anyway, and my nerves weren't helped by the fact that Worsley was sitting directly behind me. Throughout the entire flight he sat doubled over, hanging on to the meal tray, moaning and groaning. He had two seats to himself because none of the other players would sit with him. It was hard to believe that twenty-four hours later this whimpering man would be in the goal crease at the Boston Garden, with 14,000 Beantowners screaming at him, calmly staring down the likes of Phil Esposito and Bobby Orr. But that's exactly where he was, and the Canadiens won that game, 5–2, and the next one two nights later, 3–2, to sweep the series four straight.*

Phase 3 of the Gumper's career was a happy one. He and Doreen became very fond of the Minnesota area and he enjoyed sharing the goal crease with Cesare Maniago. And he especially enjoyed the various contracts he signed with the North Stars' boss, Wren Blair.

GUMP WORSLEY

About a month after I left the Canadiens I got a call from
Wren Blair. He said, "Why don't you come to Minnesota
and help us out? We haven't won in 21 games and Cesare is
worn out." I told him he couldn't talk to me because I still
belonged to the Canadiens and he'd get fined. I knew that
because I was a player rep for the union. He said he was sure
he could make a deal with Sam. He was going to Ottawa the
next day and wanted me to drive up there to meet him. I told
him I'd have to talk to the wife about it. Doreen said, "Go
talk to him." So I went to Ottawa and demanded this, and
demanded that, and he kept saying, "That's fine. That's
fine." I drove back, and when Doreen asked me how I made
out I told her, "He gave me everything I asked for." So Blair
made a deal with the Canadiens, who sold me to him, and,
a couple of days later, on a Friday, I flew to Philadelphia. I
hadn't been on skates for over a month, so I skated that
night. The game was on Saturday afternoon but I didn't
dress. We got annihilated 8–3. We flew back to Minnesota
right after the game on a small plane that had to stop in
Milwaukee for gas. You know me and planes, so you know
the shape I was in when we got there.

They had a game against Toronto on the Sunday afternoon
and Blair came up to me and told me to dress and sit on the
bench. I said, "What the hell happens if Cesare gets hurt?"
He said, "Just sit there and don't worry. We've lost 22 straight
anyway."

So I'm in the dressing room about noon putting my equipment on and I'm sweating. A newspaper guy, Dwayne
Netland, came in and said to me, "What are you doing?" and
I said, "I'm going to a masquerade party, you dummy." It ends
up we beat Toronto, 7–0. I practised four or five times and

then I played and we won that game, and by the time the season was over I'd played eight games.

I played the last game of the season, in Philly. They needed a tie to make the playoffs, and if they did, Oakland and us were out. It was a weird situation. One of our defencemen, Barry Gibbs, flipped one from centre ice on a line change. One of their guys, Ed Van Impe, tried to knock it down and missed, and the puck went right over Bernie Parent's shoulder and into the net. We won the game, 1–0, and made the playoffs. That was my only shutout all year so it was a great time to get it.

The Canadiens didn't make the playoffs that year and I had newspapermen calling me for a statement about Minnesota being in and them being out. All I said was, "That's the way it works. Some teams make it and some teams don't." They were looking for some dirt and tried to get me to say something against the Canadiens but I didn't want to get into a hassle because we were coming back to Montreal to live.

I ended up playing four and a half years in Minnesota. I tell you, if I had been younger when I went there I'd be living there today. My kids loved it. Doreen loved it. The people were just great. Each year I was going to quit but they kept talking me out of it. The longer I played, the more they paid.

My last year was when I finally wore a mask. Used it the last six games I played. Cesare talked me into getting it, one of those form-fitting kind. He said, "You're not gonna play any more after this year are you?" and I said, "No. These are the last games I'm playing." So he said, "Okay, wear the mask. You've still got your two eyes. Make sure it stays that way." But I never liked it because I couldn't see right. I lost the puck down in my feet all the time. And it was too hot. Every time the puck went down to the other end I put the mask on top of my head. I couldn't breathe. The water was just pouring off my face. I can't say it made any difference. I was almost forty-five, so what's the difference? Besides, we were out of the playoffs or else I wouldn't have worn it.

My last season was 1974–75. When Blair talked me into playing that year, he said, "Tell you what I'll do. I'll give you a five-year contract. One year as a player, and four years as a scout." So that's what I got, and it took me to when I was forty-nine. And then I scouted for them another ten years after that.

You want my All-Gump team? I'd pick Hall or Plante in goal. Harvey and Orr on defence. Béliveau, Rocket Richard, and Howe up front. Two right-wingers there, but so what? They were the best. That Howe, he had my number. It seemed that every time he needed some milestone goal he got it on me.

Bobby Hull might have been the best shooter. He'd just dare you to stop him. Bobby used to go for the far side, your glove hand, nine times out of ten. You knew what he was going to do but he'd still blow it by you.

One night when I was with the Canadiens, Bobby hit me with one of his best in Chicago. There was about thirty seconds left in the game and he came down the left side right along the boards. I didn't think he'd shoot it from where he was so I sneaked a look at who he was going to pass it to. Just as I turned back his way the puck was right there. I turned and it hit me in the ear. I dropped, and if there had been a boxing referee there he's have been counting, "110, 111, 112." They got the smelling salts and propped me up to finish the game. Know what? Nobody shot the puck at me after that. I don't know what the score was but they didn't take another shot.

Afterwards they told me I'd better go to the hospital for X-rays, so I'm walking out with one of our trainers and here's

Bobby Hull coming over to see how I was. The stars then were all like that. Like Gordie one time. He was looking for one of his big goals and there was a scramble and I was down and he had the puck right in front of me. If he had let it go full force he would have hit me right in the face. Instead, he just pushed it under me. The whistle went and he leaned over and said, "I'll get one later."

People always say goalies are different. We all have our little idiosyncrasies, but so do the guys who play forward and defence. They say we're nuts because we go in there and try to stop the puck. At least we've got the equipment. What about the defencemen who stand there and try to block the same shots? They don't have the kind of equipment a goalie does. So who's the dopiest, the goalies or the defencemen?

All the stories about me, Gump the high liver and all that, they weren't that far wrong. We had our flings. But I never took a drink the day of a game. Never. And I never knew anybody who did. When you're dumb enough to go out there sober, why go out there half in the bag and forget what you're supposed to be doing?

I had a lot of highs. The best ones? The first Stanley Cup when I got that shutout against Chicago in the seventh game. The first game I ever played in the NHL. My first shutout. And going into the Hall of Fame. They're the four biggest.

It was a good life for me. A great life. I loved every minute I was there. I think most of the guys in my era did. I'd do it all over again. Not for the money. Not for the big money. I'd just do it all over again.

3

Last of the Old-time Goalies

JOHNNY BOWER   GLENN HALL

*When hockey talk gets around to "who was the best goalie?"
the names Johnny Bower and Glenn Hall are sure to come
up. Both have become legends whose careers spanned the
old and the new of the game and goaltending. They both
arrived in the NHL in the late 1950s when goaltenders didn't
wear masks and forwards didn't fire slap shots with curved
sticks. By the time they played their final games they had
masks like everyone else and slap shots were blasting off
curved sticks at a velocity seldom seen before. Along with
Jacques Plante, Terry Sawchuk, and Gump Worsley, Bower
and Hall played in the old six-team NHL through a time
some call the Golden Age of Goaltending. Unlike goalies of
today these men did not have goalie coaches to help them
refine their craft, nor did they have the lighter, more pro-
tective equipment goaltenders now wear. They played
through the final years of the old era and into the new, all*

the while setting standards and records by which today's goaltenders are judged.

Johnny Bower was born in Prince Albert, Saskatchewan, on November 8, *1924*, and Glenn Hall in Humboldt, Saskatchewan, on October 3, *1931*. Hall's feat of playing *502* consecutive NHL games is part of his legend. Bower's claim to being only seventy years old on his birthday in *1994* is part of his. Both men have their names on the Vezina Trophy and the Stanley Cup. They played most of their careers without a mask. When they played their last games Hall was forty years old, Bower forty-five.

The first time I met Johnny Bower he was washing dishes in a restaurant he owned at the beautiful Saskatchewan summer resort of Waskesiu Lake in Prince Albert National Park. It was *1960* and I was there on a golfing holiday with Bob Turner, who lived in Regina in the summer and played defence for the Montreal Canadiens in the winter. Earlier that year Turner's team had won a record fifth straight Stanley Cup by beating Bower's team, the Toronto Maple Leafs, in the finals.

There were several hockey pictures on the walls of Bower's restaurant, including one of him playing for a Canadian Army team during the Second World War. In those days I was an accountant working for Shell Canada, so I didn't have a journalist's interest in taking a close look at how old, or young, Bower looked at the time. In later years, when his real age was a matter of conjecture, he showed his coach, Punch Imlach, a birth certificate bearing the date November 8, *1924*. Imlach pointed out that if Bower joined the army in *1939*, as he said he had, he must have done a number on the recruiting officers because he would have been fifteen years old. Imlach is reported to have said, "I knew the army was stupid, but not that stupid."

Bower still insists that he was born in 1924. But why worry? Did it matter how old Satchel Paige was when he was striking out Joe DiMaggio? What did it matter if Johnny Bower was forty-two or sixty-two when he played on his fourth and final Stanley Cup-winning team in Toronto in 1967? What really mattered was the way this amazing athlete played the game.

Men who were his teammates in Toronto all speak of Bower's competitive intensity, and how hard he worked from the first day of his NHL career to the last. And they remember how thankful he was that after so many long seasons riding buses from one minor-league city to another he finally got his chance to play, and stay, in the NHL.

JOHNNY BOWER

There was a kid who lived next door to us in Prince Albert who played with us on the open ponds, and he made me a pair of goal pads out of a mattress. He had a real pair and mine were a copy and they were pretty good. Later we had to use department-store catalogues and that's the honest-to-God truth. When we went to school we had some Eaton's catalogues and we used to pull our pants down and run one down one leg and one down the other, and they were our goal pads. That's the only thing I had to play with in the schoolyards.

The first pair of skates I ever had were given to me by a hockey player named Don Deacon, who ended up playing a few games in the NHL for Detroit. He was playing for an inter-mediate team, the Prince Albert Mintos, and we used to sneak into the arena to see their games. All the other kids had skates, so one day when he walked by me I asked him, "Have you got any old skates I could have?" He said maybe he would some day and, by golly, a couple of weeks after that he gave me some skates. God, they were big. I don't remember what size they were but I was so thrilled to get them. They were tube skates and pretty well shot. That's probably why he gave them to me. I had to put stuff in the toes so they'd fit, but I got used to them and I enjoyed having them.

I was playing minor hockey in Prince Albert when a scout for the New York Rangers, Hub Wilson, asked me if I would be interested in signing some kind of a form. I didn't want to sign anything but that excited me. Later another Rangers scout, Al Ritchie, almost talked me into it. My coach told me to check with my father before I signed. My dad was Ukrainian and could hardly speak English and he didn't know anything about contracts. So he told me to see a priest he knew. The priest advised me not to go anywhere to play hockey but to stay home and continue in school. Later I joined the army, and when I got out I was still eligible to play junior hockey. Then I got a call from a scout for Cleveland and I ended up going there with Bob Solinger. That was in 1945–46, and things worked out pretty good from then on.

I stayed in Cleveland, and then the Rangers drafted me and I played for them in the 1953–54 season. Gump Worsley had been their goalie the year before and won the rookie award. But I got the job after training camp and I played very well. The Rangers were rebuilding and coaches were coming and going at that time. I played every game and had a fine average [2.60] for a last-place team.

The following year Gump beat me out of the job at training camp. I got a little bit overweight that summer, so I ended up in Vancouver, which was where Gump had been the previous season. Vancouver had a working agreement with Providence in the American Hockey League, so I went there the next year and we won a few Cups in Providence when I was with them. A few years later I was back in Cleveland. I still belonged to the Rangers and played some games for them when Gump was hurt and I went to their training camps. I worked my butt off because I always believed in hard work, but I couldn't get along with Phil Watson. I think he really liked Gump better than me because Watson was French and Gump was bilingual. Watson got under everybody's skin. He had everybody scared. He had been a great competitor as a player and he didn't like us to make mistakes. At one time he was helping Muzz Patrick [coach and G.M.] with the coaching and he would have two-hour practices. The Rangers had some older guys like the Bentley brothers and Leo Reise and they couldn't take too much of that. I could because I was still young.

When I first went to the American League there was no way I could break into the NHL. There were only six teams and they had the six best goalies in the world, goalies like Turk Broda, Bill Durnan, Charlie Rayner, Sugar Jim Henry, all those guys. I had to sit and wait. When I made the Rangers in '53–54 I felt like my mission was more or less completed. When I finished that season I thought, oh boy, it took me a long time to get here but I've made it. Then when they sent me down the next season it hurt quite a bit. I felt, jeepers, what did I do wrong? But I didn't give up because it was my life. As a kid I wanted my name engraved on the Stanley Cup so much, and even after all those years I kept figuring that some day I was going to get a break. Finally I did.

When Bower finally left the minor leagues for good he took with him a record that makes you wonder why the brains of the NHL had overlooked him for so long.

Bower played eleven seasons in the American League and one in the Western League. He was the AHL's leading goaltender and its MVP three times. He played 595 games in the AHL and his 45 career shutouts is still a league record. He also holds the AHL record for the longest shutout streak, which took place over five games and lasted 249 minutes, 51 seconds. *He played on five championship teams, four with the Cleveland Barons and one with the Providence Reds.*

In Bower's one season in Providence, 1955–56, the Reds went from last to first place and won the championship with a four-game sweep of his old club, Cleveland. He was the AHL First Team All-Star goalie five times, including the last three seasons he played in the league. In his one season with Vancouver of the Western League his team won the championship and he was the league's leading goaltender.

Following his championship season in Providence, Bower returned to his original AHL home, Cleveland, and stayed for the next two years. It was there he got his big break.

JOHNNY BOWER

I was comfortable in Cleveland. After the '57–58 season Jim Hendy, who had been running the team there for years, told me Toronto was going to draft me. I told him, "No, I'm not gonna go. I can't help them. I'm thirty-four years old." He said, "They're rebuilding their hockey club with experience and youth. I feel you can make it. But if you don't make it I'll make sure you come back to Cleveland."

I kept telling him I didn't want to leave Cleveland and he kept telling me I could make the Toronto Maple Leafs. Then the summer was over and I had to report to training camp in Toronto. When it was over and they told me I had made the hockey club I was the happiest guy in the world. I guess I made the right decision but I have to give a lot of credit to Mr. Hendy for saying, "Hey, you go and do the best you can because this is a big chance for you. You could win a few Stanley Cups."

I enjoyed playing for Punch Imlach. A lot of players

figured he worked us too hard but I didn't. Work is a big thing and if you work hard in practice you're gonna work hard in the games too. That's the way I was brought up and that's the way I played hockey. I loved the game. I worked on fixing my mistakes and stayed out until I was ready to fall on my face. Punch once said to me, "Look, I'll keep you on my team as long as I possibly can as long as you keep working hard in the practices and in the games. You'll have some problems but I'll work something out. Just keep working. That's all I ask." He used to tell us to keep away from the newspaper guys. He said he would do the talking and we could do our talking on the ice. That's the way he was and I admired him.

I couldn't get very much money from him, but we won Stanley Cups. I remember one time I went to see him, I think it was in my third year in Toronto, and I was getting about $10,000. George Armstrong said to me, "Is that all you're getting?" and I told him that was the truth. But when I signed with Punch there were some incentives in the contract. There was a bonus for goals against and a bonus for shutouts and if I made the All-Star Team. If we won the Stanley Cup he'd match the league bonus. The defencemen were also getting bonuses for goals against. That's why our defence always stayed back and never rushed up the ice.

One time we had been having a lot of trouble inside our blue line. Punch said, "I'm sick and tired of you guys giving the puck away in our own zone. From now on anybody who does that, it's gonna cost them five dollars. I've got a guy up in the stands and he's gonna watch everybody and keep track for me." From then on every time I got the puck I just left it in front of the net or beside it because there was no way I was gonna clear it and have somebody from the other team pick it up. Do you think coaches are threatening their players these days with a five-dollar fines? [Laughs]

Punch never played goal in his life but he could tell me all about the bad goals that went in, especially the ones on the short side. That was the one thing he didn't want me to do, let a goal in on the short side. I remember letting one in there one night, in fact it was Boom-Boom Geoffrion who shot it, and I told Punch I was screened on the short side. He said, "What are you talking about? There wasn't anybody in front of you." I kept telling him I had been screened, that Allan Stanley had screened me. I tried to get out of it. Then he showed me the film. There was nobody in front of me for at least five feet. Geoffrion just picked the corner, short side. I guess I must have been dreaming when that one went by me.

I have nothing bad to say about Harold Ballard. I can only talk about the way the man treated me and he treated me fine. Sure I was underpaid, but he was a good man. He always used to ask me how my wife was and if everything was okay. And I'd say, "Yes, sir," and we'd talk about this and that. When I quit playing he kept me on as a scout and he was always wanting to know how I was doing. He did a lot for charity and a lot for hockey players that people didn't know about. He did a lot for us, the Bower family. Some of the guys disliked him. They're entitled to their opinion. In my opinion, he treated me okay.

If Bower enjoyed playing for Punch Imlach and Harold Ballard, who, along with Stafford Smythe, ran the front office at Maple Leaf Gardens during Bower's best years with the team, the feeling had to be mutual. The Leafs missed the playoffs the season before Bower arrived. In his first year in Toronto, 1958–59, the Leafs were one point behind the New York Rangers on the final night of the season. Toronto played in Detroit, fell behind, 3–0, then rallied for a 6–4 win. At the same time, the Rangers were losing, 4–2, on home ice to

Montreal. Toronto was in, New York was out, and Bower perhaps enjoyed some measure of revenge on the New York team and its coach, Phil Watson, who had shattered his first dream of staying in the NHL.

The Leafs upset Boston in a seven-game semi-final, then lost in five games to the Canadiens, who won their fourth Cup in a row. Hockey Night in Canada was firmly established on television by then, and the story of the thirty-four-year-old newcomer in the Toronto net captured the imagination of fans everywhere.

There was another Toronto–Montreal final in 1960 that the Canadiens won in four games. But the Leafs had moved up to a second-place finish in the regular season and their rebuilding program was well under way. Two years later, Johnny Bower had his first Stanley Cup, the first of three straight for the Maple Leafs, who were proving to be a great playoff team. In those Stanley Cup-winning years of 1962–63–64, the Maple Leafs played a total of 36 playoff games. Bower played in all but two. His last Stanley Cup win was in 1967, and by then the two-goalie system had started to take hold. In Toronto the job was shared by two of the greatest, Johnny Bower and Terry Sawchuk, who played three seasons with the Maple Leafs starting in 1964–65.

JOHNNY BOWER

Terry was a very quiet fellow and he had a lot of personal problems, but I got along fairly well with him. I watched his style. I liked his crouch because he would come out slowly, not like the goalies today. He used to glide out, real slow, and his reflexes were much quicker that way. I started copying him a bit and he told me to watch him in practice. Well, he was the world's worst goaltender in practice. He wouldn't stop anything. He would just stand there and if the puck hit him, well, okay, it hit him. He would come out, cut off the angles, but that was about it for him in practice.

I wasn't all that glad to see the two-goalie system come in because I wanted to play in all the games I possibly could. One time at the start of a season Punch told Terry and me that I would be starting and if I played well I'd be the steady goalie for twenty games. But if I started to falter a bit he would put Sawchuk in. So I started off and we were doing pretty well for six or seven games, then, all of a sudden, I guess I was getting a little tired because of my age so he put Sawchuk in. I ended up sitting on the bench waiting, and waiting. Then one day Eddie Shack, who had a hard shot, took a good one at Sawchuk, who was doing his usual thing in practice, just kind of waving at the puck. This time Sawchuk threw his arm up in the air and the puck hit his hand and broke one of his fingers. He didn't get back in for another ten or twelve games. I thanked Eddie for it, I really did. I said, "Eddie, you're a great guy." [Laughs]

I was always afraid that if Sawchuk got in I wouldn't get back again. He was such a good goalie and I couldn't sit on the bench. I just couldn't sit there for one or two periods and then come in and play a tremendous game. Sawchuk could do that but I never could. I had to have at least a good 30 or 40 shots in a warm-up.

I wore a mask only in the latter part of my career. I had over two hundred stitches in my face but I was lucky. Sawchuk had three or four hundred. He had a face like a road map.

I almost scored a goal one night in a game against the New York Rangers. Gumper was playing for them and near the end of the game we were leading by one and they pulled him. The puck came down into my end and I stopped it. I could see Gumper going to the bench. Bert Olmstead was close to me and he yelled, "Shoot!" So I shot the thing all the way down the ice and it missed the net by four or five feet. Olmstead just wanted me to get it out of our end. I wasn't even thinking about scoring. Afterward, I thought about it, and you should have seen me in practice for the next two or three weeks trying to score at the other end. I got a few but it was pretty hard with those gloves and everything else.

A lot of times I took the game home with me. I couldn't sleep at night when I made a mistake where, if I'd have stopped the puck, we could have got a tie or a win. I kept thinking that if we lost enough games like that Imlach would send me down to the minors. Of course there were times when we won and I would lie there thinking to myself, boy, was I lucky. Dickie Moore hit the post twice on me one night and we won the game by one goal. But I did play a lot of games over and over in my mind. Sometimes I couldn't sleep until 3 or 4 o'clock in the morning.

Goaltending is tough on your nerves. I'd be lying if I said I wasn't a little bit nervous when I started a game. I was always worried about the first shot. If I could stop that first shot I was okay, but if I let that first shot in then I'd really worry. In a home game, you've got 15,000 people on your back when that happens, and that doesn't help too much. There's always pressure on a goalie, but once you get into a game, once you're jumping around like a jumping jack and you're stopping pucks, it's great.

Where you really feel it, of course, is in the playoffs. That's when you have to go to church sometimes. Take those games we had with Montreal. That was the big rivalry. The teams didn't like each other and Montreal had won more Stanley Cups than Toronto. I remember when I first played against them I thought, oh man, here they are. You think I wasn't shaking? I used to get mad at Punch. He'd go to Montreal ahead of time and he'd tell the newspaper guys we were going to beat the Canadiens by four or five goals. I'd think, oh my God. We had a lot of good checkers but we didn't have the team to do that. I thought, what is this guy trying to do? Maybe he was trying to build our confidence but I didn't think that was the way to do it.

I'm often asked about the best shooters I saw in the NHL and I have to start with Maurice Richard, the Rocket. He was dynamite. The year I played in New York he was good for two or three goals every time we played. I think that year he scored about twelve goals on me and Boom-Boom Geoffrion had about eleven and Gordie Howe maybe thirteen. But the worst guy for me was the Rocket. I tried to size him up but I couldn't. I didn't know where he was shooting. He'd score one goal through my legs, then another along the ice, then on one side, and then the other side. He had me going crazy. The biggest thrill of my life was when he retired.

Gordie Howe was such a strong player. He had a good, quick shot and didn't miss the net too often. Bobby Hull was tremendous coming down the wing with that slap shot. Geoffrion started the slap shot and Hull perfected it. At least Bobby knew where the puck was going. I wasn't afraid to go into a half-crouch on him but when he wound up I'd straighten up a little. I was afraid of getting my head knocked off. But he was accurate and knew where the net was. I think his brother Dennis had a harder shot, a rising shot, but he didn't know where the hell it was going, and neither did I.

Then there was Jean Béliveau. Holy mackerel, what a great playmaker he was. There was many a time he should have shot. I know he saw the opening, but he would fake a move and then pass it over to his winger. They scored a lot, but often he was the one who could have scored the goal. That's the kind of a player he was.

My biggest thrill was my first Stanley Cup. We won four, and the one they seem to remember the most was the last one, in 1967. Maybe that's because Toronto hasn't won the Cup since. That was a good one, too. But the best one for me was the first one, the one I'd always dreamed of. That was in 1962. I was thirty-seven-years-old and I finally had my name engraved on the Stanley Cup.

While my first meeting with Johnny Bower over a sandwich and some dirty dishes was a pleasant one, my first with the other Saskatchewan goaltending legend was quite different.

The 1967–68 season was the first of the expanded NHL, when the league doubled in size from six to twelve teams. Glenn Hall was one of the few big names who had been made available to the new teams. The St. Louis Blues obtained the thirty-five-year-old Blackhawk goaltender in the expansion draft.

The 1967–68 season was also my first as a full-time member of Hockey Night in Canada. Glenn Hall didn't have a clue who I was but, like hockey fans everywhere, I knew a lot about him. There was his incredible record of 502 consecutive games and his habit of being so nervous before a game that he threw up. (A wise guy once suggested that if Hall carried around his own bucket it should be put into the Hall of Fame.) He also hated to be interviewed on television.

Early in '67–68 the Blues played in Montreal on a Saturday night. Their back-up goalie, Seth Martin, was to start instead of Hall that night, so Hall agreed to do a ninety-second interview before the game. I got the assignment.

So there I was, alongside the boards during the Blues' warm-up, the nervous rookie introducing myself to the hockey legend and a few seconds later interviewing him on national television. It wasn't an award winner, but even I couldn't do much damage in ninety seconds. When it was over I thanked Hall, who happily rejoined his teammates. Just then the technician working with me said, "Hold it a minute. The tape machine didn't work. Get him back because we have to do it over again." It had taken all my courage to interview Hall in the first place. Now I had to ask him to do it again. I did, and he did, although the second interview wasn't as good as the first. I was even more uptight and my interviewee wasn't too thrilled either. It was a nerve-wracking first I have never forgotten.

Since then I have had many, more pleasant meetings with Glenn Hall, on TV and off. He is now the goaltending con-sultant on the coaching staff of the Calgary Flames. For the past several years I have attended the Flames' annual charity golf tournament at the Canyon Meadows club in Calgary, and the eavesdropping is marvellous when Hall, Bill Hay, Lanny McDonald, and other players from the past get together to swap stories.

When you ask players from Hall's era to name their per-sonal all-star team, it is a rare occasion when he isn't picked as one of the goalies by his peers. In sixteen NHL seasons Hall played in 1,021 league and playoff games. With Detroit, he won the Calder Trophy in 1956, had his name inscribed on the Vezina Trophy three times, was named to the First All-Star Team seven times, and was the goaltender for the Chicago Blackhawks in 1961, the only time since 1938 that team has won the Stanley Cup. Hall's number 1 was retired in the old Chicago Stadium, and he has been elected to both the Hockey Hall of Fame and the Canadian Sports Hall of Fame.

The greatest days for hockey in Chicago came during the 1960s, the era of Hall, Bobby Hull, Stan Mikita, and a swash-buckling bunch of free spirits who were the most colourful team of their era. In those days the public-address announcer, when giving the Hawks' line-up before the game, would read

off the names of the defencemen and forwards and then con-
clude by saying, "In goal, Number One, Mr. Goalie!" It was
likely against league rules, but the raucous fans who filled
every seat and every inch of standing room in the old Chicago
Stadium loved it. For Glenn Hall, it was all a long way from
Humboldt, Saskatchewan.

GLENN HALL

I wasn't always a goalie. When I was young I played forward
until I was eleven or twelve. That's how I learned to skate and
it really helped me. I think what hurts a lot of kids today is
that they're always goalkeepers. They're six and seven years
old and they're a goalkeeper. Goalies have to skate too. If you
can't skate well, you can't play.

I was the captain of the team and that meant when the
coach didn't show up I'd tell the other guys who was going
to play what position. That's when I decided to try being a
goalkeeper. I really enjoyed it, especially when the puck was
in our end. It's a boring position when you play on a good
team and the puck is in the other end all the time. When you
are a kid and play for a terrible team, that's when you learn
to play goal.

I started in the west, in Humboldt, with their junior team
in the Saskatchewan League. I never met the guy who
scouted me because he never saw me play. Somebody simply
gave some forms to the team for a camp the Detroit Red
Wings were holding in Saskatoon. If you wanted to go you
just signed the form. I went and they had some pros there.
Gordie Howe was there, and Black Jack Stewart and Doc
Couture, the westerners who were playing in Detroit. From
there they sent me to play junior in Windsor. I turned pro
with Indianapolis and then spent three years playing in
Edmonton in the Western League.

In all that time I never had a coach. Absolutely not. The older goalies knew you were interested in their job and they did nothing to make it easier for you so you learned two ways. You learned by watching, and you learned by trial and error. If you weren't paying attention you were gonna fall by the wayside. If you didn't learn you didn't last very long.

Obviously Glenn Hall paid attention. He made his NHL debut in 1952–53 playing six games for Detroit when Terry Sawchuk was injured. Hall came out of it with a 1.67 goals-against average and turned in his first NHL shutout. Two years later he played two more games for Detroit and allowed only one goal in each.

In 1955, after the Red Wings won their second straight Stanley Cup, and their third in four years, their bombastic general manager Jack Adams decided to counteract complacency in the ranks by trading away several players. The biggest name to go was hockey's best goaltender, Terry Sawchuk, who was dealt to the Boston Bruins. Hall took his place, had twelve shutouts in his first season, and then a year later he too was traded, along with long-time Detroit star and captain, Ted Lindsay, to the Chicago Blackhawks. In the space of two years Adams had traded away two of the greatest goaltenders in hockey history.

GLENN HALL

I wasn't concerned that I was taking Terry Sawchuk's place in Detroit. When you're young those things don't bother you. I simply looked at Sawchuk as being an extremely good goal-keeper. It's more recently that I have thought of him as the best that ever played. But then I was just trying to prove to myself and everybody that I could play in the NHL.

I can suggest a couple of reasons why I was traded to

Chicago. Number one is that they didn't think I could play well enough to be good over the long haul. The other is that you should never tell the general manager to go fuck himself. The combination of the two made it easy to trade me. Jack Adams felt he was always right, and he might have been once or twice. When we were together I never looked at him. There are not many people in hockey I don't like, or didn't like. Jack Adams is at the top of the list of people I didn't like. It made it great for me in Chicago to try to prove him wrong.

I was sent to Chicago along with Ted Lindsay and being around him did a lot for my approach to the game. I had played in Windsor and I was a pretty good junior, a hotshot. I won the Red Tilson award as the OHA's best player, which is a high, high honour. What I learned from Teddy was that effort is the big thing. Talent is fine, and I think I was reasonably talented, but he taught me that if you forced yourself to play harder you'd get better results.

Most of the players who were involved with trying to form a players' association around that time got traded. That's why Lindsay went to Chicago. So did Tod Sloan, Dollard St. Laurent, Jimmy Thomson, and, to a degree, myself. Chicago was rebuilding and the big ingredient was Bobby Hull. A year or so later Stan Mikita was added. The team brought in talented players along with guys who were obviously dedicated. We did get some results but a lot of people thought we should have got more. I would probably agree, but that's hindsight.

I was in Chicago a few days ago talking to Bobby and Stan and we were recalling how much fun it was then. There was nothing Bobby enjoyed more than shooting the puck. People saw how hard he shot against the opposition and felt he shouldn't be shooting like that against his own goalie in practice. But he didn't care whose goalkeeper it was, the other teams' or his own. I like to think I was just as frightened of his shot as any goalkeeper in the league. Bobby would shoot at anything that moved. It might be the cleaning lady in the second balcony. She was in as much danger as I was.

I didn't mind practice as much as some people said I did. What I hated were long practices. In those days, before the mask, most of the time we scrimmaged. A scrimmage is just like a game, the white sweaters against the black sweaters. You'd be scrimmaging and then you would stop things and say something like, "That's exactly what happened when they scored on us in New York Sunday night." You'd look at the situation and correct it right there. I feel quite fortunate to have played in a time when the goalkeepers and the players could think for themselves.

In those days we were looking at 40 to 50 shots in a scrimmage. Today the goalkeepers look at 300 shots in a practice. They tend to get into what I call a "locked" tendency rather than a "moving" tendency. I like the goalkeeper who moves to the puck, who goes in and out. The mask changed a lot of things, including how they practice today. How many teams scrimmage? Go to a practice and it's shoot, shoot, shoot. I think for goalkeepers practice can't be as interesting as it used to be. Maybe for a forward, but not for a goalkeeper.

I'd rank Gordie Howe as the greatest who ever played. He was so great offensively, so great defensively. He would see something and react so quickly. I'd try to follow him, try to figure out what he saw before anybody else.

I think Jean Béliveau has been overlooked. When you talk of the ten best people who ever played hockey, Béliveau has got to be in the top ten. I'd place him in the top three.

One of the great days in my life was when I heard Rocket Richard was retiring. [*Compare that statement with what Johnny Bower said on the same subject a few pages ago.*] What a great competitor he was. The Rocket forced you to play the whole 60 minutes. You knew that with 58 minutes gone in the game, you had to play against him full out in the last two. He wouldn't quit.

I think it's more difficult to play goal today, against so many teams. We knew the five teams we were playing so well, knew each individual. I always had trouble with rookies, the guys I didn't know. I was always expecting them to give me a Jean Béliveau or Gordie Howe move. Howe would ring it off both posts, it would hit you in the ass and drop over the line. Béliveau was the first player I faced who I thought was capable of scoring from the blue-line. But the rookies didn't give you those kind of moves because they couldn't. They'd score some rather question-able goals on me.

There is a fear factor to playing goal. I obviously can't speak for anybody else but, boy, is there ever. I didn't know what the puck would do. What about all those forwards screening the goalkeeper? I remember one time in Toronto being screened and the puck hit me in the face. A guy was talking about it after and he said that it seemed to him the shot was a kind of a floater. A floater? [Laughs] He should have been standing where I was. When it hit me full in the face *I* didn't look at it as a floater.

It is a truism in sports that records are made to be broken. In the NHL during my lifetime there have been Maurice Richard's 50 goals in 50 games, Phil Esposito's 76 goals in 78 games, Gordie Howe's career marks of 801 goals and 1,850 points. Insurmountable we said, at the time, but they didn't last.

But there is one NHL record that will never be broken. It falls under the heading "Goaltenders," and reads, "Most consecutive games played – Glenn Hall – 502." The streak began October 6, 1955, when Hall played in Detroit for the Red Wings against Chicago in the 1955–56 season opener.

It ended seven full 70-game seasons later, and 12 games into the next, in the first period in Chicago, November 8, 1962, when a persistent back injury forced Hall out of the Blackhawk net in a game against the Boston Bruins. He was replaced by Denis DeJordy who then started in the Blackhawks' next game two nights later in Montreal. Glenn Hall didn't put on his goal pads that night and one of the most amazing streaks in sports history was finally over.

GLENN HALL

Did I want to keep the streak going? Certainly. But I probably shouldn't have played the night it ended. I knew I was hurt but you always feel, okay, the adrenalin will get going and everything. I had played hurt before. The game would progress and you got sweated up and you didn't feel it much. But that night I knew I was hurt. I thought I could play through it again, but I couldn't.

You know, they talk about that record of 502 games but it was really more than that. Prior to that I had played seven or eight years without missing a game but that doesn't show up. For example, when I was in Edmonton I went to Detroit and played a few games in a couple of seasons. So my record in Edmonton looks as though I missed some games there. That was because I was playing in Detroit. I was never hurt. I was lucky when it came to injuries.

The first time I didn't play after the streak, well, I suppose knowing the way I think I would have said it was nice, getting a chance to relax. I'm not so sure I really felt that way. I'm not accused of being hyper, but I like a hyper goalkeeper. They talk about me throwing up before a game as a weakness. I've always looked at that as one of the great strengths I had. I didn't take things home with me after a game too much. But I probably started too early for the next game. I built myself up to a point that, if I played poorly, it was because I was horseshit. I didn't play poorly because of lack of preparation, or lack of wanting to play. But if I was horseshit it was simply because I was bad.

I was really quite relaxed. I don't believe that you have to win every game. I'm a firm believer that you have to play well. Winning is a derivative of playing well. I think, okay, we played well but we lost. If we can play well again tomorrow we should win.

I didn't start wearing a mask in games until my second year in St. Louis [1968–69]. In Chicago I used one in practice that Lefty Wilson, the Detroit trainer, made, but it wasn't too solid. I called it a Lone Ranger mask. When I got to St. Louis Seth Martin made one for me that fit much firmer. But I never played like I was wearing a mask. I had total concentration. The kids now, they stand in there against a shot they can't see and they're quite comfortable, but if you can't see a shot and you're comfortable, then you're doing something wrong. You better know where that puck is. It'll go in the net if it doesn't hit you.

The first time I wore a mask was in New York. We had a bad start that night and we were down 2–0 early. I got mad at the referee and he threw me out of the game. Afterwards when they asked me about it I said, well, every time I wear a mask I get thrown out of the game.

The final chapters of Glenn Hall's career were written in St. Louis. Expansion began under a formula that guaranteed a Stanley Cup final between the old and the new the first three years. Hall backstopped a veteran team to the finals all three years. In 1968 he won the Conn Smythe Trophy as the MVP of the playoffs, even though the Blues lost four straight to Montreal in the finals. As the years went by there were times when Hall gave the impression that he didn't want to play. *He earned a lot of publicity for not showing up at training camp, claiming he had to stay home in Stoney Plain, Alberta, and paint his barn. A contract that had to be negotiated might have had something to do with it.*

Scotty Bowman, the Blues' coach, lived through that and gets a good laugh out of the story today. The way Bowman tells it, "One of our owners was in Edmonton playing in the Canadian Amateur Golf Championship and I was with him. After the tournament we visited Glenn to see if we could get him to sign early. We arrived and he was sitting on the front steps drinking a beer. We looked around for the famous barn but there wasn't one. We never did see one. As far as I know, he didn't have a barn."

Hall was in the net for St. Louis when Bobby Orr flew through the air after scoring his famous Stanley Cup-winning overtime goal in Boston in 1970. At that time Hall was sharing goaltending duty in St. Louis with another legend, Jacques Plante, who had come out of retirement the previous year. When their first season together in St. Louis was over the two so-called old-timers had allowed only 157 goals in 76 games to win the Vezina Trophy by a 39-goal margin. When they accepted the trophy, Hall was thirty-seven years old, Plante, forty.

GLENN HALL

I had no difficulty playing with Plante. I really didn't. We weren't going to teach each other anything new. We might have had a little difficulty with the way we wanted the defence to play in front of us, but it really didn't matter that one of us thought one way and the other guy another way. He was different but he was a dedicated hockey player. So often your skilled players are not dedicated, but Plante was. Plante liked to do different things, experiment, fool around with ideas. I basically did what I was told. The butterfly style was probably one thing I was told not to do but I went ahead and did it because I felt it would improve my game.

A few years after I retired I was in Jamaica for a TV taping with Bobby Orr and he says to me, "Do you remember that goal?" I told him, "You're bloody right I remember it." Then I started in on him about his temper tantrums and the way we felt so good because we forced his team into overtime. Him, Bobby Orr, the great white god of hockey, having to go into overtime to beat the poor old St. Louis Blues, and all that stuff. He got a great kick out of that.

But it was true. That first expansion was a big joke. They gave up a bunch of kids who didn't know if they could play hockey and a bunch of guys who were thirty-five or forty years old. They had no intention of trying to help anybody. But I have to say that in St. Louis they played a style that complemented the goalie. It was nice to play under those conditions. Scotty is such a great guy, and I'll tell you what, he's a great coach. All he demanded was everything you had, nothing less. You didn't have to wonder how much you had to give every night. The answer was always there: everything you've got. I loved playing for him.

There's a perception sometimes that I didn't like playing hockey, what with my so-called nerves and everything. That's an interpretation. Of course I liked playing hockey, but only one way: the game has to be played well. Hockey is too great a game to pull down. When Howe first retired they found Orr. When Orr retired, Lafleur. Then Gretzky, and Mario Lemieux is certainly in there. But it's not the individuals, it's the game, and the game is so great. The individuals that have played well have all loved the game. I don't think I've done anything to hurt hockey.

Of course I could have had an easier life. If I had to start over again I wouldn't have been a hockey player. I'd have worked in the post office. At my age right now I'd have a pension you couldn't believe. I was fortunate to do something I enjoyed, but it was tough. When it's not tough, that's no good. When you have to get down in the mud and work, that's when you can appreciate it. Maybe that's a problem with the rich kids today. When I look back at my career in hockey I figure I had to get down in the mud and work for everything I got.

4

Very Good Years

TONY ESPOSITO GERRY CHEEVERS
ED GIACOMIN

If the 1950s and early '60s represented the Golden Age of Goaltending, the years immediately following weren't bad either. As Gump Worsley, Johnny Bower, and Glenn Hall were reaching the end of their careers, future Hall of Famers Tony Esposito, Ed Giacomin, and Gerry Cheevers were among those taking their places on the All-Star teams. In the 1970s only three goalies, Cheevers, Bernie Parent, and Ken Dryden won Stanley Cups. Dryden won six, while Parent and Cheevers split the other four. The one name missing from the Stanley Cup in those years that maybe should have been on it is Tony Esposito. Still, he was a great among other greats in his prime.

The younger of the two hockey-playing Espositos, Tony began his NHL career with a brief stint as a Montreal Canadien. It was 1968–69 and he was twenty-five years old. The following season he was shuffled off to Chicago, where he proceeded to record the amazing modern-day total of 15 shutouts for the Blackhawks in his rookie year. The fans at Chicago Stadium promptly named him "Tony O." He spent fifteen seasons in Chicago and became the workhorse amongst NHL goaltenders, appearing in 873 regular-season games and 99 more in the playoffs. As might be imagined, Tony first went into the net while growing up in Sault Ste. Marie because his older brother, Phil, needed a target for shooting practice. Obviously they were good for each other: Phil certainly learned how to shoot the puck, and Tony how to stop it.

TONY ESPOSITO

I was the younger of the two of us and it seemed that I always ended up in goal. When I got into organized hockey I was better at that position than any other, so I just continued. I used to play forward, just horse around like everybody else. To tell you the truth, I'd much rather have played up front but I wasn't good enough. Right from the start I liked playing pro and the feeling of winning and all that, but there were many times I didn't actually like having to get in there and do it. I was always afraid of failure.

I played my minor hockey in the Sault. In those days there were only six teams in the NHL, six jobs for goalies, but I figured expansion was coming down the road. I was a fairly good student and the opportunity came at the right time to go to college at Michigan Tech. They offered me a scholarship. The timing was perfect because I got out of college in 1967 when the expansion started.

I turned pro out of college and spent a little while in Cleveland and then went to Vancouver in the Western League. I had never played more than 20 or 25 games a season in my four years in college. Now I'm in Vancouver and I play over 60 games my first season. It turned out to be the best experience I ever had. At that time they had a lot of older players in that league like Guyle Fielder, Kiki Mortson, Connie "Mad Dog" Madigan, old pros who were a bit kooky. A lot of guys in that league were pretty good party guys. Jim Gregory was coaching in Vancouver and he gave me a chance to see if I could cut it with them. After I started playing for them I played every game for the rest of the year. It was a great experience because every night I looked at a lot of shots. I was peppered.

Tony was signed up by one of the Montreal Canadiens' top scouts, Mickey Hennessey. Following his busy year in Vancouver the Canadiens assigned him to the Houston Apollos, their farm team in the Central Hockey League, to start the 1968–69 season, then brought him to Montreal when Gump Worsley suffered an injury. Esposito played in thirteen regular-season games and, although he didn't appear in the playoffs, his name was engraved on the Stanley Cup after the Canadiens defeated the St. Louis Blues in the finals.

By that time Phil Esposito was in his sixth NHL season and on his way to becoming a superstar with the Boston Bruins. As luck would have it, Tony made his big-league debut against Phil and the Bruins, in Boston. A couple of weeks later he faced them again at the Montreal Forum in what would turn out to be the most famous scoreless game ever played in that old building. Tony Esposito and Gerry Cheevers were the opposing goaltenders and it was the first of Tony's 76 NHL shutouts. Fans still remember it, and every year Hockey Night in Canada gets requests to replay it. Sadly, the tape of that classic game was erased years ago.

TONY ESPOSITO

My first game was in Boston. We tied, 2–2, and, wouldn't you know it, Phil got both their goals. He had no pity at all for his kid brother in his first NHL game. We went west after that and I played again, then came back to Montreal, and that's when I played in that 0–0 game against the Bruins. That was a great hockey game. Usually you think of 0–0 games as boring, but there weren't more than two minutes in that one when there wasn't action. I remember Phil had a chance to win the game in the third period. He was in alone and his shot hit me in the shoulder.

When that season was over they had to protect either me or Gump. They protected Gump, and I was picked up in some kind of a draft by Chicago. In later years, Tommy Ivan [Chicago's general manager] told me Sam Pollock owed him a favour or something.

Everybody remembers my first season in Chicago with the 15 shutouts. That was exciting, but don't forget I had a very good hockey team in front of me. Actually, the season I enjoyed the most was two years after that, the one where my goals-against average was under two. [*It was 1.77, with nine shutouts.*] That's my favourite.

Right from the start in Chicago I played a lot of games. I had nine seasons with over 60 games and two over 70. That's the way I liked it. I didn't mind all the work. What happened at the end was that they brought in other goalies. Murray Bannerman and a guy named Janecyk. They thought I was getting old. And then they started to check me at curfew time. I'd been in the league all those years and I was forty years old and they started checking me at curfew. I had planned to play until I was forty-five and I could have if they'd let me keep playing most of the games. That's why I retired at forty-one instead of at forty-five.

It was sort of the same thing when I played on Team Canada in 1972 against the Russians. I alternated with Ken Dryden and I didn't like that too much. I played okay, I guess. Not great, but not bad. We underestimated them. We weren't ready for them at all. When you played goal against those guys you had to play deep in your crease because of the way they could pass the puck so fast from one side to the other. I don't think I left my crease in the whole series. But that was a great hockey experience, for Canada, maybe the greatest hockey experience.

When I was at Michigan Tech, Phil was playing in Chicago and I used to go to their games in Detroit and some in Chicago. When I saw my first NHL game I couldn't believe the atmosphere and the tension in the building. I sat there looking around and I was bug-eyed. It sure wasn't like college hockey. That's when I learned a lot about goaltending from Glenn Hall. After the game I'd go out with Phil and some of the guys for a few beers and I'd sit with Glenn. He'd talk to me about goaltending and I picked up a lot just listening to him. I tried to copy his style. Then when I got in the league I tried to learn from Johnny Bower and the way he used his stick, and Terry Sawchuk with his concentration. At that time those guys were getting near the end of the line, but they all knew how to play goal. A guy had to be a dummy not to learn from them when he had the chance.

One way I judge good goaltenders is by how long they play. Look at Jacques Plante. He was so good for so long. Guys like him knew how to get mentally prepared. Every goalie lets in a bad goal but the good ones don't let in two bad goals. They don't let a bad goal get to them because they're mentally tough. It's the same thing when you get down 2–0 or 3–0 in the first period. Good goalies can put it together and shut the other guys down for the rest of the game, give their team a chance to get back in it. Other guys, after they let in the first two or three, they'll let in six or seven before the night is over.

On game day I never talked to anybody. I would get mentally prepared for the game from the time I got up in the morning. We'd have our morning skate and then I'd lay out my equipment in the same way, every day, and then go home. I'd eat, and rest, and at 4:15 I'd start getting dressed to go to the Stadium. I used to tell Marilyn, my wife, to be ready to leave at 5 o'clock, or else. We never talked in the car going to the game, never. Even when the kids started to drive down with us, no talking. If I was going to fail, it wasn't going to be because I wasn't mentally prepared. On the road I usually roomed by myself. But if I ever had a roommate it was the same thing. No talking.

I'll tell you a story about that. One time in Chicago there was a big snowstorm and only about 500 people got to the game. When it was over the reporters came to me and said, "It must have been tough playing out there tonight." I said, "Why?" and they said, "Because there were only about 500 people in the seats." You could have fooled me. I had no idea how many were there, 500 or 18,500. True story.

After the game though, I didn't have much emotion at all. What was done was done. Remember that 8–7 game when we beat Montreal in the finals at the Forum? The media was all over me, "What happened?" and all that stuff. Hey, I played horseshit, that's all. But we won. No excuses for the way I played, nothing to analyze. I always put it behind me, win or lose, play well or play badly.

We had good teams in Chicago but we never won the Stanley Cup. The WHA killed us. Management thought the WHA would never get started. We lost Bobby Hull, Pat Stapleton, and some other guys. Bobby was the big loss. The day he phoned Winnipeg to tell them he was accepting their offer, he made the call from my house. We were good friends.

I kept trying to talk him out of it. I told him that if he went there it would be good for me in a way because I would be able to make more money in Chicago. But I told him it would kill our team and I didn't want that to happen. He was really upset with the management in Chicago so he left.

So much of what we did centred around Bobby. The year after he went to the WHA we got to the finals but Montreal beat us. We always seemed to be missing that one final ingredient to win it all. We never really had it in Chicago.

I'm a believer in team spirit. We had a big house in Chicago and every year we'd have a Christmas party for all the players and their wives. Everybody has to fit in for a team to be successful. I'll tell you one thing. If I thought there was a player who wasn't good for the team, I did everything I could to get him off. It worked a few times.

I'm not sorry I never got to play on the same team as Phil. We were together on Team Canada in '72, but that was only for a few weeks. He had his career, and I had mine. I don't know how brothers like the Mahovliches did it. Or the Sutters. But we're together now here in Tampa. He's running the team and I've got this nice office we're sitting in and I'm helping him try to build something good down here. It's a long way and a long time from when he was shooting pucks at his kid brother in the Sault. But we're working together now, and it's great.

This is a book about goaltenders and, for the most part, in the words of the goaltenders. But I'm going to alter that formula for the next few paragraphs and bring in someone who never stood in a goal crease anywhere, anytime: Don Cherry. There were some future Hall of Fame goaltenders in the NHL during the 1970s and Grapes coached one of them, Gerry Cheevers. But he also coached a few who weren't so great, principally Hardy Astrom, who was with the Colorado Rockies during the 1979–80 season. Astrom wasn't a very good goaltender, a fact we've frequently been reminded of on "Coach's Corner" on Hockey Night in Canada. *The fact that Astrom is a Swede obviously wasn't going to help his cause as far as Cherry was concerned.*

Perhaps the softest goal I have ever seen in the NHL was scored against Astrom during a Montreal–Colorado game in Denver. Canadiens' defenceman Brian Engblom shot the puck from the Rockies' blue line, and it was likely one of those times when I said on my radio broadcast, "He didn't get good wood on it." In this case it meant that Engblom dribbled one along the ice toward the Rockies' net. For some reason Astrom was down on all fours, and when the puck got to him he slammed his catching glove onto the ice and seemed to have trapped it. Suddenly, there was the puck, sneaking along like a little black mouse between Astrom's legs and over the goal line. Astrom still had his glove flat on the ice waiting for the referee to blow his whistle. Instead, Cherry was blowing a gasket and the red light was on.

DON CHERRY

I'm holding my first practice in Colorado, and as a coach you dump the puck into one end of the rink and call a breakout. You flip it from centre ice on the goaltender, he catches it or stops it, puts it over to the defenceman who passes it up the wing and out. I was flipping it at Hardy and I scored twice. I went home and told Rose, "Pack the bags. We're gone after this year if this guy's the goalie."

Here's a true story. You know how in the old Chicago Stadium you'd come up the stairs to get to the ice. So one night I get up the stairs while the warm-up is on and here's a couple of our guys, René Robert and Bobby Schmautz, firing the puck as hard as they can at Astrom. They want to hurt him so he won't be able to play.

Another time, we're in L.A. and it's the morning skate. Hardy used to wear wooden clogs. So this morning in L.A. here's those same two guys, Robert and Schmautzy, and they've got Hardy's clogs and they're nailing them to the wall. And then they set fire to them. You know, off the ice he was really a good guy. The only problem was, he was our goaltender.

Hardy wasn't my only problem in Colorado. We're playing in St. Louis and I've got a guy named Bill Oleschuk in goal. The game starts and we're outshooting them 10–0. St. Louis comes up the ice, a guy shoots the puck from outside the blueline and it goes in. I look up at the clock, I see we're out-shooting them 10–1 and they're leading 1–0. So I yanked him. That's likely the only time in history a goalie was yanked after only one shot on goal.

When I look back on what happened to me in Colorado it was all because of the goaltending. I was coach of the year with the Boston Bruins with Gerry Cheevers and Gillie Gilbert, and I was chump of the year in Colorado. And it was all on account of we had no goaltending. I don't care if a foot-ball team has the worst quarterback, it can still win. You can have the worst pitcher in baseball, but the other guys can get enough hits and you'll win. But if you don't have a good goal-tender in hockey, you're dead.

I could tell you a lot of stories about Gerry Cheevers, but here's one. We're playing Pittsburgh in the playoffs and Cheevers beats them the first two games in Boston. We were gonna beat them for sure but at home they were pretty tough so I decide to rest Cheevers and start Gillie Gilbert in the third game. So when we get to the rink Cheevers goes out and gets a Pepsi and has a couple of hot dogs because I told him he wasn't starting. After the warm-up he's sitting in the dressing room relaxing and Gilbert suddenly breaks out in hives five minutes before the game is gonna start. So I go to Gerry and he's full of hot dogs and everythink, which he shouldn't have done, but that's Gerry. I told him, "You're playin' tonight." So what happens? He digs down, goes out, and plays the best game of his career. As far as I was concerned his game that night was better than any of the overtime games we won, or any other game. That's the kind of a guy he was. If you got up 6–1 you knew he might let in two or three easy ones late in the game. He was tough on coaches that way. But if it got to 6–4 he wouldn't let a pea get by him. He was the best money goaltender I was ever associated with.

Gerry Cheevers certainly was right on the money for the Boston Bruins when he backstopped them to the Stanley Cup in 1970 and 1972, the only two Cup wins for the Boston franchise in more than fifty years. Throughout his career he had a reputation for being "loosey-goosey," a free spirit, the kind of guy who would head for the hot-dog stand as soon as he found out he wasn't going to start in a game.

Cheevers is from the Toronto area and belonged to the Maple Leafs as a junior. He played a couple of games for Toronto in 1961 when he was twenty years old. After three years in the minors he was traded to the Boston Bruins. Except for three and a half seasons with Cleveland in the WHA, Cheevers was a Bruin until he retired in 1980. Right after he quit playing he became coach of the Bruins, a job he held for four and a half seasons.

GERRY CHEEVERS

My dad was a scout for the Maple Leafs, but I don't think he lasted too long because I may have been the only guy he scouted. In this particular year there was a big influx of good players at St. Michael's College. Dave Keon went there, Jack Martin, who became a good junior, guys from all over Canada. It was a real bumper crop. Our first game was in the Toronto Hockey League, the midget division. We played Sheldon's Grocery and we were something like 20-goal favourites. I mean, we were supposed to win by 20 goals, but it was only 1–0 with about two minutes left and they're coming at me from all angles. Suddenly there was some kind of a beef in their end and a big brawl broke out. I'm standing all by myself in the crease at the other end and everybody is concentrating on the fight. We were playing in Stouffville and in that rink, at the end I was in, the goalie could turn around and touch the clock with his stick. So I turned around and with two twirls of my stick moved the clock from two minutes to go to five seconds to go. When the game started nobody noticed the difference and we walked out of there with the win and I had my first shutout.

When I was a junior the Maple Leafs brought me up for a couple of games. Johnny Bower was hurt. I played a Saturday-night–Sunday-night double header. We beat Chicago on Saturday and lost in Detroit on Sunday. When we played the Red Wings in the old Olympia, Gordie Howe let a routine shot go and it broke my stick in half. I guess that's when they decided I wasn't ready. So that was my first stint, two games. I was twenty years old.

As far as playing for the Bruins goes, I have to talk about Bobby Orr. I remember one time early in his career when we were playing the L.A. Kings. We were up by a goal. They shot the puck into our zone as they were pulling the goaltender. It came off the back boards and I fielded it and left it for Bobby. I was starting to yell at him that they had just pulled their goalie when he turned and shot it. It never hit the ice.

It went right in the middle of the net down at the other end. So I said to myself, "I think we have something here."

He was the greatest player ever. He got your team out of so much trouble. For a while I had a little problem playing behind him because he anticipated so well. He was always one or two steps ahead of the play. He actually knew where the puck was going if there was a rebound, or if the guy missed the net. I used to want my defencemen to stay up, and I can remember having some arguments with him. I used to tell him to stay up and he'd tell me to shut up and stop the puck. At times it got a little heated, but there was never a real problem.

Bobby was fearless. He loved to block shots, and early in his career he fought a lot. He didn't pick his spots: he'd fight anybody who challenged him. He was a total team player. He wasn't selfish. Everything he did was directed toward winning, toward making other players on the team part of the team.

Then of course there was Don Cherry, who I loved playing for. There are a lot of stories about Grapes. I remember one night when I was the back-up and John Wensink got a breakaway – Cherry created John Wensink and one year he got 27 goals for us – anyway, this night he gets a breakaway and he started out all alone from inside our blueline. John tended to get a little fancy when he shouldn't have. Most of his goals were the result of him being a strong guy in front of the net with a pretty good release. Well, he had a clear-cut breakaway and this would have been Cherry's ultimate dream: Wensink on a breakaway and going in, giving the goalie a Jean Béliveau move, and sticking it up in the top corner under the crossbar. So there he is, going in all alone, and just as he gets close to the net he steps on the puck and falls into the boards. There's Wensink slamming into the boards and the puck isn't anywhere near the net. Cherry's looking at this scene and you could see the wind coming right out of his sails. It was so humorous and Grapes didn't know what to do. So he walks up and down behind the bench and says, "Anyone laughs and it will cost 'em $500. And for you, Cheevers, double." The whole bench is waiting for me to laugh, right? So I said, "Grapes, I owe you a thousand. We've got to laugh at this thing." And everybody started laughing.

I guess I was never the kind of guy Tony Esposito was when it came to playing hockey. I was never tied up in a knot. I was "loosey-goosey" as some people say. I had the knack of turning it off after a game, win, lose, or draw. But I wasn't all that different from anybody else. I fretted the day of the game but I did it privately. I tossed and turned in bed. I was lucky I was a reader because that occupied a lot of my time. They say goaltenders shouldn't read the day of a game, and they shouldn't go to the movies because it might hurt their eyesight. I think the name of the game is to do whatever you have to do to be ready at 7:30. If you have to run around the block a thousand times to get ready, that's what you do. I joked a lot, but at post time I was all business. I think I reached my peak when I was supposed to, at 7:30, no matter what I'd been doing before.

I can remember playing for the championship game in junior B against the Dixie Beehives in an arena on the east side of Toronto. The series became one of the big battles of all time. It went to the final game and everybody was nervous. When I got to the arena they wouldn't let me park my car in the parking lot. I had a big argument with them for a long time and finally parked it there anyway, jumped out, and ran inside. I was the only guy on the team who had a car and they're getting close to game time and I'm still not in the room. So I come running in and the attendant is chasing me and I'm trying to find a place to hide so he can't find me. All this is going on and then I finally throw on my gear and go out and play the game, which we won. So from early on, nothing really bothered me before a game.

I think the only high you can have in hockey is winning the Stanley Cup. When you decide to become a pro and make hockey your living, you have to try to be the best. If you decide to become a lawyer you want to be the best. In sports you want to win championships. Once in a while I sit back and feel mad or disappointed that the teams I was with as a player and a coach could never beat Montreal when we played them in big ones. But we won a couple of Stanley Cups, so I know somewhere along the line I succeeded.

The poem? It was pretty early in my career and the Bruins didn't have a very good team. We played in Montreal and they beat us 10–2. Hap Emms was our general manager and I don't care what anyone thinks of him, he was no good. There might be two people I've met in all of hockey that I'd say that about and he's one of them. I hated him. After the game he comes in, looks me in the eye and says, "What happened?" And I said:

"Roses are red, Violets are blue, They got ten, And we got two. See you later."

Ask any of the thousands of hard-core New York Rangers fans what has been the most emotionally intense night in their team's history and the answer comes easily: June 14, 1994. That was the night the long wait ended, the night their beloved Rangers won the Stanley Cup for the first time in fifty-four years. The ghosts of 1940 were finally chased out of Madison Square Garden.

As far as I know, there were only two people in the building that night who had been in Maple Leaf Gardens on April 13, 1940, when the Rangers had last won the Stanley Cup. One was Norm Maclean, a long-time New York hockey writer who, in 1940, was ten years old and had driven with his father to Toronto to see the game. I was the other one. In 1940, eight-year-old Dick Irvin, Jr., cried when the Rangers' Bryan Hextall scored the Cup-winning goal in overtime because his dad was the coach of the Maple Leafs. Fifty-four years later there were tears in my eyes again, not because the Vancouver Canucks had lost or the Rangers had won, but because I got champagne in them while I was interviewing the victorious New York players. That stuff stings like heck when they hit you in the face with it instead of letting you drink it.

Ranger fans almost unanimously agree their most intensely felt occasion before that night was November 2, 1975. That was the night long-time New York goaltender Ed Giacomin returned to Madison Square Garden wearing a Detroit Red Wings uniform just two days after the Rangers had put him on waivers. The chant "Ed–dee, Ed–dee" rocked the building all night. The object of their affection spent the evening alternately stopping pucks and wiping away tears. New York fans can be brutally hard on some home-town players, and very much in love with others. That night, in a deafening outpouring of support, they showed "Ed–dee" how much they loved him. Anybody who was there will tell you they'll never forget it.

Ed Giacomin was a late arrival to the big league. He tried but didn't make it in Canadian junior hockey, and was with Providence in the American League for five years before finally breaking into the NHL at the age of twenty-six. He played thirteen years in the NHL, the first ten with the Rangers. During that time he was voted to the All-Star Team five times and set Ranger goaltending records for most career wins and shutouts. Giacomin shared the Vezina Trophy with Gilles Villemure in 1971. He was elected to the Hockey Hall of Fame in 1987.

ED GIACOMIN

I always wanted to be a goaltender, and I played all my minor hockey in Sudbury. An old hockey player named Leo Gasperini had a team called the Falconbridge Midgets. I tried out for them but I wasn't good enough. At the same time two men named George Defilice and Mike Jelnick decided to organize another midget team with the cast-offs from Falconbridge. I made that team, and also on that team were Gary Sabourin and Frank St. Marseille. Apparently none of us were good enough to play for Falconbridge but eventually all of us were good enough to play in the National Hockey League.

In those days Sudbury was in the hockey territory owned by the Detroit Red Wings. They scouted me and I went to Hamilton to try out for the Hamilton Junior Red Wings. I wasn't good enough to beat out a guy named Carl Wetzel. [*Wetzel, a Detroit native, eventually played two games in the NHL.*] I went back home and spent that year playing in what we called an outlaw league. A bunch of us put a team together and we played teams from Bell Telephone and Ontario Hydro. I never did play junior hockey and I never did sign a "C" form with Detroit. I was what would be classified today as a free agent and I was eligible to go anywhere.

My brother was also a goaltender. He's five years older than I am. One time, when the Hull–Ottawa Canadiens came to Sudbury, he ended up playing for them. Jacques Plante was supposed to be there because the Canadiens had demoted him. Plante didn't show up so they came to town looking for a goaltender and they recruited my brother. There were many times we had only one set of goal pads between us and he'd always give them to me so I could play. He'd tell the team he couldn't play that night. My brother never left Sudbury. He gave me the opportunity and he never went anywhere.

Leo Gasperini had recommended my brother to the Washington team in the old Eastern Hockey League. For some reason they didn't have a regular goalie. A guy named Bipper O'Hearn used to play their weekend games. He came from Niagara Falls and was always travelling around to different teams. "Have pads, will travel," I guess. One weekend he couldn't make it to Washington and my brother couldn't get off work, so he sent me. I played five games for them that year and did very well. The Washington team was owned by Providence and they invited me to their training camp the next year.

That was how I came to be kicking around the Eastern League in the 1959–60 season when I was twenty years old. After the Providence camp they sent me to Commack, New York, to play for the Long Island Ducks. Things didn't work out there so they sent me to Johnstown. I spent a week there and everything was going well and it looked like I was going to make the team. But the goalie they really wanted was Eddie Johnston, who was trying out with Montreal. Johnny Mitchell was the general manager and, after the first week, I asked him where I stood and he told me to wait until 4 o'clock that afternoon. Sure enough, at 4 o'clock they got the word that Johnston had been cut by Montreal and he was coming to Johnstown. Johnny Mitchell said, "I'm sorry, son, but we're gonna have to let you go. I've talked to Providence and they want you back there. We originally planned to have you fly but it's too late. Here's a bus ticket instead." So I took a bus from Johnstown, Pennsylvania, to Providence, Rhode Island.

No sooner had I arrived in Providence than they got word that Norm Defilice, who played for the Clinton Comets, had got injured. So I went to Clinton, and I think that's where I really got it going. They had a first-place team. I always maintain that to be a good goaltender you've got to have good people in front of you. I came up with key saves and we didn't lose too many games. But then Defilice came back and they had to let me go. And guess who wanted me because I'd been playing so well? The good old Long Island Ducks.

A chap named Stanley was the general manager in Clinton. When I left, Mr. Stanley did me a favour and raised my pay to $180 a week and the Ducks had to pay me the same thing. I'd only been making $90 a week, so I got a raise of $90 for playing some games for a first-place team. I finished the year out with Long Island and went to Providence the next year.

Fernie Flaman came there to coach and he helped me a lot. I liked to roam a little bit and he took advantage of my roaming style and let me handle the puck more than goalies were doing in those days. It made it easier for our defencemen – they didn't get clobbered as much as they normally did.

I stayed in Providence five years. Then I started to hear that some NHL teams were after me. As it turned out the Montreal Canadiens, Detroit Red Wings, and New York Rangers were all trying to get me. Emile Francis was running the Rangers and he was the one who came up with the deal they liked. Providence got four players for me.

All those years I spent in the American League were important to me. Don't forget, I was twenty-six years old when I got to the Rangers. I really missed the time I might have had in junior-A hockey. I was behind maybe four years of tough competition. I really didn't get initiated in hockey the way I should have.

During all my time in Providence I never had any doubt about making it to the NHL. No doubt at all. When I was in grade seven in Sudbury my teacher was Jack Camoletti. One day he asked the class what we were going to do when we grew up. He went around the room and when he got to me I said, "I'm gonna be a goalie in the National Hockey League." And of course the kids in the room were snickering at me.

When I made it to the NHL the first letter I got congratulating me was from Jack Camoletti. He remembered I said it in his grade-seven class with such authority and was so determined he knew I would do it. Then when I made the Hall of Fame he was the first person to send me a letter. He's a supervisor of schools now in Sault Ste. Marie and says he often uses me as an example to the kids of a guy who had determination and desire, and knew what he wanted to do in life.

I started the 1965–66 season in New York. The previous year Jacques Plante and Marcel Paille had split the duties. Then Plante retired and Paille was one of the players they traded to Providence to get me. It was obvious they were giving me first chance at the number-one job.

I was getting my big chance in the Big Apple: they had traded four players to get me and I'm an excited kid from Sudbury telling myself, "This is what I've dreamed about all my life." But there was one thing I didn't do. I didn't stop many pucks.

The fans really let me know it and I ended up getting demoted and Cesare Maniago got the job. I had been on such a high that I had forgotten that a goalie is supposed to stop what the other team shoots at him. I was letting in a lot of soft goals. So they sent me to Baltimore for a couple of weeks because I wasn't doing the job for the Rangers. But when I got to Baltimore I was as excited as heck because Doug Harvey was playing there and, for crying out loud, I was getting a chance to play with the best defenceman who ever laced on a pair of skates. When I got there the Baltimore team had a week off and we spent the whole week practising at a rink in Hershey. So it was really a reprimand, a form of punishment.

After a couple of weeks they brought me back. Cesare was playing and one night in New York he got hurt fairly early in the game. He came to the bench and told Emile Francis he couldn't go any more. Emile looked at him and he didn't think he was hurt very seriously. I went in and, for some reason, that was the night I started to play well, and after the game Emile told me I was his goalie from then on. After that everything just kind of fell into place. For the next four years I missed only four games and never missed any practices.

Then the two-goalie system came in and I started sharing the job with Gilles Villemure. Let's face it, at the time I didn't want to share anything with anybody. I thought I was a workhorse. I know the media used to claim I was tired when the playoffs came, but I always figured the best way for me to play well was to play in all the games. I found it very hard to adjust. I had to work extra hard in practice to cope with the two-goalie system. I didn't think I was getting enough work. Some weeks I would play only one game, so I had to bear down harder in practice to keep myself sharp and be ready when they called on me to play. But it worked out well for us because we won the Vezina Trophy and that's one of the things a boy dreams of when he's a goalie, winning the Vezina Trophy.

There were three goalies I really liked. I think Glenn Hall was the one that I really wanted to copy, using the butterfly style. I loved Jacques Plante and the wandering he did. I tried to do more than Jacques did because I handled the puck an awful lot at that time. And I liked the competitiveness of Terry Sawchuk, who was a feisty son of a gun. I tried to put those three guys into an Eddie Giacomin. I always tried to give well beyond 100 per cent that was required because I wanted to be a leader all the time. The thing I strived for the most was the Stanley Cup. I wanted that darn Stanley Cup so bad, maybe that's the reason I never got it. Maybe I was overtrying.

We came close twice. In 1972 we got to the finals and lost to Boston. Actually we lost to Bobby Orr. He was the difference. The other time was in 1974 when we played a seven-game series against Philadelphia in the semi-finals. We had beaten Montreal in six games. We won the fifth game in overtime right in Montreal. That was quite a thrill. Then we played the Flyers and I think it came down to one punch. That was the reason we didn't win the Stanley Cup.

Before the seventh game in Philly it was almost as if our coach, Emile Francis, knew something was going to happen. That was when they had incorporated the "third man in" rule for fights, and Emile said before the game that at no time was Ed Giacomin to be thrown out for being the third man in. Sure enough, in the game there was a scramble around the crease and Dave Schultz grabbed one of our defencemen, Dale Rolfe, and started hitting him. He didn't just hit Rolfe, he pulverized him. He really did a job. It hurt me to see what was happening because I wanted to jump in. I was the closest guy and there was nobody else to come to Dale's defence. That incident took the stuffing right out of us, it really did. That was the style Philadelphia played and that's why, as far as I am concerned, we were one punch away from winning the Stanley Cup in 1974.

I mentioned Terry Sawchuk as one of my models. In '69–70 he was with us and got into a few games as my back-up. I didn't get to know him as much as I would have liked to. I know he always hated the press. He was with us when he got his 103rd shutout, which turned out to be his last. It was in New York, against Pittsburgh, and when the press came to talk to him afterwards he jumped all over them. He told them where they could all go, and yelled at them, "Where were you guys the last 20 or 30 or 40 games ?" I was in shock. When they left I told him I could never do anything like that and all he said was, "You'll understand someday." But I never got the opportunity to really understand and he was dead soon after that season ended.

Sawchuk was a great leader and a great team man. He fought for his teammates all the time, on or off the ice, and that's what he was doing in that episode in the bar. Ron Stewart was giving them heck about something and there was Terry, sticking up for his teammates.

I had been with him at the hospital. I left and I was home a few hours when I got the phone call that he had passed away. It was a sad time. There were two sad times in my career involving men who touched me deeply. One was Sawchuk and the other was Tim Horton. Tim was a super guy, a super individual. But there's something up there we can't control. One dies in an auto accident and the other one dies because of a little fight.

Tell you a story about Tim Horton. He was with us in 1971 when we played Chicago in the playoffs. I always had a hard time playing Chicago. The night before the first game, which was in Chicago, Emile Francis told Tim, "Take Eddie out tonight." There was a curfew for everybody at 11 o'clock but we went out and we stayed out. I'm gonna guarantee you that hockey players today couldn't even come close to keeping up with the old-timers when it comes to drinking. Tim could put the stuff away and the next day look like he didn't have anything. We didn't get back to the hotel until about 3:30 in the morning. Emile had told me not to go to the rink the day of the game because he knew what kind of a night Timmy would lead me on.

So I have a heckuva headache and now I'm feeling guilty. I get into the game and that night I couldn't do anything wrong. We won 2–1, in overtime. We tried it again for the next game but it didn't work because they beat us. In New York Tim didn't live near me and I stayed completely sober. In the end they beat us in seven games. But that first game, the way I played after breaking curfew and everything, that was an unbelievable night. I could never forget it.

Another incident I'll never forget was when Boom-Boom Geoffrion and I were on the Johnny Carson show in New York. First I was in goal and Boom-Boom took shots at me. Then in the commercial break Johnny put on the pads. The show starts up again with Johnny in the net and Boom-Boom rifled a shot wide, on purpose, and it went right through the scenery they had as a backdrop and made a big hole. So Johnny took his stance again, only this time he put the glove hand right over his crotch. I tried to tell him that wasn't the right position and he said, "You play goal your way, I'll play my way." It was funny as heck.

The bad news was I missed a week of hockey because of that Johnny Carson show. We rehearsed for an hour and Geoffrion took all kinds of shots at me and nothing happened. Then on the show his second shot took off and hit me right in the Adam's apple. After the show I could hardly talk and for the next few days couldn't open my mouth. But that was quite a night, and a real big highlight for me.

The Rangers missed the playoffs for the fourth straight year in 1965–66, Giacomin's first season. They then made the playoffs the next nine seasons when Giacomin was the team's main goaltender. Before the 1975–76 campaign Emile Francis, who had been the Rangers' coach and general manager through most of Giacomin's career, decided to be a full-time general manager and appointed Ron Stewart as head coach. The team struggled out of the gate, winning only four of its first ten games. Giacomin played in four of those ten games without a win, losing three and tying one. Francis decided to make some changes. On Hallowe'en night, October 31, 1975, Ed Giacomin, the New York Rangers' all-time goaltending leader in shutouts and games won, became a Detroit Red Wing.

ED GIACOMIN

Just before I was sent to Detroit, Emile Francis put the whole team on waivers. When you put a player on waivers a second time you can't recall him. As I look back, and I don't know if I'm right and I don't know if I'll ever find out because Emile Francis doesn't say too much, but I think when I was put on waivers it was already a foregone conclusion that Detroit was going to pick me up. I think it was to pay back a little debt for what happened in 1970 when the Montreal Canadiens got knocked out of the playoffs by the Rangers. Detroit came into New York the last day of that season for an afternoon game. It meant nothing to them and they left a bunch of players home. We pulverized them, beat them 9–5. We had to make sure we finished the season with more goals than Montreal. I was sitting on the bench for three of the Detroit goals because they kept pulling me to get an extra skater on, especially during power plays. Roger Crozier was in goal for Detroit and we must have had 60 shots on him. That night Montreal played in Chicago and pulled their goalie all night and got beaten, 10–2. Both teams had the same point total, but we made the playoffs because we scored two more goals. Deep down I really think that what happened to me was a pay-back to Detroit.

We were leaving Friday night to play in Montreal. We'd just finished practice in the morning and were going to catch a plane to Montreal in the evening. Emile told me he wanted to see me in his office at 7:30 that night. I asked him if I was going to go to Montreal and he said I wasn't and to be there at 7:30. I lived in Manhasset, which is about an hour's drive from where we practised at Long Beach. When I was on my way to his office that evening it was probably the longest drive of my life. All kinds of things were going through my head. Maybe he was going to ask me to retire. Maybe he just wanted to have a chat or make me an assistant coach. It never entered my mind that I was being let go.

I got there and pulled into the parking lot, which was empty, and the wind was howling because it was down by the water. The door of his office was open about an inch. I walked in and he said, "Sit down," and he started to talk. And then he said, "We put you on waivers and Detroit claimed you." Then I said to him – and I had a heck of a time saying it – "I'm no longer a New York Ranger?" And I went speechless after that. I couldn't say another word. I extended my hand and shook his, and I walked out the door.

I remember having such an empty feeling. I had given ten years of my life to that team and the worst part about it was there was nobody around. My teammates were on their way to Montreal. And here I am in this empty parking lot walking to my car, and I had visions of walking straight into the bay. I just didn't know what to think. My wife was waiting for me in the car. I opened the door and said, "I was put on waivers and we're gone. I'm a Detroit Red Wing now."

I got into the car and started to drive home and then decided I didn't want to go home right then. We stopped for a drink at a little place in Manhasset called the Library. We were sitting at the bar and the TV was on and suddenly on comes a news flash that the New York Rangers had just traded Ed Giacomin to the Detroit Red Wings. It wasn't a trade, of course, so right off the bat they were lying. I'm sitting at the bar looking at my face on the screen, and now I'm reeling. The people there were all reacting and they didn't know I was sitting there. I realized I had better phone my dad in Sudbury and tell him before he heard it on the news. So I called him and at that moment he was watching television and he says, "You won't believe it but they just flashed your picture on the screen." It was the emptiest and probably the

Lorne Chabot was in goal for Toronto's 1932 Stanley Cup victory. He was the winning goalie in the second-longest game ever played and the loser in the longest. The cap was needed to keep his head warm in the drafty arenas of the era.

Jacques Plante, goaltending's great innovator, without his mask during the Montreal Canadiens' record five straight Stanley Cup runs in the late 1950s.

Terry Sawchuk as a rookie with the Detroit Red Wings in 1950. His career record of 103 shutouts will never be surpassed.

Lorne "Gump" Worsley posing for his first picture as a New York Ranger in 1952, the start of a twenty-one-year career in the NHL.

Glenn Hall stopping Toronto's Dave Keon in one of the 502 consecutive games he played, establishing a goaltending record that will stand forever.

Johnny Bower, the ageless wonder of four Stanley
Cup-winning teams in Toronto in the 1960s.

Tony Esposito moments
after recording his fifteenth
shutout of the 1969–70
season. With him are teammates Bobby Hull and
Gerry Pinder. "Tony O"
won both the Calder and
Vezina trophies that season.

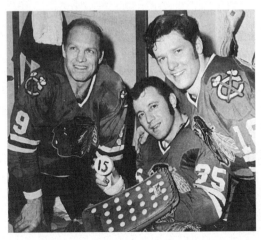

The Bruins' Gerry Cheevers (above and inset) painted
stitches on his mask every time the puck hit it. By the
time his career was over, there wasn't much space left.

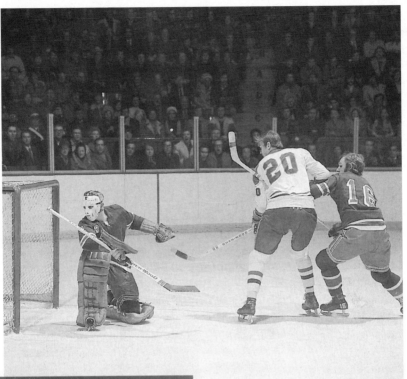

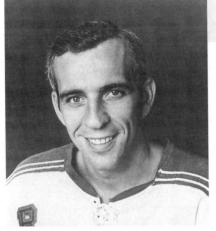

Ed Giacomin (above and left) had a Hall of Fame career with the New York Rangers. Yet his most memorable game was the first he played for the Detroit Red Wings against the Rangers.

Ken Dryden and teammate Jimmy Roberts during
a break in the action at the Montreal Forum.
Dryden's habit of leaning on his stick became one
of the trademarks of his successful career.

Hockey's most travelled goalie, Gary Smith, in a Chicago Blackhawks uniform. The Hawks were the fourth of his eight NHL stops.

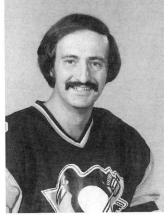

Cesare Maniago during his brief stop with the Montreal Canadiens in 1963. Coach Toe Blake wouldn't let him wear a mask.

Gary Edwards ended his career with the Pittsburgh Penguins after playing for seven NHL teams. When he was a rookie in St. Louis he shared an apartment with the legendary Jacques Plante.

The goalie behind the mask is my TV partner John Garrett. John's travels to Hartford and many other places in the WHA and NHL provided a good background for his current job as an analyst in the broadcast booth.

When the game has been won the first person congratulated is the goaltender. In this case, Greg Millen and his Hartford Whaler teammates are celebrating a victory.

Chico Resch always found time for fans and media. Here he's signing autographs at the Meadowlands in New Jersey in 1984.

most heartbreaking moment. The team was in Montreal and I had nobody to turn to after all those years.

The next day I was talking all day long on the telephone to all the reporters who were calling me. Then it was Sunday and, unbelievable as it seemed, the Red Wings were playing in New York. I still hadn't talked to Alex Delvecchio, who was their general manager. Doug Barkley was the coach. Their plane was late so it wasn't until about 4:30 that I met them at the hotel across from the Garden. They told me that Jimmy Rutherford would be their goalie that night and I said, "Look, I'm a Detroit Red Wing and have been since Friday. You paid me yesterday. At least I owe you a game because I really don't know what I'm going to do after that." So they agreed that I would play.

I hadn't eaten all day and I didn't know what to expect. I walked across the street to the Garden, and I guess the fans knew me better than I knew myself because there were all kinds of them out front waiting for me and they had signs. They seemed to know I was going to play the game but up to about a quarter to five I didn't even know I was going to play.

When we came out for the warm-up the fans went crazy. Then we came back out to start the game and they played the national anthem. I never heard one word of it. The fans were chanting "Ed–dee, Ed–dee" and they completely drowned out the anthem. I was standing there crying and all I could think was, please get the game going so I can get on with this thing. I always had a tradition that I waved to certain people in the crowd. But that night it was so hard for me to do because now I was playing against their team. I wasn't part of them any more.

When the game started the Rangers seemed to be right out of it. They had been shut out the night before in Montreal and we took a 4–0 lead in the first period. Billy Fairbairn took their first shot on me and after I stopped it he skated by and said, "I'm sorry." He actually apologized for taking a shot at me. Then Wayne Dillon, who was a rookie, scored their first goal. He couldn't help it because the puck was lying right in front of a wide-open net. And he apologized too. We eventually won the game, 6–4, but if it had lasted two or three more minutes we would have lost because I was slowly sinking into the ice. I lost thirteen pounds that night. Then, when it was over, there was just ovation after ovation from the fans. And they kept waving the signs, and everything else. I think it was the first time in New York the visiting team was actually treated like the home team.

I played another couple of seasons in Detroit, retired, and got into coaching for a while, which gave me a good look at the players of today. They train so differently now, with the weight programs, diets, and so on. They're more health-conscious. We would lose seven or eight pounds in a game and then go out and have four or five beers with the rest of the boys to put it back on. We were more team-oriented then. Today they're more worried about their health and their physique. They're making these almighty dollars and they're getting away from the team concept.

We had our stars, but they always hung around with everybody. You never saw Bobby Hull or Gordie Howe by themselves. When I was involved in coaching it seemed most players stayed in their hotel room and ordered room service. We used to sit in the lobby and chat with reporters. Today they're more programmed, more conditioned, and I think a lot of that has to do with their agents. There weren't too many agents around when I played. The agents want to make money and the only way they're gonna make their money is make sure their athletes are strong and ready to go. I guess that's common sense, but does it make for better hockey? I don't know.

The equipment is different now, much lighter. We have to be thankful to Jacques Plante for bringing in the mask. That changed our position a lot, because goaltending today is more the stand-up type. There are some, like Patrick Roy and Felix Potvin, who can do the butterfly. But the majority of them, how shall I put this, you see them looking more or less like a Herman Munster type. They just stand there hoping they have the angle on the shooter and take it full blast.

I didn't start wearing a mask until '71–72. I guess the closest I ever came to a severe injury was the time I took a shot on the jaw from Frank Mahovlich. I turned a bit at the same time so the jaw didn't break, but I felt it for months. I played thirteen years in the National Hockey League and five in the American League. I had a total of only thirteen stitches and I never lost a tooth.

I was fortunate all through my career. But the best memory is that night in New York. The love of the fans in the Garden is probably one of the biggest reasons I made the Hall of Fame. I think you make the Hall of Fame because of your record and because of Stanley Cups. But you also make it because of your popularity. When I was inducted into the Hall in 1987 I said in my speech that one of the reasons I was standing there had to be the New York fans.

After I quit playing they retired my jersey at the Garden. But nothing, nothing will ever replace that night. I wish every player could experience what I experienced that night.

5

Kenny Was Different

KEN DRYDEN

On Monday, March 15, 1971, I flew from Montreal to St. Louis to do the radio broadcast of a game the next night between the Canadiens and the Blues. Shortly after arriving I was standing outside the Chase Park Plaza Hotel enjoying some of the warm spring sunshine that had yet to find its way to Montreal when the bus carrying the Canadiens from the airport arrived. The team had played the night before in Pittsburgh. CBC Radio was still carrying Sunday- night hockey. My station, CFCF, broadcast the weekday games.

The game in Pittsburgh had marked the debut of a rookie, Ken Dryden, who was in goal for the Habs as they defeated the Penguins, 5–1. Dryden had gained some notoriety that season by playing for the Canadiens' American League farm team, the Montreal Voyageurs, while attending McGill University Law School. As the players filed past me into the hotel there was one stranger, a tall young man who was

*wearing glasses and sporting long sideburns. I pointed to
him and asked Frank Mahovlich, "Is that Dryden?" The Big
M gave me a gruff "yeah" without breaking stride. A veteran
is never too impressed by a raw rookie, even a goalie who
has just won his first NHL start. A short two months later
the young man I didn't recognize in St. Louis was riding in
a convertible in an emotional Stanley Cup victory parade
through downtown Montreal, cheered by thousands for
being named the playoff MVP the previous night in Chicago.
Ken Who?, as some mischievous media types liked to call
him then, had emerged as an improbable hero of an unbelievable playoff year. Most of the Montreal Canadiens'
twenty-four Stanley Cup victories have been predictable.
The one in 1971 was not.*

*Between then and when he retired eight years later I cer-
tainly got to know who Ken Dryden was. Ken played 509
league and playoff games for the Montreal Canadiens, and
I saw about 500 of them. During that time he became
another link in a chain of outstanding goaltenders who have
played for the Montreal Canadiens. It's a chain that began
with hockey's original goaltending superstar, Georges
Vezina; was carried on by George Hainsworth, Bill Durnan,
Jacques Plante, Gump Worsley, and Dryden himself; and
continues today with Patrick Roy.*

*One of the earliest film records of a National League
team is a brief, grainy bit of business from the early 1920s
showing the Canadiens practising on an outdoor rink atop
Mount Royal. The clip begins with the players crowded
around Georges Vezina's crease. When the players skate
away Vezina straightens up, tucks his two hands under his
chin, and leans on his stick. An early book of hockey stories
contains a thoughtful essay on the value of true sportsman-
ship, written by Georges Vezina. To my knowledge, for at
least another half-century no other Canadiens goaltender*

leaned on his stick in quite that way or published a thought-
ful essay. Then along came Ken Dryden, who struck that
same pose during games, and who wrote thoughtful books
and essays when his playing days were over. The tradition
continued, indeed.

Those of us covering the Canadiens then were well aware
that Dryden was "different," which of course didn't make
him unique among goaltenders. We were conscious of his
college background, his legal training, and his eclectic inter-
ests that extended far beyond hockey. In many ways he was
a loner in the midst of a confident, fun-loving group of ath-
letes who were the best team of their generation. Maybe the
best of any generation.

When I interviewed Larry Robinson for my book **The
Habs** he told me, *"The team was like one big happy family.
. . . I remember going to parties with Serge Savard, Claude
Larose, all the guys. Everybody hung around together. The
only one who almost never showed up was Kenny."*

*Robinson also said, "[Kenny] was taken for granted a lot
during the last few years. But you look back on some of the
saves he made in key games, he was incredible. He would
keep us in games, early, when we weren't even coming
close. We won so many games in the third period it was
ridiculous." Dryden may not have been visible at party
time, but the party-goers were very happy he showed up to
play the games.*

*If Dryden's importance to that particular dynasty was
downplayed, it was the same with Jacques Plante in an
earlier time in Montreal, and later with Billy Smith of the
Islanders, and Grant Fuhr in Edmonton. While fans and
media may be deceived, those closer to the scene are not. In
speaking of Dryden's contribution during his five Stanley
Cup-winning years as coach in Montreal, Scotty Bowman
said, "I can honestly say I can't remember him having two*

off-games in a row. Coming back after one was always a challenge to him. He was a fierce competitor and he played for only one reason – to win." The soft-spoken, Clark Kentish law student became a different man when he changed into his hockey equipment.

Harry Neale coached against Bowman's Canadiens. Harry says that Dryden is the only goaltender he has known who, when he was at the top of his game, gave the opposition the feeling they would not score a legitimate goal on him. Maybe they'd get one on a tip-in, or a deflection, or during a scramble, but that was the best they could hope for.

Because of the strength of the team in front of him, Dryden played games where his workload wasn't too heavy. After he had shut out the not-so-mighty Colorado Rockies I kidded him because the Rockies had been credited with only three shots in the third period. "That's strange," mused Ken. "I can only remember one."

An interesting version of this aspect of Dryden's play was told to me by John Davidson, who was in the net for the St. Louis Blues and New York Rangers throughout the Dryden era in Montreal. In assessing his long-time rival at the other end of the ice, Davidson told me, "Ken Dryden was the best in the business at being in games when he might get only eighteen or twenty shots and seven or eight would be classic scoring opportunities. He could keep his mind focused even though he wasn't getting a lot of work. He played the game under such control. It was like someone pushed a button and an arm came out. Then someone pushed another button and a leg came out. Everything he did was concise and for a reason. He was magnificent."

Goaltending was Ken Dryden's position from the time he began playing hockey. In explaining why he chose to play goal he once said, "The puck doesn't hurt a lot when you're little. Sometimes they're just using a tennis ball anyway,

and there's something very glamorous and exciting about
catching a ball, or a puck, and sprawling around."

Certainly another major reason young Kenny put on the
pads was the example set on the family backyard rink by his
older brother, Dave. As the Dryden boys were growing up in
Toronto, catching pucks and sprawling around ran in the
family.

KEN DRYDEN

I don't know why Dave became a goalie. If I had to guess why
I became a goalie, I'd say it was because of him and my emu-
lation of him. He's six years older, and when there's a difference of six years between kids in a family, you're not
rivals. I mean, he's too big for me to rival him and I'm too
small for him to rival me. So I think what happened was that
I became a bit of a novelty to him and he an idol to me. It's
like any kids, older and younger. If the younger kid is spunky
enough the older kid will tolerate him. I think that's what
happened to me. I was big for my age and, while I wasn't as
good as my brother, I could cope. So I was allowed to be in
the periphery of the action.

The other aspect is that in hockey your ticket into the
game is to do what the other guy doesn't want to do, and
that's play goal. When I was doing the 1988 Olympics for ABC
they did some profiles on the goalies and they asked them
why they became a goalie. There were a couple of patterns
that emerged and one was that they did what nobody else
wanted to do. They decided they would be the goalie. Mike
Richter was one of them. He had been the youngest kid on
the block and the only way they would allow him to play was
if he played goal. I suspect that's what happened to me.

The Dryden boys both became professional goaltenders. Ken attended Cornell University and was drafted by the Boston Bruins, who later traded him to the Montreal Canadiens for two players named Guy Allen and Paul Reid, neither of whom ever played an NHL game. By the time Ken played his first game in Pittsburgh, Dave had been up to and down from the NHL for almost four seasons, playing close to 70 games for Chicago and Buffalo. They had played at opposite ends of their back-yard rink in Toronto, and less than a week after Ken had played his first NHL game, they would be playing at opposite ends of the rink again, and making some hockey history in the process, at the Montreal Forum.

The Canadiens returned home from Ken's first road trip for a Saturday-night game against the Buffalo Sabres. Obviously a natural match-up was in the works, brother against brother in the nets, something that had never happened before in the NHL. Everyone thought it would be a great attraction for the fans, everyone that is except the people who were running the Canadiens.

The Canadiens' management felt that playing against his brother would put too much pressure on their rookie netminder. Punch Imlach was running the Sabres, then in their first season in the league. Imlach was a master at promotion, self and otherwise, and he correctly claimed the fans would love it if the two brothers went head to head.

The visiting coach is first to fill out his starting line-up for the official scorer. Imlach wrote in the name "Dave Dryden" as his goaltender. When it was his turn, Montreal coach Al MacNeil wrote in "Rogie Vachon" as his. So much for history. Then the unseen hand of fate entered the picture and the night turned into a memorable one for everyone who was there, especially the Dryden brothers and their father.

KEN DRYDEN

I hadn't played in Montreal yet. And so Buffalo comes into town and I know I'm not playing. I've been told that Rogie is playing. I was talking to my father on the phone and he said, "I think I'm gonna come up." I said he could come if he liked but I wasn't playing and suggested he not come up because he would be disappointed.

Anyway, he decides to come up and the game begins and I'm sitting on the end of the bench and Rogie is playing. Punch Imlach started my brother, and then after the first whistle, because I wasn't playing, my brother goes out and Joe Daley goes in to play. So my brother's on one bench and I'm on the other and we're watching the game. The first period passes and I don't think that either of us imagined that anything was going to happen except we were going to be watching this game from different benches.

In the second period Vachon gets hit. You know when goalies get hit they go down, then they always get up and play again. I mean, even at a moment like that I didn't take it very seriously. But geez, he's still down. I mean, he's not getting up. I don't know if it was Al or one of the players who said to me, "You'd better start loosening up. You might have to go in."

So I go off the bench and I guess I was loosening up, I can't quite remember. Anyway, I get motioned in and I'm going into the game. As soon as Imlach sees me go in he gives the hook to Joe Daley and my brother goes in.

So we played most of two periods against each other and the magic of it was the fact that our father was there in the stands watching the game. He had no right to imagine that anything like that was going to happen. He just took a chance, and it happened.

A night like that would normally have been enough drama for a rookie goalie promoted to the NHL to play a few games at the end of a season. But for the rookie involved that night a lot more drama lay in the weeks ahead.

I'm often asked, "What's the best game you've ever seen?" Well, I don't have one among the more than two thousand I've attended, but I do have a favourite year: 1971. Specifically, the playoffs of 1971, the year the Montreal Canadiens won a Stanley Cup we had all conceded to the defending-champion Boston Bruins. The Boston team had won the year before on Bobby Orr's famous overtime winner against Glenn Hall and the St. Louis Blues. In 1970–71 they finished 14 points ahead of their closest rival in the regular season and Phil Esposito had scored 76 goals in 78 games. They were matched in the first round against the Montreal Canadiens, a team that had finished 24 points behind them. To make the outcome of the first round appear even more secure for Boston, Canadiens' coach Al MacNeil shocked Montreal fans and media by starting the playoffs with Ken Who? in goal.

Game one in Boston ends 3–1, Bruins. Game two and it's 5–1, Bruins, with three minutes to play in the second period. The series was quickly turning into a joke, a cakewalk for the champions. But that's where the fun began. Game two final score, 7–5, Montreal. The Canadiens won game three, the Bruins took games four and five. Game six is in Montreal and the Canadiens romp to an 8–3 win. Late in the third period Ken Dryden earns an assist and when his name is announced the fans at the Forum give him a spine-tingling standing ovation, because by then he is no longer Ken Who?. His gallant stand against the best team in hockey has made him a hero in Montreal.

Game seven is in Boston on a Sunday afternoon. At the same time the Expos are playing a baseball game against the

Phillies at Jarry Park in Montreal. There are 20,000 people there all listening to the hockey game on portable radios. When the Canadiens score a big goal in the third period, 20,000 ball fans leap to their feet and start cheering. The umpires, completely baffled because nothing is happening in the ball game, call a time out and the cheers turn to laughter. Final score in Boston: 4–2, Montreal. The Canadiens have pulled off perhaps the biggest upset in the history of their franchise and Ken Dryden has played every minute of the series. Esposito, in despair and frustration, calls him a "bleeping octopus."

The Canadiens next played the Minnesota North Stars and won the series in six games. Then it was a Montreal– Chicago final, which was strictly a home-ice affair until the seventh game on May 18 in a steamy Chicago Stadium. The Blackhawks had glorious chances to win. With Chicago ahead, 2–0, in the second period Bobby Hull hit the goal post. Moments later, goals by Jacques Lemaire and Henri Richard have tied the game, 2–2. In the third period, Jim Pappin seemed to have the Cup-winning goal on its way to what looked like an empty Montreal net. But somehow Dryden stretched his right leg far enough to deflect the shot. By the time he retired it was still considered by Canadiens' fans his greatest save. From a technical standpoint it may not have been, but his timing was perfect, and the save unforgettable.

A few moments after Dryden's save on Pappin, Henri Richard swept around Chicago defenceman Keith Magnuson and beat Tony Esposito with the Cup-winning goal. Final score: 3–2, Montreal. During the series, Richard, furious after spending most of the fifth game on the bench, had created a fierce French–English media tempest in Montreal by calling Al MacNeil "the worst coach I've ever played for." Incredibly it was Richard who scored the dramatic tying and winning goals in game seven. When the game ended Montreal's rookie goalie was named winner of the Smythe Trophy as the MVP of the playoffs. A few moments later, after the handshakes were over, the Canadiens' legendary captain, Jean Béliveau, triumphantly carried the Stanley Cup off the ice to end the final game of his illustrious eighteen-year career.

So there. You see why I say 1971 was the best for me. And surely Kenny had to feel the same way, right, Ken? Wrong, again, Dick.

KEN DRYDEN

I'm sure to other people 1971 is their most vivid memory of me. It's not my most vivid memory, but I'm sure it is for others and always will be.

The Canada–Russia series in 1972 was the most vivid experience that I ever had in hockey. And the Stanley Cup that I remember the best was in 1976 when we beat the Flyers in four straight games.

As far as 1972 is concerned, I think that beyond going into the story that we both know, what makes it that way in the end is it was also my lowest low. I mean, that first game in Montreal [Soviet Union 7, Team Canada 3] and the fourth game in Vancouver [Soviet Union 5, Team Canada 3], I don't think I've ever felt so bad in my life. I just felt awful, and to be able to go from those lowest lows to the highest highs as part of the same experience over a twenty-seven-day period, it's utterly special. Boy! When you've got that low do you ever appreciate that high at the other end.

[Dryden and Tony Esposito each played four games in the series. Dryden played in the deciding eighth game, in Moscow, which was won by Team Canada, 6–5, on Paul Henderson's winning goal with 34 seconds left to play.]

Everyone remembers that series, and the 1975 New Year's Eve 3–3 tie at the Forum between the Canadiens and the Red Army. They were both defining moments. Since that time I don't think there have been any. Since then it's been moment to moment. They beat us this time but we'll beat them next time. But that's not the way it felt then. In '72 it was now and forever for us and in '75 it was now and forever for them. And of course they were completely shared experiences. That was what the fans felt, and that was what the players felt.

I was not surprised when Ken put the 1976 win at the top of his Stanley Cup memory list. The Montreal Canadiens won the Stanley Cup six times in the 1970s. The miracle of '71 was followed by the sure thing of '73, when the Habs lost only ten times in the regular season. The 1976 victory was the first of four straight Cups, all captured in years when the Canadiens were the class team of the league. But if you talk to other players who were there through all or most of those years – men like Yvan Cournoyer, Serge Savard, Larry Robinson, Jacques Lemaire, Steve Shutt – like Dryden, they speak first and foremost about the year they beat the Flyers four straight.

Dryden sat out the 1973–74 season because of a contract dispute. He based his unhappiness on the fact that he could "name six goaltenders who were higher paid than I was a year ago, and that number will increase next year." But unlike negotiations you hear about today, the Canadiens held firm that a contract is a contract. No renegotiation allowed.

The Flyers won the Stanley Cup that season, and the season after that when Dryden returned. There were some extremely skilled players in the Philadelphia line-up, including Bobby Clarke, Reg Leach, and Rick MacLeish, and they were backed by the superb talents of goaltender Bernie

Parent. But the Flyers were best known as the Broad Street Bullies, a team that used physical intimidation to get from point A to point B. They were boffo at the box office, but the hockey establishment began to worry about the criticism the team, and the game, was getting. They felt if the Flyers won a third straight Stanley Cup, the other teams would all figure, "If you can't beat 'em, join 'em," and the fistic floodgates would open wide all around the league.

The Canadiens had done some rebuilding in those two years and were ready to take on the champions, ready to match their speed, skill, and finesse against the Flyers' thuggery. The white hats were taking dead aim on the black hats.

KEN DRYDEN

The 1976 victory was a Stanley Cup of vindication. It was a Stanley Cup of triumph, of revenge, of setting things right, of responsibility self-imposed. It was a Stanley Cup of chase. We chased the Flyers from the moment we lost out the year before until we finally finished them off in Philadelphia in that fourth game. I don't think any of us had anything except them in our sights. We were going to catch them. And we did.

It began the moment training camp started. We played them in that training camp and we beat them there. We left them behind in the regular season, but the playoffs were still ahead. So every game we played during that year was a victory for then and a preparation for later. It was all in the context of later, later, later. And finally the later happened, and I can remember very vividly a few things about that.

The first part was how we were so prepared for the first game of the finals in Montreal. We knew that the Flyers liked to get the jump in a game, get an early goal to set the other team back on its heels and then use their defensive style to eke out a win. They were very successful at it.

We were so ready for them. The game starts and they have Clarke, Barber, and Leach on the ice and we've got Gainey, Jarvis, and Roberts on our side, and it's head to head, first shift of the game. We're going to set the tone and everything's going to be perfect. Twenty seconds later we're behind 1–0. I couldn't believe it. It was Reggie Leach and he did what he did through the whole playoffs: he just kept blasting away from right wing. Every shot was low to the corner, stick side. I knew where it was going but there was no way I was going to cheat on him. I just kept saying, "I'll get him the next time. I'll get him the next time." I never did get him the next time.

But we chased them and we finally got them. That was the year Larry Robinson hit Gary Dornhoefer in Montreal and bent the boards out of shape. And it was the year of Kate Smith, who the Flyers were using to sing "God Bless America" before the games at the Spectrum, and it worked because she created such a high pitch of emotion.

We won the first two games in Montreal and then our whole conversation between the end of the second game and the start of the third was, "Do you think Kate's gonna be there? Do you think Kate's gonna be there?"

Finally, blackened ice surface, the gate opens up, red carpet, spotlight, Kate Smith. I was standing beside Jimmy Roberts on the blueline and here's Jimmy, who by this time is about thirty-five years old and he's seen it all and done it all, and we're standing there belting out "God Bless America." I mean from the bottom of our lungs we're really belting it out. When it's over usually there's kind of a ritual skate. Well, Jimmy just came out of the blocks, exploded. I mean, he was Ben Johnson. There was such energy and excitement in that building at that particular moment. And we beat them.

After we had won three straight all we heard was, "It'll be four straight. It's over, it's done. The Flyers' backs are broken and the Canadiens can coast to the finish line from here." I know how I felt and I suspect most of the players felt the same way. "Are they crazy? This isn't over." I was thinking that the Flyers have their backs to the wall but this is Philadelphia. They're a good team and they're going to make one last stand. Say they win. Now it's 3–1. They feel something is building so they go back to Montreal and sneak one. It's 3–2. Then we're back in Philly and the bandwagon is really rolling and at that point there's no way you could handle them. We could lose this thing 4–3. It's entirely possible all of that could happen, a completely credible scenario.

I can remember the morning of the fourth game when I did something that had taken me a long time to work up the nerve to do. I argued with myself back and forth and I finally decided to do it. "God Bless America" had become such a big thing – Kate Smith and all that – I decided I was going to write out the words to "God Bless America" so that, if and when we won the series, I would distribute them so we could sing it. But then I said, what if we don't win tonight, and what if we don't win the series? Finally I said, I'll do it.

I wrote it out and copied it twenty-five times and I had it with my stuff in the dressing room. There was no way in the world it was ever going to appear unless we won. Finally the game was over, and we had won, and I distributed them. We sang it in the dressing room, and we sang it on the plane all the way back to Montreal.

With the completion of their sweep of the Flyers, Kenny the music director and the members of his choir had won the first of four straight Stanley Cup victories. In the process they had several people, this writer included, thinking they just might be the best team of all time.

Certainly they are statistically. In the three seasons

beginning with 1975–76 they lost 11, 8, and 10 times, only
29 defeats in 240 regular-season games. Add the playoffs
and the record stands at 213 wins, 34 ties, and just 34 losses
in 281 games. None of hockey's other dynasties has ever
come close to those figures.

In 1978–79 the Canadiens lost 17 times and finished one
point behind the New York Islanders in the overall stand-
ings. The Islanders were then upset by the Rangers in the
playoffs and the Canadiens defeated the Rangers in five
games to win their fourth straight Cup. But it was, as Bob
Gainey later told me, "a stressful season. Our team had
shown some cracks."

Two key personalities worked through the season
knowing it would be their last with the Canadiens. The
coach, Scotty Bowman, upset that he had not been named
to succeed Sam Pollock as managing director, was not
happy. And Ken Dryden, like Jean Béliveau in 1970–71,
knew he would retire when the season ended.

KEN DRYDEN

At that time there was disparity in the league, a lot of weak
teams. We had a chance to win games on bad nights not only
because we were that good, but the other teams were that
bad. It builds in the sense that we shouldn't lose. We lost
eight games. We lost ten games. Why did we lose any? We
should have won 80. We were better than anybody else.

The distinction I make between those teams and teams
from later eras – first the Islanders and then Edmonton – is
that those Montreal teams of those particular years not only
won Stanley Cups, they won everything. They dominated
seasons as well as Stanley Cups. The Islanders team, the
Edmonton team, lost a lot more during the regular season.

Part of that was a growing ethic that you don't have to win all the time.

Our domination started in training camp. It literally began September 15 and ended May 15. That was it, domination from beginning to end. It wasn't peaking here, peaking there, gamesmanship, finding the right moment, all of that. No. The right moment began in September and ended in May.

I don't buy the idea that you can't win them all. One of the great experiences I had as a goalie was playing college hockey. We only played 24 games, and when we went to the NCAA finals we played 29. You end up preparing, getting ready, anticipating, as if every game matters. Once you learn it over a short schedule you apply it over any length of schedule. It doesn't matter whether it's 29 games, or 89, or 119 games, you can do it. So those years in Montreal were a wonderful experience for me. I think there were a lot of players on that team who couldn't forgive a bad performance. That's the only way you can go through a season losing only eight or ten games. You simply feel embarrassment and humiliation over losing.

Following the 1972 Canada–Russia series, games involving high-profile Soviet teams were not kind to Dryden. In the famed 1975 New Year's Eve game in Montreal, the Canadiens had to settle for a 3–3 tie with the Central Red Army, despite outshooting them 38–13. Dryden took a lot of heat from the media and the fans for that one. Dryden admitted he let himself get mentally uptight and overprepared. That was one time he was unable to stay sharp when he wasn't getting much work.

In 1979, the NHL replaced its annual All-Star game with a three-game series called the Challenge Cup: a team of

NHL All-Stars played a Soviet All-Star squad in New York. Scotty Bowman coached the NHL team, with help from several NHL general managers. Too much help, perhaps, when all was said and done.

Dryden was in goal for the NHL for the first two games. The NHL won the first game while the Soviets came from behind to take the second. With the management types on hand all putting in their two cents' worth, Bowman made some line-up changes for the third game. Dryden was replaced in goal by Gerry Cheevers. The changes didn't work and the Soviets clobbered the NHL, 6–0.

A few days after the series I ran into Dryden at a magazine store near the Forum. I started into some small talk but the conversation ended when, not pausing to look up from the book he was browsing through, he told me, "I'm not in the mood to talk right now." I should have known better. He was still depressed over being replaced for that final game in New York.

Ken Dryden

I was really down for a long time after that series. I wasn't great in the first two games but I played pretty well. Usually you have a sense of when you might not be playing well and I had no sense of that at all. I just assumed I was going to be playing that third game. I think Scotty and I understood each other pretty well. We were good for each other. For him to be part of a decision that involved my not playing, that really hit hard.

That was also the year of our last Cup, 1979, and I was depressed through most of the playoffs. I didn't play well. I can't remember who we played in the first round [*it was Toronto*] and maybe I was okay, but I doubt I was better than that. Then we played the Bruins. We won two in Montreal. Then they beat us twice in Boston, we won at home, they won at home, and then they almost beat us in the seventh game in Montreal.

I knew it was going to be my last year. So I was facing my final playoff year and I just wasn't playing the way I wanted to play. It was a near-disaster in the seventh game against the Bruins. I let in a goal from behind the net with four minutes to go that put them ahead, and they were about to eliminate us. Then they were caught with too many men on the ice and Lafleur got his famous goal to tie the game and Yvon Lambert scored in overtime.

I remember in that overtime Don Marcotte had a wide-open chance. We got trapped behind the net, somebody dumped it out in front and Marcotte was there, all alone and he shot it. I was floundering, just floundering, but it hit me. It hit me right in the chest. If he puts it anywhere else he scores and they win. Then Lambert scores and we win.

When that game was over, I just sat in the dressing room and I couldn't even cheer. I was so relieved, so confused, it was like, "What's going on here?" I always felt in every other game I was in some measure of control, but in that one I just felt like my strings were being pulled.

Then we started the final series against the Rangers and we were down 4–0 or something at the end of the second period. I wasn't playing well and Scotty yanked me and Bunny Larocque played the third period. That was the first time I hadn't played in a Stanley Cup game for Montreal from the time I started in 1971 until that moment. The only time I didn't play was the year I stayed in Toronto. Otherwise, every minute of every playoff game. So it was crushing, but it wasn't unjust.

The thing was, that was going to be the end, my last

season. The Rangers weren't a very good team and we were going to beat them. Bunny was going to go into game two, play the same way he played in the third period, and we'd win. Then we'd go to New York, end up winning at least one of the games there, and go on to win the series. And Bunny would play it out and take my place the way I had taken Vachon's in 1971. There was this perverse circularity to the whole thing.

We were warming up for the second game and Bunny got hit in the head with a shot. He was wearing a cage mask, and getting hit in the head with a cage mask doesn't hurt. It happens all the time and it's no big deal. It was a Doug Risebrough shot, which is clearly no big deal. [Laughs] But Bunny was hurt and he wasn't going to be able to play. Holy geez, talk about strings being pulled!

I can remember being in the dressing room before the start of the game. In that situation I'm supposed to calm the troops, say something moderately amusing to cut the tension, and I was kind of acting out the role. Plays every minute, then doesn't play, gets a second chance, goes out in a blaze. Vindication. Perfect.

The fans were buzzing. That was the first thing. The next thing was they scored a goal after about two minutes. The fans were still buzzing, and then at about the four-minute mark they scored again. This was craziness. I had already figured out the last chapter of my career twice and now I didn't know what the last chapter was any more. Anyway, we came back and won the game and things settled down. I played better and we won the whole thing. With most of the other Stanley Cups I felt triumph. That one, well, I made it through. That one, I felt survival.

I had already made up my mind I would retire when I was thirty and wouldn't play that last year. But I did and I was thirty-one. I just wanted to do something else. It's easy to explain and very hard for anybody to understand. Put it all down on legal paper, pros and cons, and people will nod and say they understand. But if you give them the real reason, which was it just felt like it was time to go, they don't quite get it. But that's all it was.

During that last year I had long conversations with management, trying to work out how it could continue. We talked about my living just over the border in Ontario, in Alexandria, articling with some lawyer there, and practising and playing when I could. That's the way I started in Montreal. I was going to play about eight games for the Voyageurs, practise when I could, and do that for two years until I graduated from law school. The only stipulation was that then I give the Canadiens a full season. That's the way it was up until Christmas. Then I went to the Canadiens and said I thought I could go to law school and play full-time. So I signed a new contract as a full-time player and I had to work out the law school on my own. That's how we came to an agreement in 1970 when I had no history or background with the team.

It was different in 1979 when I was used to playing a certain role on the team and there was the fun of playing that role and having others count on you. I would have been this part-time guy coming in every so often to play. But I knew I wouldn't like it, knew it wouldn't work. So I left.

Mostly, I enjoyed life in the NHL. I liked going to different places. I'm a wanderer and I love walking, going out and discovering places. I enjoyed that part of it a lot. I especially enjoyed the things every player enjoys: the dressing room, the ice surface before a big game, or even during a big game. And the playoffs were great. In April and May we've got more energy to bring to a game. It comes out of nowhere. I thought

I was giving it all in November and February because every game was important and then suddenly I've got more to give. It was terrific that way.

People have asked me about regrets and stuff. Yeah, there are some games I would like to play again, games I would have liked to play better in. But living in Quebec in the 1970s, playing for the Montreal Canadiens in the Montreal Forum. Who would regret any of that?

6

Have Pads, Will Travel

GARY SMITH   CESARE MANIAGO
GARY EDWARDS   GILLES MELOCHE

Hockey is an itinerant trade. There's a saying, "Don't buy a house, or build one," because often the player who just bought or built gets traded. Hockey wives say, "Don't have a baby during the season," because the new father is often traded right after the blessed event. Mike Gartner played nine seasons for the Washington Capitals, always living in rented houses. Finally, he decided to build his own home. The telephone had barely been installed in the spanking new abode when it rang. The call was from the Caps' general manager, David Poile, who informed Gartner he had just been traded to the Minnesota North Stars.

David Poile's father, Bud, played in the NHL during the six-team era, and was on five of them. The only stop on the league's road map he missed was Montreal. A few years later Bronco Horvath travelled the same five-out-of-six route, bypassing Detroit. Today, a player can find himself on a lot more than five teams. Walt McKechnie, a forward, and Larry

Hillman, a defenceman, both played on a record eight teams, and are tied for that dubious distinction.

A select group has managed to play many years with one team. Gordie Howe was a Red Wing for twenty-five years and Alex Delvecchio for twenty-four. Johnny Bucyk played twenty-two seasons in Boston and Stan Mikita twenty-two in Chicago.

Goaltenders can be moved around as often as other players. Two of the greatest, Jacques Plante and Terry Sawchuk, each saw service with five NHL teams. But Turk Broda played his entire fourteen-year career in Toronto and Tony Esposito spent fifteen of his sixteen NHL years in Chicago. And then you have the Smiths (not related), Billy and Gary. Billy Smith is the all-time stay-at-home goaltender. After his rookie season with Los Angeles, Smith played seventeen years with the New York Islanders and then retired. But Gary Smith played for seven different franchises in thirteen years. One of them, the Oakland Seals, changed its name to the California Golden Seals while he was with them. A review of his NHL itinerary shows seven cities and eight teams, the most among members of the goaltenders' union. Smith established NHL residences in Toronto, Oakland, Chicago, Vancouver, Minnesota, Washington, and Winnipeg. He also played for two WHA teams, Indianapolis and Winnipeg.

Smith, who was one of the game's biggest goalies at 6'4", comes from a hockey family. His uncle, Roger Smith, was a defenceman in the NHL with the Pittsburgh Pirates and Philadelphia Quakers in the late 1920s and early '30s. His father, Des, was a defenceman in the late 1930s and early '40s for both the Maroons and Canadiens in Montreal, plus the Chicago Blackhawks and the Boston Bruins. He also played in England for the Wembley Lions, which meant that, while he may not have changed teams as often as his goal-

tending son, he travelled a lot farther to do it. Gary's brother, Brian, played forward for both Los Angeles and Minnesota in the late 1960s.

Gary Smith was given an obvious nickname. But curiously, the man who would become the most-travelled goaltender in hockey history was called "Suitcase" even before he played a game in the NHL.

GARY SMITH

I grew up in Ottawa and played both forward and defence on outdoor rinks. There was a travelling team that used to go to small places like Brockville and Carleton Place, and to towns in upper New York State like Messina, and they needed a goalie. I thought it would be fun to take those trips so I volunteered. I think I was about eleven or twelve years old. There was a scout for Toronto who lived on our street, Brian Lynch, and the next year he organized a trip to Toronto. We played a Marlies peewee team right in Maple Leaf Gardens and we got beat real bad, something like 9–0. I didn't know it at the time but the Maple Leafs were taking a look at me. Even with all those goals against me I guess I stopped a lot of shots because Bob Davidson, their chief scout, asked if I would like to go to high school at St. Mike's, in Toronto. So I finished that season in Ottawa and the next year the Leafs brought me down to St. Mike's. That's how I ended up belonging to Toronto when I started my pro career.

I didn't play many games for the Maple Leafs. That was when they had the two so-called old guys, Johnny Bower and Terry Sawchuk. They had three minor-league teams at that time. One was in Rochester, where Gerry Cheevers was the goalie, one in Victoria, where Al Millar was the goalie, and another in Tulsa, where Don Simmons was playing. After my first training camp they sent me to Rochester. Whenever anyone got hurt on any of their pro teams they would send me to fill in. That's where I got the nickname "Suitcase." Before I even played for the Maple Leafs, a sportswriter in Toronto, Red Burnett, wrote that because of the way they had me standing by to move from team to team, and with the chance that one of the old guys in Toronto might conk out, I always had to have my suitcase packed.

Bower and Sawchuk were great guys to be with, just fantastic. Let's face it, I was just a kid in pro hockey at that time, twenty years old, and these two guys were legends. But they helped me a lot. They'd come to me and say, "You're doing this wrong, or that wrong." Bower taught me how to use my stick properly. Not chopping at guys but using it to poke-check. They still call it a Johnny Bower poke check.

On a couple of road trips I was Bower's roommate and, being a cheeky kid, one time I asked him how old he really was. He said, "I never let anyone know how old I am because then they'll think I'm an old man." He and Sawchuk were my idols. The way they went out of their way to help me showed they weren't afraid of anyone taking their job. I don't think it's the same today.

The two old guys didn't conk out too often, because Gary Smith played only five games for the Toronto Maple Leafs, three in 1965–66 and two the following season. The Maple Leafs made him available in the expansion draft of 1967 and he was claimed by the Oakland Seals.

The late, great broadcaster Danny Gallivan saw a lot of strange plays during his thirty-two years in the booth at the Montreal Forum, and one of his favourites involved Gary Smith in one of his five games as a Maple Leaf. On the play, Smith started carrying the puck from his goal crease, and by the time he ended his rush he had stickhandled his way inside the Montreal blueline. I was working with Gallivan that night and, until I interviewed Smith for this book, I thought he had been looking for someone to pass to. Wrong again, Dick. The young Toronto goaltender had something else in mind.

GARY SMITH

I didn't start the game. I think Sawchuk did, and right off the bat John Ferguson was running wild against us. Early in the first period he scored a goal, and then he beat the crap out of Eddie Shack in a fight. I was sitting on the bench with a towel around my neck and I started yelling at Fergie after the fight was over, "Aw, you jerk," stuff like that. I was just trying to stay on the team. Punch Imlach was the coach and he comes over, takes the towel off my neck and says, "Go get him." I said, "What do you mean, go get him? He's in the penalty box." Punch says, "Get him when he gets out."

So he puts me in the net and they proceed to score three or four goals on me pretty quick. I figured I'd be yanked after the first period and sent back to the minors the next day. I'm standing there after one of the goals wondering what I could do to make people remember me in my first game in the Montreal Forum. So I said to myself, "I'm gonna go down the ice and score a goal."

The next time I had a shot I caught it and the wingers started peeling off and there wasn't anybody on our team near me. So I dropped the puck at my feet, put it on my stick and took off for the other end. I was gone. I was going down there to score because I thought that I had waited all my life for a chance to be in the NHL and this was it. I had screwed up in the net because they had three or four goals on me so there I was, skating down the ice trying to score.

I reached the vicinity of the Montreal zone and J.C. Tremblay was standing there, just inside the blueline.

J.C. Tremblay had never thrown a bodycheck in his life, but he stepped into me and decked me. I can remember I was spinning around off-balance and I happened to see Punch, who was pulling his hat down over his eyes. The next thing I knew, Ralph Backstrom had the puck and he was heading the other way toward our end, and I was scrambling along behind trying to catch up. Backstrom took a shot and Marcel Pronovost, who was on our defence, had gone back into our goal crease and he made one of the greatest saves I've ever seen in my life. He still had the puck when I finally got back into the net.

I was watching a game from Montreal on TV last season (1993–94), and Patrick Roy was heading to the bench on a delayed penalty call. The puck came to him right after he left his crease and one of the guys on the other team tried to check him. Patrick made a great move, deked the guy right out of his jock, carried the puck some more and then made a good pass before he got to the bench. The crowd went nuts and I heard you say it reminded you of what Gary Smith did at the Forum back in the 1960s. It was nice to hear that. They tell me that what I did that night was the reason they made the rule that a goalie can't handle the puck on the other team's side of the red line. So at least I have that to my credit in the history books.

The "Gary Smith rule" reads: "If a goalkeeper participates in the play in any manner when he is beyond the center red line, a minor penalty shall be imposed upon him." (Rule 32, section i)

Smith became a full-time NHL goaltender once he left Toronto. He played four seasons in Oakland, two in Chicago, three in Vancouver, and finally put away his suitcase after brief stops in Minnesota, Washington, and Winnipeg. There were seasons he played in 54, 65, 66, and 72 games, and he

finished with a total of 532 league and playoff games to
his credit.

GARY SMITH

I liked to play a lot of games and I had plenty of chances
when I was in Oakland and Vancouver. I never liked practice,
but when I got to play a lot I was more effective. I played in
over 70 games in Oakland and had a pretty fair year, and then
I played 72 in Vancouver, and I think that was my best
season. That was in '74–75 and it was the first year Vancouver made the playoffs.

When I was in Oakland, Charlie Finley bought the team
and he was quite a character. He owned the Oakland ball
team then and he dressed them in white shoes. When he took
over the hockey team he had us wear white skates and he
changed the name of the team to the California Golden Seals.

We didn't see all that much of him, but once in a while
he would show up. He always had some of his buddies with
him and he liked to put on a show for them. One night they
were at a game in Boston and we beat the Bruins. After the
game, Finley came into the dressing room and gave everybody
$300. He made us promise we would all use the money to
buy a new suit. We happened to be going to Montreal for our
next game. In Montreal there were clothing places that liked
to sell suits to hockey players and we went to a place where
they would sell us a suit for about $50. So we all ended up
with five or six suits with Charlie's $300.

I think I learned the most about goaltending the two years
I was the back-up to Tony Esposito in Chicago. He played a
different style than anybody else at the time. He had posi-
tioning something like Sawchuk. When he'd go down he'd
sort of do it like a box and there just wasn't a hole anywhere
to shoot at. And he was so intense. I went from playing 60

or 70 games in Oakland to about 25 each year in Chicago. But
I learned a lot from Tony. I just loved watching him play.

We got to the finals against Montreal in 1973. We had a
good team and I think, with a few breaks, we were good
enough to win it all that year. They had a lot of good players
in Chicago in those days, but Montreal had that extra something. They always had that winning attitude.

Toward the end of my career I played in Washington and
Winnipeg when they both had terrible teams and finished in
last place. Tom McVie was the coach both places and he's a
great guy. I wasn't playing much in Washington, and I kept
asking him if I was going on the next road trip and he'd always
say I wasn't. One time he said, "It's brutal when you don't
play, isn't it?" and I said, "Yeah, it's terrible."

One time when I asked him I guess he was feeling sorry
for me so he says, "You know what? I think I'll take you on
this trip." We were going to Cleveland and the Capitals
hadn't won in about 30 games. They gave me the plane ticket
that belonged to one of the other goalies, Bernie Wolfe. A guy
named Jim Bedard was playing most of the games and that
night in Cleveland he got hurt in the warm-up. So they had
to put me in and we won the game, 6–5. That was the last
game I played for Washington and I finished that season in
Minnesota.

The next season I went to Indianapolis in the WHA. Wayne
Gretzky was turning pro with that team. He was seventeen
years old. A bunch of us went there a week or so before the
official training camp to start getting in shape and he was
there. I'd heard of him, of course, but I was sort of sceptical.
I'd seen a lot of junior hot-shots come along that didn't
amount to anything in pro hockey. So we got to the first
unofficial practice and it took me about five to ten minutes
to realize this kid was the best hockey player I had ever seen
at that age.

A lot of goalies have superstitions, and I had one. Well, maybe not quite a superstition, but I would start off the season with just one pair of socks in my skates. Maybe because I was heavier or because of the way I played, whatever it was, my skates would loosen up and loosen up as the season went on. It was like they kept getting bigger. So I would put on an extra pair of socks, then after a while another pair, and then another. One year I ended up playing with sixteen pairs of socks on my feet. I think that was my record, sixteen pairs.

Everybody used to think that I was crazy wearing all those pairs of socks and they also thought I was crazy because I would take off my equipment between periods and then put it all back on again. But it wasn't a superstition. It was just to get my skates and my pads tightened up because it would feel better.

I finished my career in Winnipeg. John Ferguson, the guy who was the reason for my first big moment in the NHL, was the G.M. He and Tom McVie brought me there from Indianapolis in the last year of the WHA and we won the championship. I played ten games for them that year in the playoffs and we beat Edmonton in the finals. I played twenty games the next year when the Jets got into the NHL and then decided to hang 'em up.

I played professional hockey for fifteen years. There are always a few things you'd like to go back and do over again, but I have no real regrets. I enjoyed the game and I enjoyed the people. I certainly enjoyed a lot of the times away from the arena. You know, just hanging around with the guys. I played hockey in a lot of places, but no matter where I went there were always some great guys to chum around with. I think that was probably the best part.

Gary Smith was traded from the Vancouver Canucks to the Minnesota North Stars on August 23, 1976, in exchange for Cesare Maniago, another goaltender with a pile of destination stickers on his suitcase. Maniago played for only three NHL teams for any significant length of time, but did a lot of travelling on his way to the big leagues. A native of Trail, British Columbia, who became a goalie because he was the skinniest kid on his block, Maniago turned pro with the Toronto Maple Leafs' organization in 1960. In the next six years Maniago's minor-league stops were Sudbury, Spokane (twice), Vancouver, Hull–Ottawa (twice),Quebec City, Buffalo, Omaha, Minneapolis, and Baltimore. He played on four different teams during the 1962–63 season.

Maniago was on the move so often not because he wasn't any good. He won the leading goalkeeper award in the Eastern Pro League in 1962 playing for Hull–Ottawa. In 1965 he was named both the leading goalkeeper and the most valuable player in the Central Pro League after a fine season in Minneapolis. During all that time he played seven games for the Toronto Maple Leafs in 1961 and 14 for the Montreal Canadiens in 1963. He joined the New York Rangers during the 1965–66 season and never played another game in the minors until his retirement in 1978. Maniago spent two seasons in New York, nine in Minnesota, and his final two with the Vancouver Canucks.

Craig Billington claims **Cesare Maniago** *is the greatest-sounding name in goaltending history. Certainly Maniago was involved in history-making occasions a few times. He was in goal for the Maple Leafs in 1961 when Montreal's Boom-Boom Geoffrion scored his 50th goal of the season, to make him only the second player to score 50 and the first since Maurice Richard had reached that figure sixteen years before. Five years later, when Bobby Hull became the first player to score 51 goals in a single season, Maniago, then a*

New York Ranger, was the victim again. Stan Mikita scored his 500th career goal in 1977 against Vancouver with Cesare in the Canucks' net.

Maniago was the number-one goaltender for the Minnesota North Stars in the first few years of expansion. Jean Béliveau scored his 500th career goal against Minnesota in 1971, and "Cesare Maniago" is often given as the answer to the question, "Who was the goalie?" But Cesare had the night off: Béliveau scored his big milestone on Minnesota's rookie back-up goalie, Gilles Gilbert.

Maniago now owns a sporting-goods business in Vancouver. When I interviewed him for this book he was recovering from a broken leg he had suffered playing old-timers' hockey, as a defenceman.

CESARE MANIAGO

A lot of people kid me about being involved in all those milestones. I think the one I remember best was the first one when Geoffrion scored. I was playing that night because all the other Toronto goalies were hurt. I had played my first NHL game a couple of weeks earlier when Gerry McNamara, who was filling in for Johnny Bower, got injured. Bower came back, then he hurt his leg and they called me up again. That's why I was playing for Toronto that night in Montreal.

Jean Béliveau was Geoffrion's centre and he was trying all night to set Geoffrion up. Béliveau could have had two or three goals himself but he was always passing to Geoffrion. Late in the game there was a faceoff in our end. Big Jean won it cleanly and got the puck to Boom-Boom and he just blasted it. I didn't have a chance.

That same year I was drafted by Montreal when Toronto didn't protect me. I played the next season for their farm team in Hull–Ottawa and that's when I tried to be the first pro goalie to score a goal. Those were the days when the goalie could skate across the red line, and I used to join the rush on a delayed penalty. One time I took a shot and hit the goal post. But that all ended in a game against Kitchener. Jean Ratelle was with them and they had a pretty good team. I was carrying the puck at their blueline and somebody hit me with a bodycheck and it ko'd me. I was out like a light and went into convulsions. Imagine how that must have looked, a goalie knocked out at the other team's blueline. Anyway, I think that was the last time I ever rushed up the ice.

The year after that I played some games for the Canadiens. Those were the days when Jacques Plante was having his asthma problems. They didn't dress the back-up goalie then and I used to sit in a seat at one end of the rink right behind the general manager, Frank Selke. If Plante was in trouble with his breathing he would tell them between periods. Ken Reardon was an executive with the team and he would walk out from the corridor behind the Canadiens' bench and give me a signal, which meant I had to hurry to the room, get dressed, and go into the game. That was a terrible way to have to play. My heart would be in my throat.

Plante had started wearing a mask a couple of years earlier, and when I was with the Canadiens he wanted me to wear one too. He took me to the Montreal General Hospital for a fitting and Plante had the guy who made his mask make one for me. Toe Blake never liked the idea of his goalie wearing a mask. The day mine arrived at the Forum I carried it onto the ice when the practice started. Blake skated up to me and said, "You're not planning to wear that thing today, are you, son?" I said, "No, sir, I'm not." What else was I going to say to Toe Blake?

In my travels after that I wore one in practice. The incident that convinced me to wear a mask all the time was early in my first year in Minnesota. Gary Bauman was the other goalie and a shot hit him in the throat. He went down and started turning blue and swallowing his tongue. We thought he was dying. I was on the bench and I knew I'd be going in. I didn't have my mask with me but I turned to the equipment manager and said, "Go get my mask." I never played without one again.

When expansion came and you ended up in Minnesota, your first reaction was that you were an outcast, that nobody wanted you. But we had some guys who had been good players. Leo Boivin and Doug Mohns were two of them. On teams I had been with before there were always cliques, three or four guys going this way, three or four guys going that way. In Minnesota twenty guys all went the same way, together.

Maybe one reason was because we had "The Bird," Wren Blair, running the show. He was the coach and the general manager and we'd all be mad at him almost all the time. He'd always be putting you down, always knocking everybody. So we all had something in common. The time I spent in Minnesota was likely the best time of all for me.

I played with Gump Worsley in Minnesota when he was at the end of his career and I can't say enough good things about him. He was just great to be around. We'd heard all the stories about him and how he used to behave off the ice. But by then he was at an age when he looked after himself before the games. Mind you, if we'd just won and he knew he wouldn't play again for three or four days, then he'd let loose.

Gump had a habit of coming up with a "groin pull," or the "flu" at the last minute if he didn't feel like playing. Once I got to know him I told him that was okay with me. But I asked him to let me know. I didn't want any surprises and it worked out pretty well.

The goalies I admire today are those who focus the best. With the playoffs like they are now, any goalie who gets into the final four has to be admired. I think of Patrick Roy the year the Canadiens won ten overtime games in the playoffs. That's almost unbelievable.

I think the goalies today are facing harder shots. Bobby Hull was the guy I remember, and I'm sure anyone who played goal against him would say the same thing. Cournoyer was always tough for me. You just never knew where their shots were going.

I always respected the other goalies. I'm not saying I was glad to see the other guy come up with big saves against my team. But I wasn't glad to see him blow a soft one either. There would usually be a few words between goalies when you were skating around during the warm-up. Or you'd be standing beside each other and you'd say things like, "How's it going? I've had a good week, or a lousy week." The one guy you could never do that with was Tony Esposito. He was always so focused. You'd swear he didn't even know you were there.

Before the game is when I would say most goalies, including me, weren't just one of the boys. When it's getting near game time you want to be left alone. The other guys talk, defencemen with defencemen, forwards with forwards. But the goalie wants to be by himself.

The best part of playing goal was winning a game. I'll never forget how it felt, to go out with the guys after a big win. It's almost impossible to describe. I'll never experience anything like that again.

Another goaltender who ran up plenty of frequent-flyer points changing home teams was Gary Edwards. A native of Toronto who played junior for the Marlboros, Edwards played professionally for fourteen years, beginning in 1968. In his first three years he travelled from Kansas City to St.

Louis (where his playing time lasted four minutes), back to Kansas City, then to San Diego, back to the Blues (his playing time increased to 60 minutes), back to Kansas City, and then again to San Diego.

Edwards finally put down some roots when he began a six-year stay with the Los Angeles Kings in 1971. He played 44 games his first season in Los Angeles and, despite spending the next ten years in the NHL, never again played in as many games in one season. In 1978 he was on the move once more when the Kings traded him to the Cleveland Barons, who folded and merged with the Minnesota North Stars two years later. Two years after that he was traded to the Edmonton Oilers, who sent him back to St. Louis a year later. His final season, 1981–82, was split between the Blues and the Pittsburgh Penguins. He played fourteen years in pro hockey, had eight home towns and 286 games in the NHL, but one of Edwards' most memorable games was his first.

GARY EDWARDS

I was drafted fifth overall by St. Louis in 1968. That was the year Jacques Plante came out of retirement so they had Plante and Glenn Hall. Jacques and Glenn were like thirty-eight and thirty-nine years old and the plan was to dress only one of them for each game. I was at the training camp with two other kids, Ted Ouimet and Robbie Irons. The three rookies were going to play in Kansas City, but each of us would spend a third of the season with the Blues. The rookie would practise with the team and then dress for the games as the backup. Either Jacques or Glenn would be in the press box and the rookie would be on the bench.

I had the middle stint, around Christmas, and just after I got there we played in Chicago. That night Plante started and

Hall was in the press box. With about four minutes to go in the first period Stan Mikita let a shot go with that big curved stick and hit Plante on the head. He was knocked woozy, so they took him to the dressing room and I had to go in. It was the first time I touched the ice in the NHL.

In those days they allowed you a brief warm-up and everything seemed fine, and then thirty seconds later we got a penalty. I still haven't had a shot. The faceoff is in our end and as I look out at the Chicago power play here's what I see: Stan Mikita at centre ice, Bobby Hull on left wing, Kenny Wharram on right wing, Dennis Hull and Jim Pappin on the points. Five forwards. They're all great players with great shots and I'm thinking, what the hell is going on around here? Well, they dropped the puck and Al Arbour, who was playing defence in front of me, blocked five shots in a row. He had welts all over his body. The puck never came through to me until I caught a shot from Mikita with about twenty seconds to go in the period. My first NHL save. In those days you could bring a guy out of the press box and dress him, so by then they'd brought Hall down and he was getting ready. He went in for the second period and I was back on the bench. That was the only time I got on the ice in the NHL in my first season in pro hockey.

When I was in St. Louis I bunked in with Plante in his apartment. He was very analytical about goaltending and he would go over a lot of things with me. He kept notes on how he had done against every team, the goals against him and who scored them, and charts on everything. Staying with Plante was funny because he used to dream and talk in his sleep. But he always talked in French and I couldn't understand what he was saying.

They tell a lot of stories about Plante being cheap. I know that after the home games he would always show up at the apartment long after I got home. When a game was over

Jacques always said he had to see the owners, the Solomons, about something, and he would go to the private club in the Arena. They would invite him to stay and eat with them, so Jacques would sit with the owners and have a steak dinner, on the house, while the rest of the guys were out somewhere paying for theirs.

When I was a rookie we trained in New Brunswick. After practice a few of the boys would go to the pub and Jacques would join them. Bob Plager would order beer for everybody and then they'd go around the table and each guy would pay when it was his turn. Plante would always get up and leave just before they got to him. Then the guys caught on. The next time Plager put his money on the table and told the waitress he was ordering a round he said, "And while you're at it, bring us another round right now." He pointed at Jacques and he said, "And that guy over there will pay for it."

That same year we were in Ontario playing exhibition games and my dad came to watch. He asked Jacques how things were going with me, this and that, and Jacques said, "He's doing fine but the first thing he has to learn is how to travel." I've given that advice to some young players and they pooh-poohed it. But it's so true. If you can't put up with a bad travel schedule, loss of sleep, the whole thing, you won't last as a hockey player. You've got to perform no matter what, and you've got to learn how to travel.

There was so much done in those days that seems to be missing from hockey today. I was watching a Kings game the other night [*Edwards lives in Los Angeles*], and a goal was scored on them when a defenceman skated right in front of his goaltender. The goalie had lost sight of the puck and it was his own man's fault. But nothing happened. The defence-man skated away and the goalie just stood there. Don't players talk to each other any more?

In one of my early years with the Blues I played an exhibition game against Montreal and we tied, 3–3. In the first period a shot came through and I went to catch it and missed. It hit my pads and rebounded and somebody pounced on it and scored. I got chewed out royally by Bob Plager, like, "You're supposed to catch a shot like that. I had my man and you have to control the puck. That's what Hall would have done. You made me look bad." He was expecting me to play the shot the way Glenn Hall would have played it and so he was doing his job accordingly. What Plager did to me used to happen all the time.

Things didn't work out in St. Louis but I got a good chance in L.A. Early in my first year there they traded for Rogie Vachon, who had been a big name in Montreal but lost his job to Ken Dryden. I knew I was going to be the back-up but Rogie broke his kneecap and I ended up playing most of the games.

When Rogie joined us we were in Boston. I played that night and we scored the first goal. Then they scored the next eleven and we got beat, 11–2. As I went into the third period, they had four guys looking for a hat-trick and we got completely demolished. The next day there was a nice comment in the paper from Eddie Johnston, who had played goal for Boston. He said that I shouldn't be blamed for the final score, that I had actually played a pretty good game and stopped a lot of shots.

A few weeks later Rogie fractured his knee. They brought up Billy Smith, who stayed with the Kings for a little while and then went to the Islanders and played there forever. But I was playing most of the games and we went back into Boston, where I had lost 11–2 just two months before, and I beat them 2–0. When the game ended my guys started to crowd around me and suddenly who do I see coming through the pile to congratulate me? Eddie Johnston, who had said those nice things about me after the eleven goals two months earlier.

Nowadays they sometimes protect the goalies. They yank them so their egos won't get hurt. In those days they said, leave the kid in. Let him get run over and then put him back the next day. Then we'll see what he's made of, what kind of a heart he's got. I think that shutout in Boston was kind of a turning point in my career. I had taken it on the chin in the Boston Garden and the next time I went back there, I didn't fold. That was definitely a high point in my career.

Bob Pulford was coaching the Kings and because of him they traded for Bob Nevin, who had played with Pulford in Toronto. Nevin's been with us about a week and we go into Toronto and they are stoning us. One paper had them getting 29 shots in the second period and another paper had it as 32. We lost, 6–2, and after the game on *Hockey Night in Canada* Foster Hewitt said they normally didn't give a star to a goalie who let in six but he gave one to me. Anyway, we're in the dressing room after that second period when they had about 30 shots on me and Nevin says, "You know, guys, I'm pretty new on this team and I can see where your strategy is pretty good. I like the way we're staying out of the other end of the rink so the fog can build up around their net. Maybe in the next period we should try shooting some long ones through the fog. We might catch their goalie off-guard."

Another time we played the Bruins in L.A. and we beat them. Late in the game the play ended right in front of me, and Phil Esposito looked at one of our defencemen, Terry Harper, took his stick in his hands like he's gonna cross-check him, and said, "Here, you might as well take the damn thing because you've been hanging onto it all night." And Harp looked at him and said, "Thanks, Phil. But I don't want it because you haven't autographed it for me."

As for those two famous goals I talk about – famous to me,

that is – Lafleur's first and Orr's last, I remember them pretty
well. Lafleur's was in Los Angeles. I had stopped a shot with
my blocker and it went high into the air. It's dark in that
building. Next time you're in the L.A. Forum take a look. I
looked up and didn't see it. I turned around to see if it was
dropping behind me but it wasn't there and by the time I got
back into position he had picked it up and scored. It was like
an empty-netter for him.

Orr's last goal was in Chicago. It was in the second period
and it was a bit of a screen shot. He was in the slot and he
took a chop at the puck and it went over my left shoulder and
into the net under the bar.

There was another one, too, now that I think of it. The
first time Gretzky scored 50 he got the 50th on me. I was
with Minnesota and the game was in Edmonton. He was
standing about two feet in front of me, the puck came to
the front of the net from somewhere and he put it through
my legs.

I did a lot of travelling in my day, that's for sure. There
were times when they'd tell me I was being traded, or had
been picked up in a draft, or loaned to another team, when I
was obviously upset. But deep down you know it's part of the
business and you try your best to keep going. You have to
take the attitude that if you can't play for one team then there
must be another team that thinks you can be useful to it. I
always felt that it was my responsibility to do the best I could
to get back on the ice. If it meant playing a lot of road games
for L.A. while Rogie played most of the home games, then
that's the way it was. The guys used to joke about me being
the "road goalie." We missed the Vezina by three goals [in
1974–75].

I was never with one of the best teams, but what happens
happens. I never tried to make a big deal out of it. Looking
back and considering what people go through to play sports

and what they accomplish, I realize I was very fortunate. The people I played for gave me respect. I was always on the outside looking in when it came to playing for championship teams but I lasted fourteen years and I did okay.

If timing is everything, Gilles Meloche didn't get many breaks. Meloche moved around amongst five NHL teams, and there were two times when the whole team moved with him. His was not a case of a player who arrived at the right place at the right time. Others were luckier. In 1955 a nineteen-year-old forward named Henri Richard jumped right from junior hockey to the Montreal Canadiens and was on a Stanley Cup winner in his first five NHL seasons. Ken Dryden arrived in Montreal near the end of the 1970–71 schedule when the Canadiens were looking for goaltending help, played six regular season games, 20 playoff games, and in the space of two months found himself on a Stanley Cup winner and the MVP of the playoffs.

When a highly regarded junior goaltender, Gilles Meloche, was drafted by the Chicago Blackhawks in 1970, the timing was all wrong for him. A year earlier the Blackhawks had made a deal with Montreal for another goalie. His name was Tony Esposito and all he did in his first season in Chicago, 1969–70, was record 15 shutouts. With the Chicago goal-tending situation in good hands a promising youngster like Meloche was obviously trade bait. So while Tony O back-stopped a contending team in Chicago for the next several seasons, Meloche spent most of his working life with losers.

Meloche played in over 800 league and playoff games in the NHL. Talk to his contemporaries and they all agree that he was a heck of a goaltender saddled with a heck of a lot of bad teams. In the early 1970s he was playing for the not-very-mighty California Golden Seals. One night during that time I was in the visitor's broadcast booth in the Oakland Coliseum, home of the Goldens, when they were playing the Montreal Canadiens. The occasion was memorable because late in the third period Meloche became the only goalie I have ever seen receive a standing ovation after he gave up a goal.

Montreal was completely in control. It was one of those times when the Zamboni driver didn't need to resurface the ice in the Canadiens' zone because the play was rarely there. Yet, amazingly, with just a few minutes to play in the third period, California was ahead, 2–1, because Meloche had been absolutely brilliant. I wish I could remember the shot totals but the Canadiens must have had at least 50. Then, as must have happened to Meloche often with that team, his defencemen forgot to play defence at a critical moment and Yvan Cournoyer broke loose from centre ice. The Roadrunner scored, and the game was tied. A few seconds after the goal some of the fans began to applaud Meloche. What started as a mild expression of sympathy quickly picked up emotional momentum, and soon everyone in the sell-out crowd was on their feet cheering the home-team goalie for his gallant one-man stand. It sent shivers up my spine. I was hoping the Canadiens wouldn't score again. They didn't and the game ended 2–2. Meloche didn't win it, but he certainly didn't deserve to lose it.

Gilles Meloche didn't win many honours during his sixteen-year NHL career. The closest he got to the Stanley Cup was with Minnesota in 1981 when the North Stars reached the finals and lost in five games to the New York Islanders. But he is the NHL's all-time leader in one goaltending statistical category: he was scored on 2,756 times. That's not fair. A good guy like Gilles Meloche doesn't deserve that dubious honour.

GILLES MELOCHE

Even though I was a French-Canadian kid from Montreal I wasn't upset that Chicago drafted me. Glenn Hall was my idol. The first time I played goal I was about ten. I had been playing forward in an outdoor league, so the goaltender's position wasn't too popular on cold nights. One game our goalie didn't show up so I put the pads on and got a shutout. I thought it was great and pretty soon I was pretending I was Glenn Hall. When it came time for me to be drafted I was happy to go to Chicago.

In my first year of pro, I played in Flint, Michigan. I had a good training camp and the Blackhawks told me if one of their goalies was injured they would call me up. Gerry Desjardins was backing up Tony Esposito and he broke his arm. So I joined the big team and played two games. My first was in Vancouver and we won, 6–4. We went to L.A. and Tony played there, then to Oakland where I played again and we won, 5–2.

Your first game is something you never forget. When I played mine the coach, Billy Reay, never told me I was playing until after the warm-up, so I didn't have time to worry about it. The game went pretty well for me. In those days Chicago had a good team. We're talking about 1971 so it was quite a thrill just being around Mikita, Hull, Stapleton, and guys like that.

Those were the only two games I ever played for Chicago. In the next summer they made a two-goalie trade and sent Gerry Desjardins to Oakland for Gary Smith. I went to the training camp and was still with the Blackhawks when the season started. But Desjardin's arm hadn't healed and Oakland wanted to cancel the deal. Instead, Chicago took him back and sent me and a defenceman, Paul Shmyr, to Oakland.

When we were told about the trade Shmyr grabbed me in the dressing room and said, "Hurry up. Get your wife and meet me at my house. We're driving to Oakland. Don't see the manager, don't talk to anybody. Just do what I say." He'd been a pro for a couple of years and I was a rookie and I didn't know what was going on. I rushed to the hotel where my wife was and we threw everything into our suitcases and took a cab to Paul's house. The phone was ringing all the time but he never answered it. They had wanted us to fly to Oakland and play in a game the next day. But Shmyr wanted to have his car there. So we hit the road in his car and we took three days to get to Oakland. By then they had a search party looking for us. It was in all the papers and people thought we didn't want to play for Oakland because they had a bad team. They said maybe we had retired or had gone to Vegas. They never found us until we arrived. It was quite a trip.

Oakland didn't have a very good team for most of my time there, but those were good years for me because I was in my early twenties and playing 50 to 60 games a year. I just wanted to play the game. Actually, when I first got there the Seals weren't all that bad. Charlie Finley was the owner by then and when he had some contract problems with a few guys they threatened to go to the new league that was being formed, the World Hockey Association. Finley didn't believe the WHA would get off the ground so he didn't pay them what they wanted and we lost nine regulars the next year. Add up what all those players wanted extra from him and it came to about $45,000. We were flying first class everywhere, eating in the best restaurants. He was giving us money to buy clothes, throwing money around like crazy. Yet he wouldn't pay nine guys a total of $45,000 and it wrecked what was becoming a good team.

After we lost the nine guys to the WHA, playing there was

kind of a nightmare. When you're losing three games out of four, four games out of five, it's easy to lose your confidence. But I was getting great press and the fans were always with me. I just enjoyed playing the game and I was having fun so I really didn't mind my days in Oakland. I was in the NHL and that was all that mattered.

One night we were playing the Rangers in New York and we scored on the first shift, just twenty or thirty seconds into the game. There were eleven more goals scored that night and the Rangers scored all of them. 11–1, final score. When the game ended, our captain, Joey Johnston, asked the coach not to go into the room because he wanted to have a private meeting with the team. So we all troop in and Joey closes the door and he starts into a big speech. He talked about what a disgraceful game we had played, how we should be embarrassed to call ourselves professionals, and he went on like that for a minute or so. We were all sitting there with our heads down looking at the floor. Then he said, "I called this meeting because I'm confused. Who was the asshole who scored that first goal to make them so mad at us?" [Laughs]

We had some interesting coaches in Oakland. One was Vic Stasiuk. Whenever we played in Toronto or Montreal he would give us a pep talk about how the game was being seen coast to coast on *Hockey Night in Canada*. That meant friends and relatives of the players would all be watching so it was a chance for the guys to show off for them. We found out later that sometimes the games would be seen only in Toronto or Montreal, and sometimes they wouldn't be on TV at all. He knew that but he always gave us the same pep talk anyway.

Another coach we had was Fred Glover. Fred used to put full equipment on and practise with us. All we would do was warm-up the goalies and then scrimmage. That way he got to play hockey. We'd let him score two or three goals and as soon as he did the practice was over. Then he'd be pretty happy for the next couple of days. It didn't matter if we won or lost as long as he scored in practice.

The team finally folded in Oakland and they moved it to Cleveland and we were the Cleveland Barons. But nothing changed. In fact it got worse. Nobody went to the games. It didn't feel like the National Hockey League with only 5,000 or 6,000 fans in the stands. We'd go on a road trip and play in places like the Montreal Forum and the Boston Garden where the atmosphere would be just great. Then we'd go home to Cleveland and it was like being back in the minor leagues. It wasn't run like a big-league team and it was the only time I went into a team's office and asked to be traded. But they wouldn't move me.

We'd get paid every two weeks. One time we were almost a month behind in salary and they told us there wasn't enough money to meet the payroll. There was a by-law that said if a team skipped two paycheques every player became a free agent. We were supposed to play a home game against Buffalo and it had been almost a month since we'd been paid. We had a meeting that afternoon in a restaurant and, as far as we were concerned, we weren't going to play the game that night. So we sat around eating and having a few beers. All of a sudden the president of the NHL, John Ziegler, walked in the door and Alan Eagleson was with him. They told us the league was taking over and would be running the team and paying the players. So we played that night, but the Sabres were obviously in better shape to play than we were. They beat us, 9–0, right in our own building.

Things finally ended in Cleveland and they merged the team with the Minnesota North Stars. So we moved to Minnesota and, for me, it was the best time in my career. The North Stars had finished in last place overall the year before and they ended up picking Bobby Smith, Steve Payne, and Craig Hartsburg in one draft. My first year there we missed the playoffs by three or four points but we made them the next six years and they were great years.

We beat the Montreal Canadiens in 1980, the year they were going for their fifth straight Stanley Cup. We beat them in the seventh game right in the Forum. They always said about me, you're a good goalie but you've never played with a lot of pressure in the playoffs. So we came into the Montreal Forum and I remember the first game when I shut them out, 3–0. Those years you played two games in two nights and the next night we beat them, 4–1. I was in seventh heaven. We went back to Minnesota and they won the next two and then they beat us again in the fifth game in Montreal. So we were down, 3–2, and went back to Minnesota and beat them, 5–2. Then there was a great seventh game in Montreal. We won it, 3–2, when Al MacAdam scored the winner on Denis Herron with about two minutes left in the game. That was the greatest thrill of my career. [*Meloche's goaltending in that series rates among the best I have ever seen in the playoffs.*]

We lost to Philadelphia in the semi-finals, but the next year we made it to the finals against the Islanders. They had a powerhouse. You know, you get into a series where you don't think you have too much of a chance to win and that's bad because the mental edge has something to do with it. We weren't really in the series but it was still a thrill. I remember losing on the Island and seeing the Stanley Cup on the ice. You know then why it's something everybody dreams about.

I played out my option in Minnesota. My last year there was '84–85. I couldn't get along with Lou Nanne when it came to my next contract, so after the playoffs I got traded to Edmonton. I talked with Glen Sather but I couldn't get along on the contract with him either. So I stayed in

Minnesota and forced Sather to trade me. I went to Montreal that summer and spoke to Serge Savard. They were looking for a goalie because Doug Soetaert was looking elsewhere. I had visions of finishing my career back home and playing in the Forum. But Soetaert decided to stay. The Canadiens also thought they had a pretty good young goalie coming up, and they were right, because it was Patrick Roy.

Finally Sather made a deal with Pittsburgh and I was there the last three years of my career. They weren't bad years but the divisional alignment wasn't really fair. We had over 70 points for three straight years and in one of those years we had over 80, but we never made the playoffs. Eddie Johnston was the G.M. and Mario Lemieux was just starting out, so they were building a pretty good team.

I had never seen Mario play as a junior, and in my last year in Minnesota, which was his rookie year, he had played just one game against us. When I started practising with him I was just amazed. I didn't believe anybody could be that good. I played against Gretzky for ten years and I played with him in Europe in the world championships. I played against Lafleur and Bobby Hull, but no one I've seen has individual talent like Mario has. Everything comes so easy for him. Whatever he wants to do, it works.

When my contract was over I was supposed to have a deal with the Penguins to stay as a goalie coach. But over the summer management changed. Tony Esposito came in and brought his own crew. So I just sat in Pittsburgh for a year. Then Craig Patrick took over and he hired me as goalie coach and scout and I'm still working for him.

They always say goalies are different, like being a loner and things like that, but I don't think I was. Everybody I played with said I was different because I wasn't a weirdo like most of the goalies they had known. Craig Patrick told me I was the most normal goalie he ever knew. But I played with some strange ones. I played with the Cobra, Gary Simmons. He slept all day and stayed awake all night and came to the games on one of those big, high-powered Harley-Davidsons.

I remember rooming with Tony Esposito during the short time I was with Chicago. I was just twenty years old, a raw rookie, and the whole afternoon of a game he would walk back and forth in the room, sweating, saying that he hated the game and that he wished he was doing something else for a living. Then he'd get into the game that night and they couldn't put a pea past him. He couldn't stand practising, and I just loved going to practice and getting peppered with a couple of hundred shots. I loved it and he couldn't stand it. But he's one of the best goaltenders who ever played.

When it comes to the shooters I faced, well, I practised with the Blackhawks and Bobby Hull was scary. They had the big curved sticks at the time and Stan Mikita had the puck moving two feet up or down from the red line or the blueline. Dennis Hull was dangerous because he was after your head. You just never knew where his shot was going and I don't think he knew either. Reed Larsen in Detroit could pepper it pretty good too. I never played against Bobby's kid, Brett, but he can smoke it.

I always told everybody I never worked a day in my life because I couldn't wait for the next day to go to the rink, get on the ice, and practise. From the day I started to the day I ended my career I was the first guy on the ice and the last one off. As long as there was somebody left out there who wanted to shoot the puck, a kid or a veteran, I'd just stay out with them because I enjoyed it so much.

I never won a Stanley Cup and I have feelings about that, especially when I saw the thrill of the Islanders winning it against us. I was close to coming to Montreal and the Canadiens won it that year. I said, "Maybe that's just my luck. I guess I'll never see it." Then I get the job as coach and scout with Pittsburgh and we won in '91 and '92, so I have two Stanley Cup rings. It's not the same as winning it as a player, but I was on the ice with the Cup and did all the celebrating that goes with it. It came after I played, but I'm pretty fulfilled.

7

Philosopher-Goalies

JOHN DAVIDSON JOHN GARRETT
GREG MILLEN CHICO RESCH

During the 1995 Stanley Cup playoffs Hockey Night in
Canada *looked like a goaltenders' convention. John Garrett,
Greg Millen, Brian Hayward, Kelly Hrudey, and John
Davidson were front and centre with their colour comments
and analysis, either in the broadcast booth or the studio. If
goaltenders are "characters," they also are insightful when
it comes to talking about the game they play. I speak from
experience because many of the best between-periods and
post-game interviews I have done have been with goaltenders. Maybe it's the perspective they get from the crease.
Whatever the reason, a lot of them love to talk and, when
they do, they know what they're talking about.*

*Ken Dryden may, at times, be the most visible ex-goal-
tender in Canada, and the same can be said for John
Davidson in the United States. Big J.D. has moved his 6'3"
frame, with its accompanying 200-plus pounds, from the ice
into the broadcast booth to become NHL hockey's busiest*

commentator. He has parlayed his knowledge of and love for the game into a successful career in the television booth.

There is no secret to his success because John Davidson is probably the hardest-working broadcaster in hockey. When he isn't at a hockey game he's at home watching one, or two, or three a night via his satellite dish. If I happen to be in New York for a Sunday-night game, he can tell me things we said on Hockey Night in Canada *the night before. He's watched the game, live or on tape, in order to do his homework on the Canadiens for his Sunday-night broadcast from New York.*

Davidson's visibility isn't lost on the hockey establishment. Our conversations for this book took place during the NHL contract negotiations in the fall of 1994. J.D. had to postpone one of my calls when Commissioner Gary Bettman phoned him to get his views on the situation. (Naturally I expected the Commish would also be calling me but there must have been a problem getting through – I'm still waiting.) In 1992 J.D. was interviewed for the job as general manager of the Hartford Whalers. I have a feeling he may yet end up in one of hockey's executive suites.

John Davidson was in the crease for 332 NHL games through seven full seasons plus parts of three more before a series of knee and back injuries ended his career. He played his minor hockey in Calgary and in 1973, at the age of twenty, became the first goaltender to jump directly from junior hockey into the NHL.

JOHN DAVIDSON

I was a left-winger until I was fourteen but I wasn't very good. Not quick enough. Then the kid playing goal for our team got hurt and I gave it a try. I liked it right from the start and stayed there.

The first full year I played goal I ended up playing in three leagues at the same time. I played in a city midget league and for a team sponsored by the *Calgary Herald*. I was a *Herald* delivery boy. I also played for a team run by the father of one of my friends. He worked for the Burns meat-packing company and they always needed a goalie. So I played for them too. So it was kind of a saturation, a lot of ice time in one year. And having some success I stayed with it.

I worked at Safeway as a kid, making $1.91 an hour. I saved enough money to pay for half a trip to a hockey school in Nelson, British Columbia. My parents paid the other half. I took a Greyhound bus to get there. Someone told me that Glenn Hall had once taught at that school and I expected him to be there. It turned out he hadn't been there in ten years. But Seth Martin, who played with Hall in St. Louis, was there, and so was Brian Spencer, of all people.

The night I got home I found out that the Calgary Centennials junior team was having a tryout camp. I showed up there the next day, which happened to be the last day of the camp. Their coach was Scotty Munro, who was a legend in junior hockey in the West. He spotted me that last day and invited me to go to the team's training camp. I stayed with the Centennials the whole season but all I did was practise. I played about three minutes. I brought my own equipment but didn't have a chest protector and was too embarrassed to ask for one. When I was in the dressing room getting ready I'd turn around and throw my jersey on over my head and nobody ever noticed. I had quick hands so I would keep my hands in front of my chest all the time. I guess I was just too naive and too shy. More likely, I guess, too dumb. [Laughs]

After that year I became their regular goalie. One of the big moments for me in those years was when we were on a trip to Minnesota and we saw the North Stars play the Boston Bruins. That was my first chance to see an NHL game in person. Eddie Johnston played goal for Boston and Cesare Maniago for Minnesota, and did those guys ever put on a show. Boston won the game, 2–0 or 2–1, and I thought the goalies were unbelievable. The building was packed and afterwards, let me tell you, I had a few dreams about playing in the NHL.

I was drafted by St. Louis in 1973. That was the year Denis Potvin was the first pick by the Islanders. Lanny McDonald went fourth, just ahead of me. There was a pretty good first round that year with guys like Tom Lysiak, Bob Gainey, Rick Middleton, and Ian Turnbull.

My first NHL memory is from an exhibition game we played in Flint, Michigan, against the Detroit Red Wings. Their first shot on goal was a snap shot from the high slot by Marcel Dionne. I moved to stop it and I basically missed it but the puck hit the outside of my pad and went wide. I didn't have a clue how quick a shot like that could come at you. He had it, and then *zingo*, there it was. Welcome to the NHL.

During that camp the older players would play cards at night. Connie "Mad Dog" Madigan was there. He had played some games for St. Louis the year before as the NHL's oldest rookie when he was thirty-nine years old. He made so much money during those card games he left town with a new Cadillac convertible. I'll never forget it. We're all on the balcony of the hotel looking down at him and he's honking his horn and driving away in a big white Cadillac.

In my first game against the Canadiens at the Montreal Forum I stopped Henri Richard on a breakaway. He came down and he faked to my right, then went to my left, and went back again to my right. I was pretty well out of it but I came back with my stick in my blocker hand and jammed it down on the ice next to the goal post. The puck hit the shaft of my stick and stopped about an inch from the goal line. I came down so hard with my right index finger caught underneath my stick I thought I'd chopped it off. I ended up losing the nail on the finger, but I stopped him. I'll never forget that one.

That whole night was really something for me. When I was growing up I was the only Montreal fan in our family. The rest all cheered for the Maple Leafs, so we had bitter wars in our house. Saturday night was always *Hockey Night in Canada* for us. In those days the TV started a half-hour after the game did so we'd be praying for a fight or something to hold up the first period so we could see more of the game. Then, there I am playing against the Canadiens at the Forum, and it's Saturday night and you learn how the locker rooms are so close to the ice, and then they play the national anthem, and you see the way the people dress up for the hockey game, the whole build-up. It was pretty amazing.

I played almost exactly half of the games my two years in St. Louis. Wayne Stephenson was the other goalie and he was a great guy for a kid to break in with. I had a questionable second year, kind of a sophomore jinx, and they sent me down to the minors a couple of times. In retrospect I think it would have been smarter if I had spent more time in the minors. I had some early success in St. Louis, then got beat up with injuries. I didn't really understand how tough a full year in the NHL could be.

After my second year they traded me to the Rangers. Eddie Giacomin was there and that was when Emile Francis put him on waivers and Detroit picked him up. That happened very early in the season and I inherited his job. Dunc Wilson was my back-up. It was a busy year. The Rangers were in transition and I played 56 games.

That was also the year Emile lost his job. It happened about halfway through the season. We all lived out in Long Beach, off Long Island, and it was just a dreadful area in the winter. In the summer it's all beach and tourists and it's beautiful. In the winter all that is gone and there's nothing but bookies and drunks and it's so desolate. Anyway, Emile got fired so I went over to his house to say goodbye and he was in the shower. So I went home and an hour later he knocked on my door. He is such a classy guy.

John Ferguson took over. Fergie didn't like Manhattan, and in particular he didn't like the players who liked Manhattan. That's one reason he and Rod Gilbert didn't get along. They finally really got into it after Fergie had been there a couple of years and Gilbert retired. That was a real nasty scene.

Another guy Fergie had a problem with was Dunc Wilson, a real character. One night we lost to Pittsburgh at home, 6–2. Dunc was in goal and the fans were really giving it to him, calling him names and booing the hell out of him. After the sixth goal they're really letting him have it so he skates out about fifteen feet in front of the net, drops his stick, takes off his gloves, and very slowly starts to roll up his right sleeve. Then he takes his right arm, holds it up, sticks the middle finger up, and does a 360-degree pirouette giving everyone in Madison Square Garden the finger. It was hilarious.

Fergie traded him to Pittsburgh in the off-season and he played very well there. We'd be in an airport going somewhere and Fergie would be looking through the paper at the hockey results and then he'd roll it up and start bashing it around and throw it on the floor. The players would look at each other and say, "Guess Dunc had another good night in Pittsburgh."

We had a wild bunch, guys like Ron Duguay and Don Murdoch. Holy smokes! I was a western Canadian beer-drinking kid and I wasn't "one of the boys" with those guys. I never hung out in Manhattan or anything like that.

That first year with the Rangers was a tough one for me. It was a horrible transition coming from western Canada, then to St. Louis, then to New York. Calgary was a small hockey community, and while St. Louis is a big American city it was suburb-ish and the people were nice. Then I go to New York and, my God, I'd never been subjected to hockey fans like that. When you don't do well it's like they're going to cut your heart out. At a hockey game in Calgary they voice their opinions but you see how quiet it really is. Here in New York they'll blow your car up. There were a lot of kids on the team and we didn't make the playoffs a couple of years. It was tough.

I started taking the games home with me. I'd be mad at everything. As the saying goes, some nights after a game I wanted to give the dog a kick. To be honest, there were times when I asked Fergie to trade me. We had a number of run-ins, but slowly I learned to accept things. It took me about four years, but once you are able to co-exist with New Yorkers then, geez, anywhere else is boring. You've got to get back to New York.

When you do well and get to know the people, and they get to know you, they're really loyal. I found that out in 1979 when we got to the Stanley Cup finals. That was the big highlight for me. When I was a kid growing up the Yankees were winning the World Series and you'd see them on TV getting ticker-tape parades. It was kind of a fantasy land. Then we got to be part of something like that in '79 and, my goodness, I'd never seen an explosion like that. I'd get up in the morning and there would be gifts on my front doorstep. Shoes, belts, books, all kinds of things. It was absolutely amazing.

The big series that year was when we beat the Islanders. They had finished the regular season first overall but we beat them in six games. We won the last one, 2–1, and that was the first year they had great hockey in New York since the Rangers made it to the finals in 1972.

The Canadiens had won three straight Stanley Cups and they almost lost to Boston in the semis. That was the year they beat the Bruins in seven games when Grapes was caught with too many men on the ice late in the last game. I still think we could have beaten Boston, but there was no way we could beat Montreal. We won the first game and had them down, 2–0, in the second. But they came back and won four straight. They were so good, such a special team.

That playoff year was a highlight for me, but I think it was also the start of the end of my career. I played eighteen games in a very short space of time. I had damaged my knee halfway through the Islanders series and it didn't get better. I'll never forget the goal Jacques Lemaire scored on me in the last game in Montreal. He let it go from just outside the blueline. I went to drop to the ice to clear the puck into the corner and my knee just gave out. It collapsed on me.

I played 41 games the next year but by then I was pretty well banged up. It was either my knee or my back. When you have a bad knee the other leg starts to compensate for it, then your spine gets out of whack. I ended up having six knee operations and two back operations. At the end it was just painkillers and tape, and "When's my next operation?"

I played ten games one year, then one game the next, and two the year after that. I remember my last game was a win over Philadelphia, at home, 5–2. I was picked as one of the three stars. I had felt good, had worked really hard in practice. The day after that game, in practice, Walt Tkaczuk came in on me, made about four dekes, and I went with him. I felt a big *pop* in my back, and that was it for me. The end, right there. The disc had popped right out. There was no way I was going to come back.

As I look back, I don't think I ever committed myself

physically the way I should have. I think I was a good team guy, I worked hard in practice and games, but off the ice I had too much beer and too many laughs. To be a champion you've got to commit yourself off the ice as much as on it.

I realized when it was over that I had better get that part of it together if I was going to stay in the game somewhere. I found that way through television. I did one year here in New York and it worked out pretty well. I remember the first thing they had me do was interview Bill Torrey. I was holding the microphone in my right hand and it was shaking so much I must have chipped a couple of his teeth. I was a wreck. But he was a champ, and steered me right through it. Then I did some colour as third man in the booth, and some studio work between periods and after the games.

Don Wallace was the executive producer of *Hockey Night in Canada* and he got me to join the show. I was there for two years. My first game was in Toronto. I stayed at the Westbury Hotel and I swear I never slept a wink the night before. I was a basket case just thinking about it. When the game started I must have sounded pretty rough during the first ten minutes or so because the next thing I know Wallace is with us in the gondola giving me a massage on my shoulders and my neck, trying to get me to relax. During the game I took my first shot at a player when I said something derogatory about Rick Vaive. So then I didn't sleep that night either worrying about what Rick Vaive was going to say to me when he heard about it. [Laughs]

I remember working games with you in Montreal and the 1986 final between the Canadiens and Calgary. After Montreal won the last game you were in their dressing room and they sent me to interview the Flames. I had to stand outside in the hall and when Lanny McDonald came out for an interview, he was crying.

Naturally, in my job today I study the goaltenders. Habit,

I guess. It's changed. I don't think there is any fear any more because of the equipment they have. Our position was the last to be taken care of in that respect. I remember Donny Edwards used to wear pads so flimsy I wouldn't have worn them even as a kid. He used to say he wanted to feel the puck.

Here's a story for you. We played Philly in the '70s, back-to-back Friday and Saturday, and lost them both, 5–3. I had about 105 shots in the two games combined. After the second game I was walking through the medical room at the Garden and the doctor stopped me and said he wanted to see me the next day. I asked him why and he told me they had counted sixteen big bruises on my body. He wanted to do a blood test on me because when a person bruises easily he might have a blood disease. He thought I might have leukemia.

We were constantly just beat up. We used to have fear every day in practice and every night in a game that we were going to be killed.

During my chats with John Davidson I digressed to ask about another goaltender and former teammate, Gilles Gratton. When strange characters – flakes – in hockey are discussed, Gratton's name always comes up.

I had a brief encounter with him in the early 1960s on a Montreal TV show called "Montreal Minor Hockey." The twelve-year-old goalie on the team representing Ville la Salle was Gilles Gratton. Eight years later he was playing in the World Hockey Association for Ottawa. He then spent two years with the Toronto Toros, one more with the St. Louis Blues, one with the New York Rangers, and quit hockey at the age of twenty-four.

Gilles Gratton is remembered as much for what he claimed he had done in previous lives as for what he did in his current one. Like Shirley Maclaine, Gratton firmly believes in reincarnation. He tended to tell different far-out stories about his other lives to different people. He claimed to have stoned people to death in biblical times and said that being bombarded with hockey pucks as a goaltender was his punishment.

Gratton once refused to play goal because the moon was in the wrong place in the sky. He walked around the ice before and after some practices wearing nothing but his jock strap, if that, and threatened to do a complete striptease in the final minutes of the last game of his last season. When the time came and the game was nearing its conclusion, his New York teammates were urging him on as the clock ticked down, yelling at him and banging their sticks on the boards. But they were disappointed: Gratton's skates, goal pads and jock strap stayed on.

Gratton wore one of the first truly colourful masks, with a fierce-looking lion's face painted on it because he had been born a Leo. In Gratton's final season in hockey, 1976–77, he and John Davidson shared the Rangers' netminding duties almost 50–50. He is high on J.D.'s list of unforgettable characters.

JOHN DAVIDSON

We used to call him Jingle Bells. When we were living in the house in Long Beach, Jingle Bells used to walk right in without warning. He'd just walk in, drop his coat on the floor, and go right over to the piano. He could play classical piano and he had never taken a lesson in his life. And I mean heavy classical music. He could also play a twelve-string guitar. He practised it a lot.

Guys would take slap shots at him from the blueline and he'd catch them behind his back. But I swear to you, he hated to play the game. Fergie would come into the dressing room about 6:30 for a 7:30 game and he'd have a puck in his hand.

He'd throw the puck to me, which meant I'd be playing, or he'd throw it to Jingle Bells. If he threw it to me Gratton would jump up and down and start yelling, "Yeah, yeah, yeah!" and dance around the room. But if Fergie threw the puck to Gilles, he'd walk to the middle of the locker room and collapse on the floor, pretending he had fainted.

The whole team went to the Garden one day for a luncheon with all the big sponsors like Coca-Cola and American Express, big-time corporate boys who were spending a lot of money on hockey and basketball. The Knicks were there too and Marv Albert was the emcee. He had each of us come up to the microphone and answer a few questions.

Jingle Bells was there. He had another nickname too, the Count, and Marv asked him why he was called the Count. So Gratton grabbed the mike, looked at everybody, and said, "Well, I've got something to tell you. In my last life I was a Spanish count and one of the things I loved to do when I was a count in Spain was take all the commoners, line them up against a wall, and throw rocks at them." And all the big business guys are looking at each other asking, "What the hell is this guy all about?"

He was a pretty good goalie, a pretty talented player. But he was a piece of work, all right. A real piece of work.

John Garrett also traded in his goal pads for a microphone. Like Chico Resch, John is nicknamed after a popular comedian, in his case Cheech *of Cheech and Chong. A native of Trenton, Ontario, he played junior hockey in Peterborough, with a side trip to Montreal. Once he turned pro, Garrett hit the road big time, stopping off in a variety of exotic hockey locations.*

Garrett's travels began in 1971 with the Kansas City Blues. The next season he played for both the Richmond

Robins, in Virginia, and the Portland Buckaroos, in Oregon. He then spent six years in the World Hockey Association, starting with the Minnesota Fighting Saints. When they folded in the middle of his third season there he was off to play for the Toros in what was to be their final few weeks in Toronto. The next season that franchise became the Birmingham Bulls. After two years in the deep south he was traded to the New England Whalers, and finally arrived in the NHL in 1979 when that franchise became the Hartford Whalers. In December 1981 he was traded to the Quebec Nordiques, and a year later went from Quebec to Vancouver. He retired two years later, shortly after the Canucks sent him to their farm team in Fredericton.

John is still lugging his suitcase around the hockey trail in his current role as a colour commentator and analyst for Hockey Night in Canada *and sundry mid-week telecasts featuring Canadian-based teams. I have had the pleasure of sharing a broadcast booth with Cheech on many occasions. I interviewed him for this book while we were working together on the New York Rangers–New Jersey Devils playoff series in 1994.*

JOHN GARRETT

My older brother was a pretty good hockey player who was once asked to play junior A in Hamilton. He's a lawyer now in Trenton. He needed someone to shoot at and I was the designated target. I got a pair of ball-hockey pads and after a while he said, "Why don't you try out for a team as the goalie?" I was about eight or nine. It was a novice league and I liked the idea of being able to play the whole game. I think that had a lot to do with it.

As you get older the shots get harder. When you get to be twelve or thirteen, that's when you can weed out the guys who have potential to be a goalie and those who don't. When they start raising the puck and taking slap shots and you're not afraid, you can be a goalie. If you flinch when the shots get harder, then you'd better think of being a defenceman or a forward.

I didn't have a mask until I was thirteen. We used to have those little Cooper helmets, leather things that just covered your temple. Goal skates were a luxury. You wouldn't get them until you were in midget when you were about fifteen. The blockers had no fibreglass in them and you were continually breaking your fingers because they'd be pinched in between the stick and the felt-padded blocker. The catching glove was a glorified first-baseman's mitt. You'd get a first-baseman's mitt and put a cuff around it to protect your wrist and that would be your catching glove. It was designed for the baseball to go into the webbing but the puck didn't always go there and you'd be crunching the palm of your hands. And we had the old-style leather goal pads. I remember weighing my equipment one time and it was around 45 pounds and I only weighed 150.

I used to play defence in house-league games and sometimes just for a lark I'd be blocking shots. So I figured, just play goal. It's like being a pitcher or a catcher in a baseball game. You're not a fringe type. Your personality is such that you want to be the focal point, be out there the full sixty minutes. You have to be mentally and physically involved in the entire game. I think that's the main personality trait of most goaltenders.

I was in the Ontario junior-A draft and got picked by Peterborough. Roger Neilson was the coach. I was just going into grade 13 and my dad was the principal of the high school. I got offered a scholarship to Cornell where Ned Harkness was running the hockey program. Right after I was drafted by Peterborough I drove down to Cornell with my parents.

It's not far from Trenton to Ithaca. Ned met us and said, "We've got a tradition of strong goaltenders here and you're honoured to be even thought of to join our team." Typical Harkness. After about ten minutes he got up and said, "I have to go and coach the lacrosse team. I'll get somebody to show you around." That kind of bugged me.

This was in the late '60s and the Vietnam war was going on. There were protesters and black activists on campus. Somebody had just taken over the student union. The football players tried to go in and they threw acid on them. It was a completely ugly scene. This is Cornell, an Ivy League school. My mother looked at all this and said, "What are you thinking about, bringing us down here? You're not going to this school."

Cornell offered me a scholarship worth about four grand but I would have had to get a job sweeping out rooms at a fraternity to make up the balance. At the same time Roger Neilson offered me a full ride at Trent University, in Peterborough, and said he'd make sure the practices were worked around my courses. So I took a generalized course majoring in English, and they paid for it.

I had no coaching whatsoever. Practices were a complete joke for goalies then. Roger's weren't bad. He would have the guys shoot from farther out but no teams worked on things specifically to help the goalies. Nothing involving game situations like you see in some practices now. Teams are using goaltending coaches now. But it's raw talent that gets guys into the NHL. In the minors I had John Choyce in the Central League and he never talked to me. Gord Fashoway in the Western League and Larry Wilson in Richmond, same thing. I played 35 straight games for Larry and all he ever said was "You're it. Go."

The first year I played in Peterborough we played the Toronto Marlies in the playoffs. They had the best line in junior hockey, Steve Shutt, Dave Gardner, and Billy Harris, but we finished ahead of them because we had Roger Neilson as our coach. We played a tight-checking defensive style, like he has the Florida Panthers doing now, for 60 games in junior hockey and I set a record for the best goals-against average. I had it under three for the first time in about forty years in the OHA and I did it both years I played there. I'd get 30 to 35 shots a night but not many tough ones. Most came from the perimeter, no rebounds. We had Bob Gainey, Craig Ramsay, guys who became outstanding defensive forwards in the NHL. But then in the playoffs the teams with the gunners like Shutt would turn it up a notch and we didn't have anything to pick up. We didn't do anything different and they beat us.

The Montreal Junior Canadiens beat the Marlies to get into the Memorial Cup finals. Both teams had nothing but gunners and every game was 8–7 or something like that. In those days the OHA team could pick up a goalie for the finals and in 1970 they picked me up. It was their second year in the finals and the year before they had picked up Jimmy Rutherford. So I go to Montreal, and on this team there's Richard Martin, Gilbert Perreault, Ian Turnbull, Jocelyn Guevremont, just an unbelievable team.

Wayne Wood was their regular goalie. Talk about practices. It was nothing but offence and more offence. I thought I was going to be killed. They had no rules at all. Richard Martin would be teeing it up about five feet in front of you and going for the top shelf every time. Perreault and Guevremont could really shoot the puck too. It was brutal to have to stand there and take shots from those guys. No wonder Wood was shellshocked by the time the season ended.

We played Quebec and they had Gilles Meloche in goal and Guy Lafleur, a good team. In the first game of the series we were down, 5–1, at the end of the second period so the coach, Roger Bedard, comes into the room and says, "Woody, sit down. John, you're going in." So I'm in and in the third period Gilbert Perreault decides he'll take over. What a show he put on. It was like he said, okay, enough of this stuff. He just owned the puck and we beat them, 6-5. Then we beat them easily the rest of the series and I played all the games. In the next series we played Sault Ste. Marie and in one game beat them 20-2, or something. It was just a mockery. Then we played the west and beat them easily too and won the Memorial Cup.

The St. Louis Blues drafted me. I was the second goalie taken that year and when I got to their camp I had lots of company. Glenn Hall and Jacques Plante had both retired. Peter McDuffe had been the minor-league player of the year and he was going to be their guy. But they also had Ernie Wakely, Jacques Caron, Chris Worthy, and a bunch of others. They had let Scotty Bowman go, and Sid Abel had taken over. His son-in-law had played goal at Michigan State and he was there. All told there were thirteen goalies in camp.

I played in Kansas City that year and then got called up to St. Louis for the playoffs, but I just sat around. By that time Al Arbour was the coach. Abel started, then quit and gave the job to Bill McCreary and then he fired McCreary at Christmas. It was quite a mess. McDuffe and Caron were the goalies and Ernie Wakely was still there. Ernie got shafted.

I went to their camp the next fall and Abel came up to me one day and said, "I have bad news for you." I immediately thought something had happened at home but he said, "We've just traded you." Okay, fine. Who to? He told me I was going to Chicago. Tony Esposito was coming off a big year and Gary Smith was his back-up. Chicago sent me to Portland, but I didn't get to play every game which is what they wanted me to do out there. So they brought me back to Chicago, told me they didn't have a place for me yet and I went home to Trenton. But within a week I was sent to the Richmond Robins and that was a break for me because there I got to play all the time.

Chicago brought me up to be the third goalie in the 1973 playoffs so it showed they had some respect for my ability. But I had no chance to make it in Chicago with Tony there. Their coach, Billy Reay, said to me, "What are you worrying for? You'll never make it as a goalie until you're twenty-seven or twenty-eight years old." I had been drafted by the Minnesota Fighting Saints in the WHA. I was twenty-two and the WHA was offering me better money than I had in my NHL contract. So I signed with the Minnesota Fighting Saints.

I played a lot in Minnesota, but by my third year there the team was in all kinds of trouble and we started calling it the Minnesota Folding Saints. I don't think anyone can imagine what it's like to go through something like that. Your cheques are coming in regularly and all of a sudden they aren't there. We tried very hard to stay focused and we played well. We went six weeks without being paid and during that time had the best record in the league. The North Stars had a bad team and we were outdrawing them.

Harry Neale was our coach and Glen Sonmor the general manager. Some of the things that went on because we weren't being paid were hilarious. Like the dress code. They wanted us to look like a professional team but we were getting on the plane wearing jeans and running shoes. Harry would say, "Come on, you guys. You know we have fines for that." "Sure, Harry. Take it out of our next paycheque."

In the NHL when teams got in trouble, like Oakland and Cleveland and Colorado, they'd move them. In the WHA they would hang on and hang on. Like the New York Golden Blades who became the New Jersey Knights. They played at a rink in Cherry Hill that held about 3,000. There were no dressing rooms, so the visiting team had to dress in their hotel. We'd be staying at the Cherry Hill Hilton, nice hotel, nice rooms, and we'd be walking through the lobby with our equipment on and skates over our shoulders. Then we'd come back after the game and walk through the fancy lobby again still in our equipment but now it's all sweaty and smelly and some of the guys are bleeding.

But the WHA was good for me. I think I probably played as well as I did at any time in my career when I was in Birmingham. The competition got better, they started signing some good young players like Gretzky, Messier, Mike Gartner, and Michel Goulet. They had unlimited curves on the sticks and the puck would dip and dive, and that made you stay sharper as a goaltender. Don't forget, Bobby Hull was in that league. They didn't pay much attention to defence. The good defencemen were well-paid to stay in the NHL, so you had the John Arbors and the Rick Smiths, guys who would be the fifth or sixth defenceman in the NHL, and they were the first or second on WHA teams.

Gordie Howe scored his 1,000th professional goal on me. He had 999 and about ten games went by and he didn't score. He was with New England and I kept watching the summaries, and it would be no goals for him, then Howe was hurt and didn't play, then no goals again. All kinds of media were following him around waiting for him to score. We played them in Birmingham and Gordie was standing in front of the net and the pass came to him, a one-hopper, and he picked it off about three inches above the ice and nailed it. I got a picture of the play with the puck in the net behind me, and Gordie signed it, "Thanks for all the help."

We played some NHL teams like Atlanta in exhibition games, and we won a few. But our management would say, "Don't get cocky. They didn't care." I was with New England when the league folded and the NHL took in four teams. We were one of them and we made the playoffs the first year. We had a lot of experience on that team. Gordie was there, and Dave Keon and Mark Howe, Blaine Stoughton, Mike Rogers, and those guys really came through.

Here's a story for you: I'm playing for Hartford and we're in Chicago and they score on me in overtime. In the old Chicago Stadium at the end I was in you just went out the door behind the goal and down the stairs to the dressing room. The puck goes by me and I'm mad and I just want to get out of there. I spun around and started banging on the door for the guy to open it. It must have been stuck because he worked at it for a bit and then it opens. I'm really pissed off so I charge through the door, miss the first step and down I go. I'm sliding all the way down the thirteen or nineteen steps, or whatever it was, and end up lying at the bottom of the stairs. And I just started to laugh. The rest of the team starts coming down and they all have sad faces because we've just lost and I'm on the floor killing myself laughing.

The trade from Hartford to Quebec was hard to take. Larry Pleau had been on the Whalers but had to quit playing because of a blood disorder. They made him an assistant coach, then they fired the head coach, Don Blackburn, and Pleau got the job. Three games later he wanted them to get rid of the general manager, Jack Kelly, and they did, so he got his job too. Larry wanted to get rid of the guys he'd played with and give the team a whole new image. So the writing was on the wall. He traded me to Quebec in December.

There's no better place to play than Quebec. You're the only game in town and the fans eat, breathe, live and die the Nordiques twelve months a year. There's a dozen pages about it every day in the papers. We were an English-speaking family in a French city. I could read the papers and get by but my wife couldn't and our kids, who were quite young, couldn't. So that made it difficult. It was a tough off-ice experience but a good one on-ice. We had a pretty good team and one year went to the Stanley Cup semi-finals.

I didn't mind going from Quebec to Vancouver. Harry Neale was the general manager and a good friend of mine, and Roger Neilson was the coach and I had played for him in junior. When I got there I was the back-up to Richard Brodeur and played about 50 games in two years. That was tough.

The next year Harry's contract wasn't renewed. Jack Gordon took over and Tom Watt became the coach. Brodeur was getting to the end of the line and they wanted a younger goalie to be his back-up. They didn't want two thirty-three-year-olds sharing the job. They had Frank Caprice and Wendell Young coming up.

That was probably the toughest year I ever had. I don't think Tom understood what it was like for a professional athlete to go months and months without playing, without feeling like you're a part of the team. Their farm team in Fredericton had some injuries and ran out of goalies so Tom told me I had to go down there as an emergency replacement. We argued about me having to be put on waivers and finally I told him I was going home and I'd call him back in an hour. Coaches who have never played the game, like Tom, Mike Keenan, Roger Neilson, don't understand the mentality of a professional athlete, a man who has been in the game for ten years. You've got pride, a big-league mentality, and those guys just have no idea.

I went and played three games. Once I resigned myself to going there it was all right. But from the Canucks' standpoint it was like, just do it. You owe the team something. I felt like saying, "Well, what have you done for me this year?" But by then I had made up my mind to retire.

I think one of the biggest improvements for goaltenders these days is the advent of goalie coaches. They can work with a goalie who isn't playing very often to help him stay focused.

Regular coaches won't do that and the other players won't do it either. Nobody understands the position who hasn't played it. Even if you're Mario Lemieux or Wayne Gretzky, you can have games where you don't show up and your team still wins. They can have a bad game, make five brutal errors in the first period, but if the goalie or the defence plays well nobody remembers. But if the goalie makes five brutal errors the score is 5-0 for the other team. Hockey is a team game but for a goalie it's more like an individual sport.

I guess if there is one thing people might remember about my career it's the story of how I almost won the car as the MVP of the All-Star Game.

I got traded from Quebec to Vancouver on a Thursday and joined the Canucks when they played in Toronto two days later. With about three minutes left in the game Dan Daoust let a high shot go and it hit Richard Brodeur on the side of the head and broke his eardrum. We played in Pittsburgh the next night, Sunday, and the All-Star Game was on Tuesday in Long Island. Richard had been the only Canuck picked to play in the All-Star Game and they had to have a Vancouver guy in the line-up so I went in his place.

I'm on the Campbell Conference team with Gretz, Messier, Coffey, and all those Edmonton guys. Murray Bannerman was our other goalie and he started the game. I went in halfway through the second period when it was 2-1 for them. I started to make a lot of saves and it was 3-2 for us going into the third period.

They had a good start to the third period but the pucks kept hitting me and they didn't score. I had about 15 saves total up to about the six-minute mark of the third period. I knew Lanny McDonald from playing with him at the World Championships one year and he kept talking to me after I'd make a save: "Hey, Cheech, you got the tires . . . the glove compartment . . . hey, great stop. Now you've got the steering wheel." Then about the six-minute mark Gretz scores and makes it 4–2. On his next shift he scores again. 5–2. Lanny comes back to me after each goal, "Oh-oh, There go the tires . . . Oh-oh, there goes the steering wheel." The very next shift 99 scores again. Now he's got the hat-trick. And then he gets another goal on his next shift. I mean, he takes four shifts and scores four goals. Guess what. I didn't win the car.

Another former-goaltender-turned-broadcaster is Greg Millen, who spent all but a few games of his fourteen-year professional career with five different NHL teams. Millen is now an analyst for Hockey Night in Canada *and has the same job on telecasts of Ottawa Senators games.*

Greg Millen played in 663 games. His is a story with some unusual twists involving snowstorms, contract brinkmanship, and the birth of a baby. Millen ran the gamut when it came to ice time. He had years with Pittsburgh and Hartford when he was in the crease in more than 60 games. He also spent an entire season with the Chicago Blackhawks during which played exactly 58 minutes.

GREG MILLEN

I was a small kid. I'm 5'9" now but back then I was too small to play anywhere but in goal. I was with the Toronto Marlies' minor organization and was drafted by Peterborough. I played for Roger Neilson and Gary Green was the assistant coach. I was drafted in the sixth round by Pittsburgh in 1977. I went to their camp where the goalies were Dunc Wilson, Denis Herron, and Gord Laxton, who was considered the up-and-comer. They sent me to Kalamazoo in the IHL and that lasted about five days. I was in two games, played poorly, and they sent me home. At Christmas I enrolled at Guelph University. I was ready to continue my education and forget about hockey. Then, lo and behold, just after Christmas I got a call from Angelo Bumbacco, who was running the Sault Ste. Marie Greyhounds. Peterborough wanted to trade me and he asked if I would go and play a final year of junior hockey. I decided I would. Basically, that saved my whole career.

Wayne Gretzky was playing there then, and so was Craig Hartsburg. I would pass the puck to Wayne behind my net and say, "Come on, Wayne. We need one now," and he'd take off and go through the whole team. He was only sixteen years old and he was that good.

Buzz McPherson was the coach and he got fired. Angelo didn't want the job except during the games so I was running the practices because I was the over-age goalie. Finally we went to the executive and told them we were walking out. The next day they hired a coach, Paul Theriault, but we had basically quit so for a while things were reversed: They had a coach but no team.

But then we got going again and it's well documented that Theriault is the only coach who ever benched Wayne Gretzky. He benched him in the playoffs. Didn't play him very much. We ended up doing quite well but I'll always wonder how much better we would have done with Wayne taking a regular shift.

The next season I went back to the Pittsburgh camp. Dunc Wilson had retired and there was a job open. It was between me and Gord Laxton and I ended up making the team. So I never really went to the minors before starting in the NHL. The only place I had any coaching was at the Haliburton Hockey Haven. Johnny Bower, my boyhood idol, was an instructor and he taught everybody how to poke-check. They had some pro players there to shoot on us and I remember poke-checking one of them and he took a header into the boards. Everybody was laughing. You went for fun and a holiday but it turned out to be a great experience. When I got to the NHL and played against Bernie Parent, I remember I said to him during the warm-up, "You taught me how to play goal at Haliburton and now I'm here." And he said, "Thanks a lot, kid. But I'm not that old, am I?"

When I got to Pittsburgh Baz Bastien was the general manager. He's gone now but there are still plenty of Baz Bastien stories going around. I was there when he made a trade with Montreal for a minor-league player named Rod Schutt. Baz thought he had traded for Steve Shutt, who was an All-Star. When Rod Schutt arrived Baz came into the room and announced how great it was to have Steve Shutt on the Pittsburgh Penguins. They didn't even spell their names the same, and for sure they didn't play hockey the same. Rod Schutt never did make it in a serious way.

After my second or third game, we played the Red Wings at the old Detroit Olympia and they bombed us. They had us down, 5–0, after one period and I was awful. Now I'm scared to death that I'm gone because that's the way it was. Sure enough, the next day I get a call to go and see Baz in his office. He was an old-time goalie from the pre-mask days and lost an eye when he was hit by the puck. When you had a meeting in his office he was in a chair that was raised up pretty high and you would be sitting on a couch so you had to look up at him. Baz was famous for his lectures. One of our players, Steve Gatzos, used to stuff cotton in his ears whenever he went in for a lecture. Baz had all kinds of old expressions and he starts in on me, "You've got to get on the John Daly . . . you've got to grab the post on your short side because it's just like home." He started raising his voice and he grabbed the side of his chair, like it was a goal post, only he forgot that the chair was on rollers on a plastic pad. The chair started to roll and it went halfway across his office and when he tried to stop it he fell on the floor. I was just a young kid who had played two or three games in the NHL and I didn't know whether to laugh or cry. There I was sitting on the couch and the general manager's lying on the floor.

One of my favourite games was a double overtime we played in St. Louis in the playoffs in 1981. It was the fifth game in a best-of-five and it was an incredible game. The adrenalin was really flowing. Mike Crombeen hadn't played much that night and he scored the winning goal for them. I can still see the play. The puck jumped over Randy Carlyle's stick and Crombeen picked it up and, *bang*, it was in the net. We had a post-game meal and Baz comes up to me and says, "Kid, you could have been a hero tonight but you blew it." I'll never forget that either. Right in front of the whole team.

When the season was over I was a free agent subject to compensation. At the summer draft Hartford gave my agent an offer sheet and we told the Penguins about it right away. We told Baz we'd like to stay with the organization, but instead of going back to Pittsburgh, Baz went golfing. We never heard a word from them. I was at Roger Neilson's cottage near Peterborough when Larry Pleau called from Hartford. It was on a Saturday night and they wanted to do the deal, go for the compensation and hold a news conference on Monday. So we went there Sunday and signed. The next day, at the press conference, I got a call from Paul Martha, who was the president of the Penguins. He said there was a rumour I had signed with Hartford. I said, yes, because we never heard from you. He said, "What do you mean you never heard from us? We gave you an offer." But that was when Baz had gone golfing and he never told us about it. Then Martha said, "Greg, what if we offer you U.S. Steel?" I told him I'd love to have U.S. Steel but it was too late. Pittsburgh got Pat Boutette and Kevin McClelland as the compensation and I was a Hartford Whaler.

One of my favourite stories about Hartford is the time we had our first child. There was a big snowstorm and we had a game in Long Island the next night. The team went there but they let me stay behind and my wife, Ann, delivered at 2 in the morning. I was at the hospital and when it was over I couldn't get home because of the storm. So I had to sleep on a couch in the hospital, and of course I didn't get much sleep. In fact, none.

I finally got home around 8 in the morning and right away started to drive to Long Island with Bob Crocker, our assistant G.M. It's normally about a two-and-a-half-hour drive but because of the storm and all the traffic we got there about 6 o'clock. To this day I don't know how we made it. I'm going on zero sleep and of course I'm thinking I'm not gonna play. Well, sure enough, I start the game. It was tough enough in those days playing the Islanders with Mike Bossy, Bryan Trottier, and that bunch, so I'm thinking this is going to be interesting and I'm scared to death. But we end up tying the game. The next day we had an afternoon game against Toronto. I played in that one too and we won it.

The point of this story is that, for the first time in my career, I realized just how mental goaltending is and how important it is to focus. I had no business even playing that night in Long Island and yet I had one of the best games of my career. I was on a high from having our firstborn. Then I went home, saw the baby again in the morning, and played again in the afternoon. You could have counted the hours of sleep I had in those two or three days on the fingers of one hand.

From that day on I worked on changing my personality when I played. I'm a mild sort of guy and I think you have to have a bit of a mean side to play goal. A competitive side. After that I found that the older I got the harder it was to come down off this thing. I found myself walking the halls at 3 or 4 in the morning after tough games. It took a lot of energy to get me into the state I needed to be in to play goal and it took as much energy to get out of that state.

During the '84–85 season Hartford traded me to St. Louis for Mike Liut. I spent five years with the Blues and it was the best time I had with any team. At the same time things were tough and the franchise was constantly in trouble. There were times when guys didn't have sticks because the purchase orders weren't filled out. When Harry Ornest owned the team he sent us on terrible road trips, flights with four connections in one day, just to save $40 on each ticket. In '86 we went to a seventh game in Calgary to see which team would play Montreal in the finals. We lost and Harry cancelled our charter home after the game. There was a snowstorm in Calgary so the guys had to take all kinds of different commercial flights to get back home. It was just a mess.

Adversity always brings teams together. We had Barclay Plager as one of our coaches and at the end he was dying of cancer. We were almost carrying him around the airports at the end but he refused to give up his job. He was the best hockey man I ever met. He taught me so much. He had the ability to give you heck and when he walked away you felt good about it. Not many guys can do that. Then there was Dan Kelly, our broadcaster, who also died of cancer. He was very close to the team.

Jacques Demers was the coach when I first got there and Ron Caron was the G.M. and he was always fun to be around. Rick Wamsley and I were the goalies. One night after Rick got pulled Caron was so mad he ripped the phone off the wall in the press box and left a big hole in the drywall. After that any time one of us got pulled or had a bad game we said that he won the AT&T award.

I had three shutouts in a row playing in St. Louis. I was in

a groove. Most goalies thrive on attention. The more attention they get, the better they play. A momentum builds up,
not only for you but for the team around you. I've always said
a shutout isn't an individual thing, it's a team shutout.
Everybody used to say, yeah, that's a cliché, you've got to say
nice things about your teammates. But we had a checking
team and played a defensive style. Bernie Federko was my
roommate and I remember him saying that I was in a different zone. That's the word that comes up at a time like that,
zone. How you get there is a mystery.

The streak ended against Montreal when Mike Keane
scored. He shot it from the right boards early in the game so
it was over in a hurry. I hated playing Montreal. I don't know
what it was but I never had any success against the
Canadiens. Maybe it was just the intimidation of playing
Montreal. It drove me nuts my whole career. Of course I
never told anybody about it. The coaches kept playing me
because they never knew how I felt when I played Montreal.

The first two times I got traded I was in Madison Square
Garden when they told me. The first was with Hartford and
the second with St. Louis. What happened in St. Louis was,
the Blues had Curtis Joseph in the wings so they were
looking to trade me. There's a great story about the trade.
Two weeks before, we were in Quebec City and Jeff Brown
was in the doghouse there. He was skating all by himself and
I was there watching him with our coach, Brian Sutter. I said
I thought Brown was a pretty good player and if we had a
chance to get him we should. Two weeks later they got
Brown and I was gone, to Quebec City. But that was a good
trade for them. Jeff Brown's still playing in the league and
I'm here talking to you.

I didn't go to Quebec right away. It's a part of my career I
don't really want to get into. There were some promises
made in St. Louis but that's history. In Quebec there was the

unknown of the education our kids would get there, a lot of questions. But they treated me very well. Sometimes I think they are too good to their players. They try to make up for the fact that a lot of people don't want to play there. But I couldn't help that team in Quebec. It wasn't working. I wanted to finish my career with a chance to win a Stanley Cup and there was no chance there. I explained my feelings to them and suggested they try to trade me and get a couple of good kids in return. Maurice Filion was very good about it. He asked me what teams I wanted to go to and Chicago was one of them. So he made a deal with Chicago and I'll always admire him for that.

There were ten games left in the season and there I was, in Chicago, playing for Mike Keenan. With Mike, for a goalie, it's a totally new experience. There isn't a goalie in the world who wants to get pulled in a game, ever. In my career I was accustomed to playing. If I had two bad goals I would keep playing my way and maybe make ten good saves to make up for the two bad ones and maybe we would sneak a win. Well, with Mike, one bad goal or even if he didn't like the way you warmed up, you could be gone. This was very different for me, but at the same time very challenging.

We went to the final four and played Edmonton. Mark Messier stole the Cup from us that year. There was one night they say Messier might have played his greatest game. It was in Chicago and I saw him sitting with John Muckler during the morning skate. I glanced at him and I made sure I didn't look at him again, because he had that look in his eye and I thought, right away, we'd better be ready for this guy tonight. I played that game. Messier two-handed some-body right off the bat. He was on a mission. They beat us, 3–2, and he was in on all three goals. I thought we had a good chance for the Stanley Cup but Mark Messier took it away from us that night.

My next year in Chicago is an amazing story. I was never big on physical fitness but I had trained all summer long. With Mike, you had to report fit. We had a five-mile run before camp and, if you can imagine it, a goaltender came in third. Me. Then I couldn't stop a thing the first week of camp so I said I'd never do that again. We had an exhibition game in Milwaukee. I played one and a half periods, let in one goal, and felt terrific. And that was it. There was no question Ed Belfour should have been the starting goaltender. But Jacques Cloutier became the back-up and I sat in the press box all year. I didn't know how to get to any press box so I was asking directions all season on the road. I had a great seat in the organ loft for the home games in Chicago. I played 58 minutes in Minnesota. It was 3–1 for them. They weren't bad goals, but I was done. I never saw the ice again.

I went everywhere with the team, had my own room and no curfew. But I never played. It was an incredible challenge. The guys on the team were great. E.J. McGuire was an assistant coach and he kept me going. E.J. kept telling me, "Be ready, be ready, just in case." I was the third goalie so they pounded me in practice. I never could practise properly but I learned how to practise that year. Keenan never spoke to me. I didn't know exactly what the situation was other than that the other two guys played very well.

That was the year I really learned about the hockey business because I had all that time to watch and study. The biggest lesson I learned was that it doesn't matter how you play goal as long as you stop the puck. Ed Belfour doesn't have the greatest style but he stops the puck. Dominik Hasek plays tremendous hockey, and nobody thought he was going to be a success in the NHL the way he stopped the puck.

I also watched the coaches and how they motivated people. Coaches like Mike always say a team wins together. Well, you lose together too and Mike was part of that. But don't get me wrong. Mike taught me some things. One day he took the whole team to a grocery store and we're all snickering and wondering what he was doing. He had us read the labels on food boxes and packages to get us to understand what was good for us to eat and what wasn't good. I'd be 500 pounds now if I hadn't learned that from him.

The next season I spoke to Mike but there wasn't a chance there for me. Neil Smith, the Rangers' G.M., called me from New York so I became Rangers' property and they sent me to San Diego for a couple of weeks to get in shape. I was just awful down there, couldn't stop a thing. I couldn't get used to the undisciplined style of minor-league hockey. Guys were dressing in the parking lot because they didn't want to lose a minute of sun-time. I called Neil and asked him to get me out of there. So he sent me to Maine where E.J. McGuire had a team in the AHL. E.J. was great and helped me get my game back. Later on they sent me to Detroit because they wanted some insurance. I played ten games, had a 2.80 average, and felt good again about my game and myself. I thought I could keep going, but every athlete feels that way. I got a call from the Philadelphia Flyers who were looking for a third guy and part-time coach. But the money wasn't there, a commitment on my part wasn't there, and Ann was pregnant with our fourth child. Then the television opportunities came along and I thought, well, the game is trying to tell me something. So that was it.

It took me a year or two to finally get over the Chicago thing, to really get over wondering how it happened, why it happened. But things are okay now. I'm lucky because I'm still in the game. Sure, I miss the routine, miss the guys, the friendships, the life style. It's the easiest life style in the world. For all those years there were so many days when I was through work at 2 in the afternoon and had my family with me from then on. The problem is, you don't realize at the time how great that is. Now I'm into fitness. Me, a guy who hated it all the years I was a pro athlete and now I'm paying money to a fitness club to stay in shape. But I'm feeling good about myself. I love hockey. Imagine, getting paid to play a kids' game. It was great.

Glenn "Chico" Resch didn't make a career in broadcasting, but he probably could have. He was one of those athletes found in any sport who the media tend to seek out in their eternal search for a meaningful quote at the end of a game. As a journalist, you learn quickly who they are, the players who appear never to have met a microphone they didn't like. You also learn about those who wish we would all go away, and stay away.

It always helps when a mega-star is in the first category. Wayne Gretzky is almost always available. His patience with the crush of reporters covering the playoffs or an All-Star Game is amazing. Mario Lemieux is in the second category. When he's able to play Mario gives the impression he's trying to surpass Bobby Orr as hockey's least-interviewed superstar. Orr made a career of hiding from the press.

In recent years, especially in the playoffs, it has become almost obligatory for players and coaches, whether they like it or not, to meet the media after games in a designated area away from the dressing room. Lemieux tolerates it, at best. I often wonder how Orr would have handled it. I know Chico Resch would have handled it just fine.

Chico was in goal in over 600 games in the NHL from the time he broke in with the New York Islanders in 1973 until he retired from the Philadelphia Flyers in 1987 a couple of months short of his fortieth birthday. Between those two teams he played in Colorado for the Rockies, and in New Jersey when the Rockies moved and became the Devils. He was a fan favourite everywhere he played, and a media favourite too, because Chico loves to talk. No hiding for Chico. After practices and games he would sit and chat as long as we had questions to ask him. Usually his answers made more sense than our questions.

He became "Chico" because his teammates thought he bore a resemblance to the late actor Freddie Prinze, who was Chico in the TV show "Chico and the Man." Since then nobody has called him Glenn. Resch became the Islanders' number-one goaltender in the mid-1970s until the team was poised to win its first Stanley Cup in 1980. Then they gave the job to Billy Smith, a switch that so devastated Resch that he almost quit hockey.

Chico first turned up at an NHL training camp in 1971 as one of the last of a breed that has now disappeared, a player from an organization sponsored by an NHL team. He had played minor hockey in his native Regina for the Pats, who were sponsored by the Montreal Canadiens. In those days NHL teams followed the premise, "Get 'em young and train 'em." Chico Resch became a member of the Montreal Canadiens' system when he was only twelve years old.

CHICO RESCH

My age group was the last of the old sponsorship system. I had played all my minor hockey for the Regina Pats. The Canadiens had sponsored them and I had signed a card at twelve. That's how I ended up at the Montreal Forum for my first pro training camp, in 1971, the year Guy Lafleur was a rookie. The Canadiens had won the Stanley Cup the previous spring when Dryden came up so he was the hot-shot at camp. I was twenty-three and had been playing college hockey at Minnesota–Duluth. We played against Cornell in the NCAA championships when Dryden was their goalie. They beat us, 1–0, in double overtime.

They had several NHL goalies at the camp. Guys like Rogie Vachon, Phil Myre, Wayne Thomas, and Michel Plasse. Scotty Bowman was in his first year as coach there. He was wearing one of those roly-poly sweatsuits that were just coming in. I'd never seen a coach dress like that. There was quite an aura to the whole scene and it was intimidating to a rookie like me. You know, the mystique of the Montreal Canadiens and all that stuff. But it was really there, believe me.

They split the camp into four teams. You started playing scrimmage games right away and they kept track of all the stats. There were summaries printed in the papers the next day, which I found quite incredible. I was having a pretty good camp and it came to the end of the first week, Friday, and I was skating around thinking I'd soon be playing in some exhibition games against American League teams. I didn't expect to make the Canadiens but I thought I'd be staying a while longer. So I was skating around and Scotty came to me and told me to go upstairs to see Claude Ruel after the practice. Claude was Scotty's assistant and was sort of in charge of the younger players there.

When Scotty told me that, I thought for sure they were going to sign me to a contract. I remember that Rogie had the best goals-against average and I was second for the first two days of the four days of scrimmage. So I go upstairs to see Claude Ruel. He's sitting behind a big desk and starts telling me how pleased they are with my play and I'm getting even more excited. As he talks I can hear the dollar signs ringing up on the cash register. I'm starting to see myself playing for their American League team in Halifax. He's talking and I'm listening and I think it's just awesome. Then, as I'm sitting there with all these dreams going through my head he says, "You're just not ready to play pro. We're going to send you to Muskegon."

In those days I was pretty shy and quiet and, like I said, I was really intimidated by the Canadiens and the Forum. At that moment I don't know what got into me – maybe it was because of the sudden despair I was feeling – but anyway I started talking. I was rambling all over the place. I said, "Come on, Mr. Ruel, give me a chance. I'm playing well."

I kept going on like that and Claude was getting a little nervous. He finally put his hand up and says, "Glenn." I was Glenn then, not Chico. He says, "Glenn, I know this is hard for you but I wouldn't lie to you. If I'm not telling you the truth about not being ready to play pro, then may God take my one good eye."

Claude had lost an eye playing junior hockey, and there he was talking about God taking his good eye. When he said that I stopped. The guy has only one eye and you can't argue with that, right? What else could I say? I'm thinking that if I go to Muskegon for sure I won't get called up that year because, if I do, that would mean I'm ready to play pro and Claude loses his good eye. I actually ended up chuckling a few minutes later. I was wondering how many kids he used that line on.

He wanted me to leave the next morning. The Canadiens were playing Boston at the Forum the next night so I begged him to let me stay one more day so I could see the game. He said he'd think about it. He called me later and said I could stay until Sunday morning, so I got to see my first NHL game at the Montreal Forum. It was just an exhibition but Kenny Dryden and Derek Sanderson got into a fight, if you can believe that.

One thing about that camp, I really studied Rogie Vachon. For the five days I was there I watched him all the time, and when I was in the minors I kept remembering how Vachon played and I tried to do the same.

Bob Turner, who played defence for the Canadiens when they won those five straight Stanley Cups in the '50s, had been my junior coach in Regina. I hadn't really played that much and when I did I hadn't played very well. I figured I'd better get an education and so I applied to Minnesota–Duluth for a college scholarship. When Bob heard about that he tried to talk me into staying and told me he would guarantee he'd put me in the NHL. I told him he had more confidence in me than I did.

Anyway, I went to college and then I was playing in Muskegon and having a pretty good year. By then Bob was doing some scouting for the California Golden Seals and as fate would have it Bill Torrey was working for them too. Bob told him if he was looking for a long shot as a goalie he should try to get that Resch kid out of Muskegon. A couple of years later Bill was the general manager of the Islanders and made a trade with Montreal. I was a throw-in and that's how I ended up on Long Island. It was really because of Bob Turner and I'll always appreciate what he did for me.

My first full year with them, my rookie year, was 1974–75 and it was incredible. Until then Turk Broda had been the only goalie to bring a team from three games down in the playoffs and win the series. Now that's one of my claims to fame because that's what happened to me in my rookie year. It was the Islanders' third year in the league and the first time they had made the playoffs. First we played the Rangers in a best-of-three and beat them, and that was a massive upset. That's what really started the rivalry between those two teams. Then we played Pittsburgh and lost the first three games. Billy Smith was the other goalie and we both played early in the series. But I played the last five games and I was there all the time for the comeback. We won the last game,

1–0, right in Pittsburgh. Then we played Philadelphia in the semi-finals. They were the champions, the Broad Street Bullies and all that, and of course they had Bernie Parent in goal and he was awesome in the playoffs. They beat us the first three games. In the third game they beat us 1–0 and we only had thirteen shots on goal. They completely shut us down. Then we started another comeback and, wouldn't you know it, we won three in a row.

I was playing in the seventh game, in Philly, and when it started an awful thing happened. They scored on the first shift. Gary Dornhoefer shot one that was just about ankle-high. I couldn't reach the puck with my glove and it hit my stick and caromed up into the net. There was a chip in the blade of my stick where the puck hit it. You should never let anything like that happen right at the start of a game and we never recovered. They beat us, 4–1, with an empty-net goal. But we were that close to getting to the Stanley Cup finals.

The Islanders got a lot better as the years went on but we kept coming up short in the playoffs. In 1978 Toronto beat us out in seven games when Lanny McDonald scored the winner on me in overtime. That really propelled his career. But at that time I felt things were really starting to roll for me.

The next year was when we finished first overall but lost to the Rangers in the playoffs. Our coach, Al Arbour, had a theory that whoever was hot at the end of the season got to start in the playoffs. That year Billy Smith and I were both playing well and in the Ranger series we alternated. In the first four games, Smitty won two and I lost two. Then Al had a talk with us and said that Smitty is playing very well and Chico you're playing okay but, you know, and I knew what he meant, that Smitty would play and I said it was all right with me. Smitty was sitting there really quiet, not saying anything and I was wondering if he has a problem. I had the feeling he didn't want to play in the game, which must sound strange to anyone who remembers Billy Smith and the way he was so competitive during all those Stanley Cup years. But I was right because later he said to me, "I'll play. But if I lose I'm not playing the next game."

We lost that game, 4–3, and now we were going back to the Garden and Smitty was saying he won't play. So we went in there and I played and we lost, 2–1, and the series was over. He should have played because in that fifth game he was awesome even though we lost. He was really our hot goaler but he wouldn't play. At the time some people said he was a loser but the next year we won the Stanley Cup and he was awesome again. That's what I tell young kids, that sometimes you can find yourself thinking like a loser but you can overcome that and start thinking like a winner. I give Smitty a lot of credit because that's what he did.

That next year, when we won the Cup, I was really hot at the end of the season. I went my last ten games undefeated and thought for sure I was going to start in the playoffs. I still remember to this day, after our last regular-season game Al said to me, "Smitty is going to start tomorrow night." I thought, what's going on? We were playing Los Angeles and we won the first game, blew them out, 8–1. I started the next game and this is the thing I hated about goaltending. I can't say that I was great and we were down, 4–2, after the first period, but all their goals were breakaways. They got two shorthanded goals. I mean, the whole team was just awful after beating them in the first game, 8–1. So I got pulled after the first period and Smitty went back in. We lost that game, 6–3, and I only played a little bit for the rest of the playoffs.

A lot of things changed in my life because of that. I actually became a Christian, a committed Christian, through that experience, because when all of that was happening I realized my life was out of control. I remember being on the bench just about in tears because I couldn't play. I couldn't say anything to the press but I was really wondering if it was the end. I couldn't see how it could go on for me. I would go home and be in tears. I just could not understand why it was that I had waited my whole life for this moment, to help my team win the Stanley Cup, and I couldn't do anything about it.

At a time like that you want to feel sorry for yourself. Instead, I learned that my hockey career and my life were not under my control. I had to be the best person I could be and if that meant being on the bench and encouraging the guys, then so be it. It was one of the toughest experiences of my life. To be candid with you, there was more to it than the hockey situation because at the time my marriage wasn't going well. All of it was piling up on me. Now as I look back I think of my faith and how my perspective on life changed, and the fact that we won the Stanley Cup. I can say the Cup was part of it because even though I wasn't a big part of that playoff year it was tremendously exciting. Many good things came out of what I thought was a tragedy. It was actually the greatest spring of my life, although it didn't seem like it at the time. In the final analysis, I didn't give up on myself.

Late in the following season, 1980–81, the Islanders traded Resch to the Colorado Rockies. After one more year in Denver the Rockies' franchise moved east and became the New Jersey Devils. Resch certainly wasn't spending much time on the bench in those days. He played 65 games in his one full season with the Rockies, and 61 his first year as a Devil. He was with the Devils for another two and a half seasons, and spent another one and a half with the Philadelphia Flyers before retiring.

Resch's swan song was as the back-up to Ron Hextall with the Philadelphia team that reached the 1987 Stanley Cup final before losing in a dramatic seventh game to the Edmonton Oilers. The Flyers had defeated Montreal in six games in the semi-finals.

Game six was played in Montreal. In those days two Canadiens, Claude Lemieux and Shayne Corson, would stay on the ice after the pre-game warm-up and shoot pucks into the empty net the opposition would be defending when the game began. The Flyers didn't like that. In Philadelphia they had turned the net around. That night in Montreal they did more than that and, with friendly, mild-mannered Chico Resch playing a key role, the two teams staged a pier-six brawl before the Zamboni had even cleaned the ice after the warm-up.

CHICO RESCH

Athletes are the most superstitious people in the world. For a lot of guys what they do before a game is very important and Claude Lemieux liked to score into the empty net. The game before we thought we'd beat them in Philly and clinch the series. Before that game we turned the net around on him, but he went down and put the puck in anyway. Then in the game itself the Canadiens beat us and Lemieux scored a goal. That whole thing got to be such a big deal that when he'd come in after the warm-up the Canadiens would ask Lemieux, "Did you score?" and our guys would ask the last guys to come in, "Did you stop him?" People ask, "What's the big deal?" but you have to understand how athletes feel about things like that to catch the mood of what happened that night in Montreal.

Before the game the coaches told us, "You know how this guy Lemieux likes to score into the empty net and the other night he scored in the game and they beat us. So tonight, do whatever you have to do to stop him."

Ed Hospodar and I were the ones who got caught up in trying to stop him. Ed didn't play much and I was the back-up so that was like our contribution to the game. The mistake we made was not staying on the ice when the warm-up was over. Lemieux and Corson left but we knew they were coming back. They had a lookout to tell them when to come back. If we'd been standing by the net they would have seen us and would have gone back in. We made the mistake of going to our bench. When Corson and Lemieux came back out they saw our net was open so they jumped over the boards and raced to the net and Lemieux had a puck. I came back on the ice but I wasn't gonna jump those guys or anything so I did what we do in practice sometimes to stop a guy who has an open net: I threw my stick to try to knock the puck away from him. I was still in the mood that it was just fooling around.

Hospodar took a different approach and he charged at Lemieux and jumped him and started pounding him on the back. I skated over and yelled at him, "Ed, what are you doing?" And Lemieux looked up and he says, "Yeah Ed, what are you doing?" But by then the word had reached the dressing rooms about what was happening so here were all the other guys pouring out onto the ice. Some even came running out in their bare feet and it turned into one of the biggest brawls I'd ever seen.

Afterwards, guys on my team would say to me, "I can't believe you, of all people, would help start something like that." Hey, I didn't mean to start a major brawl. It wasn't like that was what was planned. Everything that could go wrong went wrong leading up to it and I must say that when it was over, I was embarrassed.

Chico Resch has stayed in hockey since his retirement. He had a brief stint as coach of the Tri-Cities team in the Western Junior League, and has served as a goaltender coach and consultant with two NHL teams, first the Minnesota North Stars and currently the Ottawa Senators. He still loves to talk about goaltenders and goaltending.

CHICO RESCH

Goalies are different, no question about it. It takes a special kind of guy to go through what a goalie goes through prac- tice after practice, game after game. It's an individual posi- tion where no one really has any empathy for you, even the guy you're sharing the job with. Smitty and I got along great. When the other guy is not playing well and you are and you're getting the starts, you might feel for him because he's strug- gling. But the reality of it is you're playing great, you're playing the games, and you're going to do everything you can to stay in there as long as you can.

You're really playing an individual game as opposed to the other guys. What do they analyze most on TV? The goals. How many times do you see a highlight package on the news that shows great saves? It's always the goals going in on the goalie. It's the one position where there is no let-up, even in practice. Maybe in the past players like Gump Worsley and Smitty didn't practise all that hard. That's changed. Today there's no horsing around. A goalie has to pull his mask down and get his head into it or he'll get nothing out of it except aggravation. Maybe that's why a former goalie like Ken Dryden and a few others don't put on the pads with the old- timers. You're always struggling to get goalies for those games because it isn't much fun. The guys had too much of it when they were playing.

When I scout now I look at how a kid reacts under

pressure, severe pressure with the game on the line. How does he react after a quick goal to start a big game, or after giving up a bad goal? Does he break down and self-destruct?

Great goalies all have one thing in common. Under pressure the puck doesn't go through them. Under pressure they continue to play up to their standards. Nine out of ten times the good goalies are going to make the shooter beat them with a good move or a good shot. They say Patrick Roy goes down in the butterfly all the time and it's true. He's giving you a few inches at the top of the net and he's saying you can beat me up there, but under pressure that's a tough shot. You'll never score on him through the five hole or under his arm. Ken Dryden may have given up some bad goals but, when you think back, when he did give up a bad one they never got a second. Grant Fuhr was like that too. The great ones don't self-destruct. They stay focused and in control of their game and their emotions. That's as simple as it gets, but getting that across to goalies is a tough thing.

When I became an NHLer I realized the perception I had of the glitz and the glamour was wrong. It wasn't what I had imagined and at times I almost wished I hadn't made it. But when you retire and look back on the people you got to know, the tough times you overcame, and the highs you experienced, you can look back with great satisfaction.

8

Goalie Coaches

STEVE WEEKS RICK WAMSLEY
BOB FROESE PHIL MYRE

When you talk to the men who played goal in the National Hockey League before the 1980s there is a recurring theme: "I never had a goalie coach." That applies to many of the all-time greatest, people like Sawchuk, Worsley, Hall, Bower, Esposito, Dryden. They were all self-taught – their coaches didn't help them at all. I remember as a youngster being shocked when my father, who coached in the NHL for twenty-six years, told me he didn't know the first thing about coaching a goaltender. I thought he, of all people, knew everything about hockey.

Those days are gone. Today it is rare for an NHL team not to have a goalie coach or consultant on its payroll. When they are not working with the big team, these coaches are travelling through their team's minor-league system working with the youngsters in the organization. It is a trend that has allowed many who spent countless nights in the crease to remain in the game. Others who never played in the NHL, like

François Allaire, who has been Patrick Roy's coach for many years, become coaches through intense study of the position. In another area, the growth of summer hockey schools has included many devoted exclusively to goaltending.

One old-timer who did try to teach his goalies a thing or two was Eddie Shore, the greatest defenceman of the 1930s, who became the long-time autocratic and controversial owner, manager, and coach of the American League team in Springfield. Jacques Caron, a professional goalie for nineteen years and now the goalie coach for the New Jersey Devils, spent seven seasons playing for Shore.

"We had to play his style, or not play at all," recalls Caron. "He didn't want me going down on the ice or doing the splits to make a save, so he tied my knees together in practice. Then he made me do what we used to call a chop-chop drill, doing little steps back and forth across the crease so I would get in the habit of being square to the shooter. I'm a tall guy with long legs, so that was tough. If he thought you were roaming out of your net, getting caught out of position, he'd tie you up to the crossbar with a rope so you couldn't go much further than the edge of your crease. If he thought you were getting too deep in your crease he would put a steel bar across the net between the two posts. Eddie Shore taught me a lot but I think he changed my natural talents. I would never do that to my goaltenders."

Caron had a disappointing taste of "non-coaching" when he played junior for the Toronto Marlboroughs. The legendary Maple Leaf goaltender Turk Broda was the coach. "I was all excited about playing for Broda," says Caron. "I thought it would be a chance to learn from one of the greats. Instead, all he ever said to me was, 'Watch the puck like you're a cat watching a mouse. Whatever way the puck goes, you grab it.' I was hoping to learn a lot more but that's all he ever said to me."

Goalie coaches are considered important not only because of their knowledge of the technical side of the position. They also work on the mental aspect, getting their charges into the right frame of mind to prepare for future games, and providing solace after bad ones. That's another thing the older goalies will tell you: they never had anybody to talk to. Today's goalies have the benefit of someone who will share their troubles.

Steve Weeks, an outstanding goaltender in college hockey with Northern Michigan University, played ten seasons in the NHL with four different teams. He seemed to be jinxed by goalies waiting in the wings. When he was with the New York Rangers John Vanbiesbrouck was on his way up. He was settling in with Hartford when they traded for Mike Liut. When he arrived in Vancouver Kirk McLean was ready to become a regular. A native of Toronto, Weeks is now the goaltending coach for the Hartford Whalers.

STEVE WEEKS

The first time I was in a meeting with a hockey team was when I was six or seven years old. It was with a house-league team and we were there to find out who was going to play what position. My father was sitting beside me. The coach came in and said, "Okay, who wants to be the goaltender?" Nobody put up their hand and everybody's looking around, so finally I put up my hand and said, "I do." My father looked at me and said, "Are you sure?" I told him I was. That was the first time I played organized hockey and from that day on I never left the position.

I played minor hockey in the Marlies' organization and had a cup of coffee with their A team for about twenty games when I was seventeen. I heard about a college program opening up at Northern Michigan. I talked to the coach and it sounded pretty interesting, a chance to get an education. I didn't know if I would make major A the next year so I decided to go to Northern Michigan. After my second year there I was home in the summer and I got a call from the New York Rangers telling me they had drafted me in the eleventh round. I thought that was great, something I could tell my grandkids, that I had been drafted by an NHL team.

Up to then I had never figured on a career as a pro goaltender. Maybe it was a dream, but not a practical one. Then in my senior year it started to become more of a reality. I was thinking, hey, I might get a contract. That fourth year we lost in the NCAA finals to North Dakota. They were ranked number one and we were number two. That was a great year. Looking back, if I had played major A I would have been done after two years and that would have been it. I would have ended up paying to go to university somewhere.

I went to the Rangers' camp the year I graduated, 1980. I had an awful camp and they sent me to New Haven. Near the end of the season, at the trading deadline, the Rangers brought me up. I hadn't been playing outstanding but, after practice one day in New Haven, Rod Gilbert, who was one of our coaches, called me in and said, "They want you in Quebec City for the game there tonight." I was shocked. He told me I had to grab my stuff, go to New York and fly out of La Guardia to Montreal. So I do that and there's a limo waiting to take me to Quebec City. The driver had to stop for gas and then he got kinda lost trying to find the rink. We finally got there and I end up running through the lobby with my goalie sticks in one hand and my equipment bag over my shoulder and I can hear the national anthem being sung.

I put on my equipment and when I got to the bench they told me to go to the scorer's table at the penalty box and have them put my name on the game sheet. By now it's halfway through the first period. So I start watching and, wow, you know, this is a lot faster than anything I had seen before. After the game we got on a charter plane and went right back to New York. I was up for the rest of that season. I played in one game in the regular season and a part of one in the play-offs. We beat L.A. and St. Louis in the first two rounds, then lost to the Islanders. Steve Baker was our number-one goalie.

The one game I played was against the Islanders and of course there was the big rivalry between the two teams. I'll tell you, I couldn't sleep a wink the night before. I went out to a movie in the evening but all I could do was think about the game. I was so nervous. We ended up losing, 2–1, on the Island, but it was pretty exciting for me. I got in one period in the series against L.A. and that was exciting too. Just seeing the calibre of play, the excitement, the playoff atmosphere. You're just going, wow, this is where I want to be.

I played 49 games the next year and it was kind of funny. We had a lot of goaltenders. J.D. was there but he was hurt and only played one game. Wayne Thomas retired, Doug Soetaert got traded, and Steve Baker pulled a hamstring or a groin badly two or three games into the season. I just had to stay healthy and I did. I played a lot and things worked out pretty well.

I was with the Rangers the first time I played against Wayne Gretzky. The first chance he had to score against me he was cruising just above the crease when the pass came to him. You were always wondering where he was and I knew he was there that time. I get to the top of the crease and I figure I can't be in a better position. This is where I want to be and, if you ask me, I've got him. So I'm at the top of the crease, he's got the puck, and I'm watching. He stops and then puts the shot right off the crossbar. It hits the bottom of the bar and comes down about three inches behind the goal line. I just went, wow! There's nothing more I can do. Talk about instant respect.

I was with New York a couple more years but was mainly the back-up. Glen Hanlon came there and Vanbiesbrouck was their guy for the future. They traded me to Hartford and that was great. Greg Millen was there, but shortly after I got there he was traded for Mike Liut. When I went from there to Vancouver Kirk McLean was being groomed for the future and better things.

My philosophy was always that no matter how many games I played I just played as well as I could for those games. I think I had the reputation of being able to come in when called on whether I had been off two or three weeks, or whatever. I prided myself in being ready to do that.

It was always interesting playing against the guys I used to play with. One time I was in Hartford playing for Vancouver. Ray Ferraro got a breakaway on me about fifteen seconds into the game. We always used to have fun with each other in practice when I was his teammate on the Whalers, going one on one for bragging rights. So now we're on different teams and he's got a breakaway and he gives me a couple of dekes, this way and that way. I got all twisted up and went down and he ended up hitting me on the back, right between the numbers. I froze the puck and when they lined up for the faceoff I could hear him banging his stick on the ice and talking to himself. He looked me right in the eye and I started laughing, and then he cracks up and he starts laughing.

Working with the goalies now, one of the big differences from when I started is handling the puck. The majority of guys play the puck well. I think when Hextall started playing the puck as aggressively as he does it really brought it into focus. You have to impress on the kids the value of making the right decisions when you do that. Right now I would say

Tom Barrasso is maybe the best at that. He really makes good decisions with the puck. Kirk McLean is very good too.

Another thing I try to teach them is the importance of working your way through a bad time. There were nights when I was certainly frustrated and mad at myself when I played. If I had a bad night I'd feel I had let everybody else on the team down and embarrassed myself. But there's no sense moping. The biggest lesson you learn through experience is not to get too full of yourself when you're on top or too down on yourself when you're down.

Rick Wamsley has always been a favourite of media types covering the National Hockey League. Wamsley arrived in the league with a ready wit and an impish smile and he has lost neither. He had a ten-year goaltending career in Montreal, St. Louis, Calgary, and Toronto. In 1982, while with Montreal, he shared a Jennings Trophy with Denis Herron.

A typical example of Wamsley's humour in adversity occurred when he was playing for the Montreal Canadiens. Wamsley was hurt in a goal-mouth scramble. At that moment the members of the team's training staff were in the dressing room tending to a couple of previously injured players. The coach asked the team's equipment manager, Eddie Palchak, to go onto the ice and see what was wrong with Wamsley. When Palchak arrived the fallen goaltender looked up and said, "Eddie, what are you doing here? I don't need a new stick, I need a doctor."

After retiring in 1992 Wamsley became the Maple Leafs' goaltending coach and then became a regular assistant coach in 1994. Unlike Steve Weeks, who shyly put up his hand when his first coach asked a roomful of tykes who wanted to play goal, Rick Wamsley didn't need to be asked.

*When he was seven years old he pleaded with his coach to
let him put on his first pair of goal pads.*

RICK WAMSLEY

I grew up in Port Dover, a small town in Ontario. When I was
in grade two I played forward and got two goals in my first
game. I loved playing hockey. But for some reason I don't
understand to this day I really wanted to be a goalie. The next
year, before the first game, I waited beside the door for Mr.
Bill Barker, the coach. As soon as he walked in I begged him
to let me play goal, like, "Can I play goal, Mr. Barker? Please,
Mr. Barker, let me play goal." For fear of his own life, or just
to get rid of me, he said, "Okay, we'll try you today and see
how it works." The organization was providing the goal
equipment so all I needed was skates, socks, pants, and a
sweater. I just loved rummaging through all the old goal
equipment they had. I picked out some stuff and I've been a
goalie ever since.

I played junior in St. Catharines and Hamilton my first
two years and played my last year for the Brantford
Alexanders, arguably the second- or third-worst team in
Canada. I hurt my knee in training camp and didn't play
until Christmas. My average from then on was 5.30 or there-
abouts. I didn't have any great expectations of playing in the
NHL, but I got drafted in the third round by Montreal in 1979.
I went to their camp and played pretty well and they signed
me. I played my first two years of pro in Halifax.

In my second year I got called up and that was the real-
ization of a dream. Bunny Larocque and Richard Sévigny had
been injured at the same time. Denis Herron had played the
game before I got there and he lost when Edmonton scored
the winning goal with just two seconds left in the game.
Claude Ruel was the coach and he always changed goalies

after the goalie lost. So I was next in line and he started me December 23, 1980, in Quebec City. We ended up playing a 2–2 tie. They pulled me in the last minute and Bob Gainey scored for us with just four seconds left in the game. There was no overtime at that time. The Stastny brothers, Anton and Peter, scored for them. I've always said that if the Stastnys hadn't defected to Canada I would have got a shutout. [Laughs]

Because we tied I started the next game against Washington, in Montreal, and I was very nervous. Mike Palmateer was in goal for the Capitals. We won, 7–4, so that meant he had to play me again. We played the next night in New York and won, 5–2. So he had to play me in the next game, which was in Montreal against L.A., and we won 4–0, my first shutout. Then we went to Hartford. We were leading 1–0 in the first period when a shot from Blaine Stoughton hit me in the shoulder. The puck went up and got me in the ear. I was wearing an old-style helmet that didn't protect the ears and I had to leave the game. Bunny Larocque was back from his injury so he played the rest of the game and we won, 3–1. He was in goal when we scored our second goal so he got credit for the win. And then they sent me down. I had played in five games, had a shutout and a 1.90 average, and they sent me back to Halifax. That was like, "Welcome to the Montreal Canadiens, kid."

Truth to tell, up to that point my year in the minors hadn't been going very well. When I was called up it was understood I wasn't there to stay but my time with the big club refocused me. I went back to the minors and played well. I think of all the games my father saw me play he was the happiest about my first game back with the Voyageurs after my NHL stint. We played in Rochester, got outshot very badly, and won, 3–1. Dad wasn't a real sports guy who would sit down and discuss theories and philosophies of sports. He was more into stocks and bonds. But he was very happy that night because I showed him I wanted to get back in the NHL, that I wasn't going to sulk and pout because they had sent me back to the minors. I showed him that night and he let me know about it. He could see I was willing to work hard, pay my dues, and hopefully make it back one day.

Playing in Montreal was special. I don't think I would have wanted to start anywhere else. You are aware of the guys that have tended the net before you, from Georges Vezina to Jacques Plante to Ken Dryden. They've got their portraits in the dressing room, you see them every day. It's the tradition of the Canadiens, passing the torch. Being a hockey player and understanding what the Canadiens mean to the people of Montreal, to hockey, and to the NHL makes it a very special place to play.

When I started in Montreal they were a defensive-minded team. It was a treat to play behind a defence with Larry Robinson, Guy Lapointe, Rod Langway, and Brian Engblom. They cleared away rebounds and they cleared away bodies. It was easy for me to play behind those guys.

One of my favourite stories is from around that time. We played in Montreal and I guess I was feeling my oats because I had wandered out of my net quite a bit, into the corners, living dangerously and all that. After the game Toe Blake came into our dressing room. He was such a presence when he showed up, that old tradition thing again. He came up to me and said, "Do you mind if I ask you a question?" I said, "Of course not, Mr. Blake." Then he said, "What I want to know is, when you're in the corner with the puck, who's playing goal?" I got the message.

While he was playing for the Montreal Canadiens, Rick and his wife, Lori, suffered the tragedy of losing their infant son, Ryan.

RICK WAMSLEY

Ryan was born in April, just after we were eliminated from the playoffs. He was in the Montreal Children's Hospital the whole summer and he passed away September 19.

The easy part for me was that when Ryan was in the hospital the last few days of his life training camp was on. The Canadiens were very good about it. Bob Berry was our coach and he told me, "You do what you feel you have to do. If you want to come to practice just show up. If you're not here we'll understand." For me, playing hockey and being with the guys for two or three hours was a way for me to deal with what was going on across the street. [*The Children's Hospital is across the street from the Montreal Forum.*] On the other hand my wife, being the way she is, was there every minute, every second. So it was a lot tougher on her. Ryan was our firstborn. You know, you find out you're pregnant and it's a great day. You buy the crib, start painting the bedroom, you get all the presents. Then, the day he was born there was trouble.

Today I feel Ryan helped my career because I found out what was important to me. Early in my career I was so focused on the game. If I was playing that night I had to sit in my chair, watch my program on TV, eat at 12:30, go to bed at 2:30. I was so regimented because the game meant everything to me. Then you have a family and somebody like Ryan is taken away from you and you realize what's important. Your career is important but in the end it's your family and your friends you have left. Enjoy them while you can.

The Canadiens traded Rick Wamsley to the St. Louis Blues in the summer of 1984. On March 7, 1988, he was dealt to Calgary with Rob Ramage. In return, St. Louis received Steve Bozek and Brett Hull. Early in January 1992, Wamsley

became a Toronto Maple Leaf, along with Doug Gilmour, as
part of a history-making ten-player trade. He finished that
season in Toronto, then retired and joined the Maple Leafs'
coaching staff.

RICK WAMSLEY

When Mike Murphy moved on to the Rangers I got his job
as assistant coach in Toronto. It's a step in the right direc-
tion. I was involved in the game as a fan when I was a kid
and as a player in my early adulthood. Now I guess I'm
heading into my late adulthood and I'm a coach. Coaching
is the closest you can get to the game without being a player.
The possibilities are still exciting whether it's as an assistant or as a head coach somewhere. Who knows where
you're gonna go?

The day I was traded by the Canadiens was the day they
held the 1984 draft at the Forum. I was staining the fence in
our back yard. I had three sections done when my neighbours came over and said they'd like to go down to the draft
and I say okay. I don't really clean up. I'm wearing cut-offs
and sandals and I throw on a shirt and we drive down. About
ten minutes after I left the house the phone rang. The
Canadiens were trying to reach me to tell me I'd been traded
but I was on my way downtown.

So I walk into the Forum and it's jammed because that was
the year Mario Lemieux was going to be picked first overall.
I'm going to play tour guide and show my neighbours around
when an usher runs up to me. He's out of breath and says,
"Serge Savard wants to see you." I go, "Oh-oh." My neighbours are looking at me and I'm saying, "This isn't good,
guys." It all changed in about thirty seconds when Serge
informed me I was traded to St. Louis. I hung around until
they announced the trade. I was brought to the Blues' table.

I met the owner and the G.M., Ron Caron, put a Blues sweater on me. It was the first time the draft was televised. They interviewed me and I'm standing there in cut-offs, wearing sandals, with paint stains on my hands. They asked me how I felt and I said, "The most upsetting thing about being traded is that I just started painting my fence. I don't know whether to finish it, or leave it in case the new owners don't like the colour."

At 5:30 a.m. on Sunday, November 10, 1985, Pelle Lindbergh, the number-one goalie for the Philadelphia Flyers, left a restaurant in Voorhees, New Jersey, with two companions. They piled into Lindbergh's Porsche 930 Turbo and Lindbergh got behind the wheel. Ten minutes later the car failed to negotiate a turn in Somerdale, New Jersey, and rammed into a three-and-a-half-foot high concrete wall. The two passengers in the car escaped with minor injuries but Lindbergh suffered serious brain and spinal-cord damage. He was taken to John F. Kennedy Memorial Hospital in neighbouring Stratford where an examination determined he was brain dead. Lindbergh remained on a life-support system until his father arrived from Sweden to join his mother who was already visiting her son. After his parents authorized the removal of their son's organs for transplant purposes, one of the National Hockey League's best goaltenders was allowed to die. At the time of the accident Pelle Lindbergh had a blood-alcohol level of .24 per cent – .14 higher than the legal limit. He was twenty-six years old.

The previous season Lindbergh had been voted winner of the Vezina Trophy as the NHL's outstanding goaltender. His back-up on the Flyers was Bob Froese.

BOB FROESE

I was at church when I found out. I got a call from Dave Poulin's wife who told me that Pelle had been in an accident early that morning. I went to the hospital and the first person I saw was Dave Poulin, who was my best friend on the team. Dave was crying. He wasn't an emotional guy but he was crying and I knew instantly. Dave got into my car before I got out and said, "Pelle's dead."

A couple of hours later we all met at our practice rink. It was gut-wrenching. There is no feeling like losing part of your team. That Philadelphia team maybe wasn't the most talented but I think of all the teams I've played with, it had the closest bunch of guys. Maybe it was like in school when you have a stern schoolmaster. We had Mike Keenan and we were a very close-knit team.

Mike talked to me that day and so did Bobby Clarke, our general manager. I always had a good relationship with Clarke. Then we went out to practice and I got hit in the cup. In fact the cup was shattered. I tried to stay in the net but I was bleeding internally, although I didn't know it at the time. There was no way I wanted to bail out on the team. When I came off the ice and took my stuff off they realized something was wrong. I was back fairly soon, but I couldn't play the next night against Edmonton. Darren Jensen was brought up from the minors. It was such an emotional night. I still don't know how the guys did it, but we won.

For the balance of the 1985–86 season, Bob Froese and Darren Jensen shared the Flyers' goaltending duties. When the season was over they shared the Jennings Trophy, awarded to the goaltenders on the team with the fewest goals against. It was Froese's fourth season in the NHL and he would play four more. Darren Jensen never played another NHL game after their award-winning year.

Bob Froese, who is now the goaltending coach for the New York Islanders, is a native of St. Catharines, Ontario. He played junior A in St. Catharines, Oshawa, and Niagara Falls. Froese paid his dues on his way to the NHL by spending four years in the minor leagues before joining the Flyers at the age of twenty-four. Before that he had an unusual hurdle to overcome on his way to a career in professional hockey.

BOB FROESE

Both my parents were Mennonites and I married a Mennonite girl from back home. There was a large Mennonite population in the little area where I grew up and we weren't allowed to do anything on Sunday. Sports was definitely taboo. I forget how old I was when I finally got to play hockey on Sundays. Then when I started dating my wife, in high school, I was playing home games on Sundays and that was taboo in her family. She didn't come to the games very often. Her parents were a lot more strict than mine. But eventually she started coming to all my Sunday games and I think that my in-laws now watch hockey on Sundays.

I was drafted by the St. Louis Blues in 1978 when they were going bankrupt and couldn't afford to sign many new players. I went to their camp and had a pretty good one, but when it was over they sent me to the Saginaw Gears in the International League. In the next four years I played there, and in Milwaukee and Maine. You face a lot of rubber down there and you learn to endure when things don't go your way. I am thankful I had coaches like Don Perry, in Saginaw, and Tom McVie, in Maine. They both instilled a good work ethic in me. They appreciated guys who worked hard. I can't stress enough how important it is for young goalies to get that kind of training.

I was always determined to make the NHL. In my final year in the IHL in Saginaw I tore up my groin in the first game of the year. It was a bad one and I thought for sure I was gonna go home and be a truck driver. But I came back at Christmastime and played the rest of the games, every one of them. We ended up winning it all. We lost only one game in the playoffs.

I was with Milwaukee for a few months and that was Philly's team. The coach there was Gene Ubriaco and he suggested to the Flyers that they give me a shot. I had been let go by St. Louis so I signed with Philly. Once I got to Philadelphia I was basically a back-up. In my second year Pelle had an off year and I played close to 50 games. There's a story about that. My best friend owned a gas station and early in the season we were talking about how many games I might play. He said he thought I'd play about 50 per cent of the schedule. I told him that if I did I'd pump gas at his station for a week. So I played over half the season and I held good on my part of the bargain. I worked for a week pumping gas. I had a blast.

The following year Mike Keenan came in as coach and he had it in his mind that Pelle was gonna be the goaltender. Mike always has been good with his goalies in the sense that they perform for him. We both played well but Pelle had an outstanding year. Then the following year Pelle died early in the season. I went on to play the bulk of the games after that.

There aren't too many funny Mike Keenan stories. I wish there were but he was very militant in his attitude and we became that way on the ice. I think every team takes on its coach's personality and we became like Mike.

There is one story, though. It happened in Mike's first year. We were in Quebec in the playoffs and there was a big table in our dressing room. Mike came in and he was really mad at us and he tried to kick the table over. But the table was made out of four-by-fours and it was one heavy piece of furniture. I think he thought he'd broken his foot. We were all trying not to giggle because we respected the man. Well, I don't know if we respected him, but we sure lived in fear of him. If ever there was a time we thought we had a reason to giggle in the dressing room, that was it.

I got traded the next season on December 18. Ronnie Hextall had come up and was playing almost all the games. We had a good relationship. I went about my business, I remained a good team guy, but I wanted the opportunity to play and they knew it. So they traded me to the Rangers.

I had more fun playing for the Rangers than anywhere else. The first year I was there we were playing the Flyers in the playoffs at Madison Square Garden. Lindsay Carson had run me into the net and I knew that was a Flyers ploy. He had knocked my stick away and I was skating to the bench for an extra attacker and I saw Lindsay. I was gonna say to him, "Sucked in, eh, Lindsay?" and I guess he thought I was gonna jump on his back. So he turned around and swung. He missed me but I went into a dive. It's been on a few blooper tapes. I get to the bench and Phil Esposito, who is coaching us, is yelling "Nobody laugh! Nobody laugh!" Wayne Cashman was the assistant coach and he said to me, "Why don't you go down one more time." So I dropped again, just for effect. Then I sat on the end of the bench and our trainer, who was a little guy, is pretending he's giving me smelling salts. We were always kidding around so as he's doing this he's asking me if I liked him and would I like to marry him. So I lifted my mask up, grabbed him, and kissed him on the lips. He went ballistic and was screaming about how everyone was going to think this and that about him and the whole bench was howling.

I was with the Rangers in 1988 when Guy Lafleur came out of retirement and played for us. Michel Bergeron was our coach. The first day of training camp in Three Rivers Chris Nilan, who had played with the Flower in Montreal, told me to be careful because when he comes down his wing in practice he puts it right by the goalie's ears. We're having our first scrimmage of the camp and the arena is packed to see the Flower again. So down he comes and its the first shot of the scrimmage, the first shot. I straighten up and I've got my hands ready to go up to my ears and he slides one along the ice and it goes into the net. I'm still on my tiptoes and Nilan comes by and I say, "You didn't tell me if he did it every time or just sometimes." [Laughs]

That year didn't end well for us. That was when Espo fired Michel Bergeron just before the playoffs, with two games to go in the season. It was April 1 and we were in Pittsburgh. I remember waking up that morning, looking in the mirror, and reminding myself to keep my head up because it was April Fool's Day. Before practice Bergie came into the dressing room and started talking about getting let go and I thought he was joking. All of a sudden he started crying and I realized the guy wasn't joking. He left through one door and Espo, came in the other as the new coach. There were some guys who were close to Bergie and they felt they'd been left high and dry. There were others close to Espo so it split the team right down the middle and, boy, teams don't need that. We lost in straight games in the first round.

I finally had to retire because of my shoulder. It was hurting the last couple of years of my career. I had hurt it originally in Philly but never wanted to take myself out of the line-up. I think they appreciated me in New York but I think I lost focus on my own personal job because Espo always wanted me to be a good team guy. Then along came Roger Neilson and he had me room with Mike Richter. We became very close and I think working with Mike started me towards what I'm doing now as a goalie coach.

There was one reason my wife was glad I retired. I had a few superstitions and one of them was I didn't change my underwear if I was on a winning streak. One time near the end of a season I went eleven games unbeaten and she told me more than once during that time that I should gas that superstition.

There's a real bond between goaltenders. I remember when Al MacInnis first came into the league. He shot one from centre ice that hit Mike Liut right on the head and knocked him flat. The word got around to all the guys right away: Look out for this guy. He can really shoot.

Grant Fuhr is the best goalie I've ever seen. I remember the year I was with Philly and we played Edmonton in the finals. We had four-on-one breaks on him and he still made the save. But Grant plays his best when he thinks he is the best. I think that's what happened to him in Buffalo when Hasek came along. I think he started to have doubts because the other guy was playing so well.

Through the years some goalies have had the reputation of being flaky, or whatever, but it seems that now there are fewer and fewer personalities. Take a look, there are fewer and fewer nicknames. It's more a business. We've got a goalie on our team now, Tommy Soderstrom, who likes to put on this facade of being loosey-goosey. But that's all it is, a facade, because when he gets in the net he's got to be focused and play with passion.

I think the biggest characteristic a goaltender needs is passion for the position. A guy has to enjoy it. You have to enjoy being the one who the rest of the team is looking to as their man. I hate to see a goalie who looks like he's not enjoying what he's doing. It's so obvious to me when you see a guy who is enjoying it and then you see someone who is doing it because someone else wants him to, or because he feels pressured. Worst of all, I hate seeing someone who looks like he's doing it just for the money.

Phil Myre first played for the Montreal Canadiens during the 1969–70 season when he appeared in ten games. The following season he was sharing the goaltending duties in Montreal with Rogie Vachon when the team decided to give Ken Dryden a late-season look. Dryden had been playing for the Canadiens' American League farm team, the Voyageurs, who were splitting their home games between Montreal and Halifax. After a Sunday-afternoon game in Halifax in mid-March, Dryden was told he was being called up by Montreal. When I talked to Ken for my book The Habs, *he explained: "I flew to Montreal that same day. The Canadiens had played an afternoon game in Philadelphia and my plane landed the same time theirs did. I ran into the players walking through the airport. Phil Myre looked at me and did a real double-take. I could see the expression on his face meant, 'What are you doing here!'" What Dryden was doing there was taking the first step in a process that would eventually cost both Myre and Vachon their jobs in Montreal.*

PHIL MYRE

When I turned pro after playing junior in Niagara Falls, Tony Esposito was also breaking in with the Montreal organization. Rogie and Gump Worsley were with the big team. They sent me to Houston in the Central League and I had a good year, made the All-Star team and won the league's top-goalie award. Then they moved me up to the Montreal Voyageurs in the American League. That was the year Gumper retired from the Canadiens and I ended up playing ten games behind Rogie. That really was difficult for a twenty-year-old kid, not to be playing. I needed to play. The Voyageurs had a good team and going up to the Canadiens set me back quite a bit. I should have played more in the minor leagues.

In my second year there Rogie and I pretty well split the season. Then Dryden came in and the team won the Stanley Cup and he won the Conn Smythe Trophy and you knew that was the end of Rogie. Early the next season he got traded. He always teases me and says he was the first guy to go to Sam Pollock and ask to be traded away from the Montreal Canadiens because he knew he wasn't going to play much behind Dryden. When they traded him to L.A. I ended up sitting on the bench playing behind Kenny.

Those were tough years for a young player. I know it set me back but at the same time it was great being with the Montreal Canadiens. I had the opportunity to play with Jean Béliveau, John Ferguson, Frank Mahovlich, Yvan Cournoyer, Jacques Lemaire, Henri Richard, all great players. I didn't get much on-ice experience, but I certainly learned a lot from those people in the dressing room. I think it made me a winner, made me realize what it takes to win. I know it helped me when I went to other organizations having played with those people.

Myre would tend goal for five more organizations in a fourteen-year career in the NHL. He left Montreal when he was drafted by the fledgling Atlanta Flames in the 1972 expansion draft. Myre spent just over six seasons with the team that introduced the NHL to the deep south of the U.S.A. From there he went to St. Louis, Philadelphia, Colorado, and Buffalo. While with the Flyers, Myre was a

key member of the team that set a league record of 35 games
without a defeat during the 1979–80 season.

PHIL MYRE

I feel proud of the time I spent in Atlanta. Dan Bouchard and
I were the two goaltenders and we never finished worse than
sixth in goals against. For six years we were the only two
goalies who ever dressed for a game when we were partners
there. We hid our injuries because we had a real good competition going. We knew if one guy had the chance to take
over the other guy might not get back for a long time. So we
both played hurt, we both played sick, but for six years
nobody else ever dressed for a game. The most one goalie
played was 47 games. We pretty well split things right down
the middle.

The first year the Flames played in Atlanta some funny
things happened. People would clap and cheer at the wrong
times. For the first few games every time Danny or I stopped
the puck when the other team tried to ice it from the other
end of the rink they would cheer. Scared the heck out of us
the first few times it happened. You'd make a save on a
routine shot from the blueline and they'd cheer. But it was
a fine city. It had a lot to offer and the weather was great. I
really felt bad when the team left there.

One of the most exciting times in my career was when I
was playing for Philadelphia and we went 35 games without
losing. We didn't have a great team but we felt good about
each other and we won together. The Flyers' team record
before that was 22 or 23 without a loss, and when we beat
that we were excited. But we didn't think we'd beat
Montreal's NHL record which was 28. But then, there we
were, and we played in Pittsburgh in the game that would tie
the record. Greg Millen was in goal for them and he almost

beat us singlehanded. They were ahead of us late in the game and then Behn Wilson went end to end and scored for us and we got out of it with a tie and we had tied the record.

Then we went into Boston and our coach, Pat Quinn, told me I would play. The Flyers hadn't won in Boston in five years. It was just before Christmas and we won the game, 5–2. To me, it was the highlight of my career. It meant a lot to play in that game. There was no way they were going to beat us. That year Pat played me in a lot of pressure games, tough games on the road. Pete Peeters was my partner. Pete was a first-year man so in many cases I was getting a lot of the tougher games. I liked that kind of pressure.

I think goaltenders are better today. There are a lot more kinds of shots today. The one-timer didn't exist twenty years ago. The shots are stronger. But the goalies have better equipment. In practice now the other guys shoot at the goalies' heads because the equipment is better. Before, they used to take it easy. We used to have about a half-inch piece of felt on our shoulders and arms. So there used to be a lot more physical awareness of getting hit. I go out now with the team I work for, Chicago, wearing today's equipment and when I take a shot on the arm or the shoulder it doesn't hurt. I think that's a major difference.

We had to deal with getting hurt a lot more than they do now, but they have to live with a lot more different situations and tougher practices. I think most goaltenders are better athletes than they used to be. If you remember guys from the old days, Bruce Gamble, Turk Broda, the Gumper, they didn't exactly look like well-conditioned athletes. It's different today. Ed Belfour may be the best-conditioned athlete on the Chicago Blackhawks.

I'm very interested in coaching and I run goaltending schools for kids. I don't run a regimented school. I want the kids to have fun. Parents come in and ask me if I think their ten-year-old son has a chance to make it as a pro. I can't tell them that. But I can tell them if he's got some ability and I tell them if he likes to play then let him play and let him have some fun. I think that's important. We try to have drills that the kids can have fun with and make them look forward to coming back the next day.

Does teaching kids help them? I think so. Look at how many good young goalies are coming into the NHL today. They seem to be learning quicker. I became a better goalie when I worked with Jacques Plante in Philadelphia, but by then I was thirty-one years old. I had never had a coach before that. Jacques's game was a game of inches. He would say, "Just be at the right place at the right time." My way of teaching today comes basically from him.

I grew up with Jacques Plante and Terry Sawchuk. Obviously, growing up in Montreal I would admire Plante. But I idolized Terry Sawchuk. Whenever I would play hockey, whether it was on an outdoor rink or on the street, I was always Terry Sawchuk. I used to go down to our basement at 6 o'clock in the morning and throw balls against the wall and when I stopped them coming back I was always Terry Sawchuk. Now, let me tell you a story.

When I was brought up by Montreal I played my first game in the NHL against the Rangers in Madison Square Garden. Terry Sawchuk was with the Rangers. He was backing up Ed Giacomin. I remember in the warm-up sneaking glances at Sawchuk. I couldn't believe I was on the ice at the same time as he was, in the same game. Giacomin played that night and we got beat, 2–0. I felt I played a pretty good game. There I was, twenty years old and playing my first game for the Montreal Canadiens, and I felt like I had played well.

In those days in New York both teams went out the same gate to get to their dressing room. When the game ended I was skating down the ice to go out the gate and I see Terry

Sawchuk standing there. I didn't realize it right away but he was waiting for me. I had never talked to Terry Sawchuk and he didn't know he had been my idol. So he waited for me and when I got to the gate he patted me on the ass with his stick and said, "Good game, kid. Keep playing that way and you'll be a helluva player." I couldn't believe it. It was one of the greatest moments of my life and it was so motivating for me. The sad thing is, I never did get to properly meet and talk to him. He died a few months later.

I consider myself very lucky to still be in hockey. I talk about hockey every day. I've been involved in coaching now for eleven years. That's my life. Some people join the army as a career. I'm in hockey as a career guy. It's what I'm going to do for the rest of my life.

9

Shootouts in Faraway Places

BILL RANFORD   SEAN BURKE

While European forwards and defencemen have had a major impact on the NHL, the same can't be said about goal-tenders. Other than Pelle Lindbergh, Dominik Hasek, and Arturs Irbe, no Europeans have had success in the NHL. In fact, it's been a bit the other way around. At the 1981 World Championships in Helsinki, Wayne Gretzky was among the many NHL players representing Canada. They played Italy and what was supposed to have been a laffer turned into a 3–3 tie. The star of the game was the Italian goaltender, Jim Corsi, a Montrealer who had played briefly in the WHA and NHL with Quebec and Edmonton. Corsi, who stopped 53 shots in the game, spent several years playing and coaching in Italy.

Roberto Romano and Mike Zanier are former NHLers who also played goal in Italy. Daniel Bouchard spent some time with a team in Switzerland. Jacques Plante conducted goaltending schools in Europe. Vladislav Tretiak sometimes coaches for the Chicago Blackhawks, but even he hasn't been able to bring a European style to the goal creases of the NHL.

While European goalies haven't been taking jobs away from North Americans in the crease, another aspect of their game hasn't made it to the NHL: shootouts. I don't imagine goaltenders are too anxious to see that arrive either.

"Should the NHL use shootouts to decide tie games?" That question usually gets a pretty good going-over right after we've been exposed to a major international competition where games and gold medals have been decided that way. Recent cases in point include the 1992 and 1994 Winter Olympics and the 1994 World Championship tournament. While some minor leagues in North America employ the shootout, the basic answer from the NHL is "no way."

Bill Ranford and Sean Burke are two high-profile NHL goaltenders who have been involved in pressure-packed shootouts when playing for Canada at the international level. Ranford emerged as a hero on a couple of occasions when his country's hockey ego was on the line. He backstopped Team Canada to victory with an MVP performance in the 1991 Canada Cup and was chosen the outstanding goalie at the 1993 World Championships in Germany where he had a 5–1–0 record with two shutouts and a 1.83 goals-against average. At the 1994 World Championships in Milan, Italy, Ranford won all six of his starts and had an amazing GAA of 1.17. Best of all, he made the most dramatic save of the competition to win the gold medal for Canada. The championship "winner take all" final game between Canada and Finland was tied at the end of regulation time so there was a shootout. Luc Robitaille scored to put Canada ahead. About thirty seconds later Ranford came through with a heart-stopping save against Finland's final shooter and Canada had won the gold medal.

Bill Ranford first played in the NHL with the Boston Bruins. He was only nineteen when the Bruins called him up from New Westminster in the 1985–86 season. He played in four games, winning three. They brought him back for the playoffs and he started twice against Montreal in the first round. The Canadiens swept the best-of-five series, but every game was close and the Bruins' unknown rookie goalie was outstanding. That was my first look at Bill Ranford and I wasn't the only one who felt the Bruins had finally found their goalie of the future. But it didn't work out that way and I was always curious to know why.

BILL RANFORD

I guess it was a personalty conflict. Butch Goring was the coach when I first got there. Early the next year they fired Butch and Terry O'Reilly took over. I didn't have the style he wanted in a goalie. It was frustrating but it was probably the best thing that happened to me. They sent me down to Portland, Maine, the next season. We had a good year in Portland and I was playing every night. It was a great learning experience. Then they dealt me to Edmonton for Andy Moog right at the trading deadline. I played in six games and backed up Grant Fuhr in the playoffs and we won the Stanley Cup. I didn't play in the playoffs but it was nice to feel I was a part of it.

I was an army brat. My dad was in the armed forces so we moved around a lot. Even before I played organized hockey I had goaltending equipment. My dad used to take shots on me down in the basement. I think when I was a little kid I was fascinated by the equipment and I just kind of carried on with it.

Ken Dryden was definitely my hero. The thing that was important to me then was combining hockey and schooling. He was able to do that. I finished my high school and then I went to university. That's where I was when I got called up to play Montreal in the playoffs. From then on, though, it's been all hockey.

When I came to Edmonton, I joined the team late in the season and went through a complete Stanley Cup run, which we won. That was 1988 and that summer I got invited to the Gretzky wedding and did the whole spiel with the guys. Everything happened in such a short space of time. Then Wayne gets traded. To see a guy that's such a big part of not only the hockey team but the whole city traded away meant a huge adjustment for everybody. Gretz had been the leader for so many years. It put that weight on other shoulders and we were fortunate that we had a guy like Mark Messier who was able to take it. I mean, winning a Stanley Cup two years later was totally unexpected.

In that 1989–90 season the Oilers finished with 90 points, second to Calgary's 99 in the Smythe Division. The year before, Number 99 had led the L.A. Kings to victory over the Oilers in an emotional seven-game series. Ranford didn't play a minute in the playoffs that year. Again, he sat on the bench as Grant Fuhr's back-up. In '89–90 Ranford played 56 games as Fuhr was plagued by injuries. Fuhr, who had been so spectacular so often in the Oilers' glory years, was unable to suit up for the 1990 run to the Cup. Again in Edmonton they looked for another set of shoulders to carry the load. In 1990 Bill Ranford did it brilliantly.

In the first round of the playoffs the Oilers barely made it past Winnipeg while Los Angeles was upsetting Calgary. The Oilers then got some revenge on Wayne and his new team by sweeping the Kings four straight. They went on to defeat Chicago in six games and Boston in five to win Bill Ranford's "totally unexpected" Stanley Cup. Ranford played in all but two of the 1,403 minutes of the Oilers' playoff year. Minutes after the Stanley Cup had been won Ranford was named winner of the Conn Smythe Trophy as the playoff MVP.

The toughest series was the first one against Winnipeg, who had finished just five points behind Edmonton in the final standings. The Jets won the first game, in Edmonton, 7–5, and after four games led the series, 3–1. In the words of Oilers' coach John Muckler, quoted in my book Behind the Bench: *"They beat us pretty good in the first game. Bill Ranford was just horrible. Our back-up goalie was Pokey Reddick and I remember Peter Pocklington coming in after the game and asking why I hadn't pulled Ranford at the end of the second period. I told him I didn't think we could win the Stanley Cup with Pokey, and I was going to stick with Billy and go all the way with him." Good call, coach.*

Muckler called Ranford's performance in a 3–2 triple-overtime win in Boston in the opening game of the finals "unbelievable. The only other performance I can compare it with was when Grant Fuhr shut out the Islanders 1–0 when we won our first Stanley Cup."

BILL RANFORD

After my bad start against Winnipeg a lot of the veterans helped me out. Guys like MacTavish, Lowe, Kurri, they all came to me and said, "Don't worry about it. We know what you can do." Glen Sather pulled me aside and said, "Hey, just play the way you've got to play and you'll be all right." We came back from down 3–1 and made one of those incredible comebacks. In the fifth game we were leading, 4–3, and I made a save on Dale Hawerchuk on a breakaway with just a minute left. If it goes into overtime who knows what could have happened. Everything seemed to start from there. I kind of got on a roll.

Bill Ranford replaced Grant
Fuhr in Edmonton and
promptly won the Conn
Smythe Trophy as the playoffs
MVP when the Oilers won the
Stanley Cup in 1990.

Sean Burke's career has had
its ups and downs. Now, in
Hartford, Burke is emerging
as one of hockey's premier
goaltenders.

Life in the crease of the Ottawa Senators is never easy. Here's Craig Billington under fire in a 1993 game against the Hartford Whalers (below) and in a calmer moment (left).

Ron Tugnutt, who faced 73 shots in the Boston Garden playing for the Quebec Nordiques, the second-highest one-game total in NHL history. Tugnutt stopped 70 to earn his team a 3–3 tie.

Ron Hextall (above) the instant he became the first NHL goaltender to score a goal by shooting the puck into the net. Hextall did it at the Philadelphia Spectrum, December 8, 1987, against the Boston Bruins. He scored again against Washington in a playoff game, April 11, 1989. He takes a bow (right) as the first star in a game at the Philadelphia Spectrum.

Patrick Roy demonstrates his familiar style against
Bernie Nicholls. In his first eight years in the NHL
Roy won four Jennings trophies, three Vezina
trophies, and was MVP in the playoffs twice.

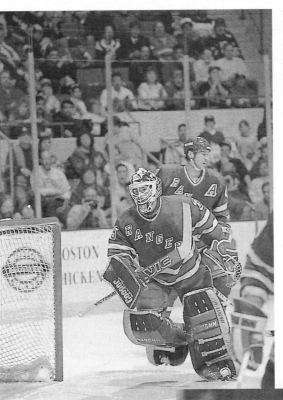

Today's goaltenders must have quick hands and quick feet. Mike Richter proved he had both during the New York Rangers' dramatic run to their 1994 Stanley Cup victory.

Felix "The Cat" Potvin quickly became a high-profile goaltender with the Toronto Maple Leafs. In 1994 Potvin had three 1–0 playoff shutouts against Chicago.

Mike Vernon was at the top of his game when he out-duelled Patrick Roy as the Calgary Flames defeated the Montreal Canadiens in the 1989 Stanley Cup final series.

Brian Hayward had to adjust his approach to the game when he went from being number one with the Winnipeg Jets to backing up Patrick Roy in Montreal.

Martin Brodeur and his father, Denis, who was the goaltender for Canada at the 1956 Olympics. Two years after this picture was taken, Martin was rookie of the year in the NHL with the New Jersey Devils (left).

The Irvins, Wilma and Dick, pose with Patrick Roy, June 10, 1993. Also in the picture is the Stanley Cup, won the night before by the Montreal Canadiens, and the Smythe Trophy, won by Patrick as the MVP of the playoffs.

Something like that, when you're on that kind of a streak, can be really weird. It really gets hold of you when you get into a playoff run. Everything is totally focused on hockey.

I didn't go through any kind of special preparation, not really. At a time like that I just try to stay as relaxed as possible. I think that until you've experienced it people don't realize what it takes out of your body. I know by the time we won the real question was if I was going to make it all the way. There's the weight loss and everybody was tired and we had the flu going through us in the Boston series. Everybody was worried we weren't gonna make it.

In the last few years I've had lots of work, played lots of games. The last couple of years it's been tougher because we haven't been winning. I guess when you play for teams that don't win a lot of hockey games you've just got to go out there each night and play as hard as you can. You've got to battle and try to keep your team in it as long as possible.

I was playing against Wayne in Edmonton the night he scored to break Gordie Howe's record for most career points. The only real disappointment about the whole night was that we had played a great hockey game and with a minute left the people in Edmonton started chanting, "Gretzky! Gretzky!" It's tough to take when your own fans are cheering for the other team in a big game with a minute to go.

Here in Edmonton I played for a Stanley Cup team in '88 that had Wayne and all the veterans and then a surprise winner in '90 with a mixture of veterans and a lot of young guys who weren't supposed to win anything. With the Oilers through those years and now what the team has been going through there have definitely been peaks and valleys. You've just got to play through it. I've been fortunate enough to have a Canada Cup and a World Championship along the way.

The atmosphere when you play in those international tournaments is different. With the Stanley Cup playoffs the media exposure is larger and longer. You have to be at your best for two and a half months. The World Championship lasts about two and a half weeks. The thing a lot of people in Canada don't understand is the huge adjustment you have to make to survive the style of game over in Europe with the different ice surface.

The World Championships in '94 with the shootout at the end was certainly one of the highs of my career, no doubt about that. I was kind of in that mode again, like in 1990, when you're so focused on what you have to do. The pressure's there but at the time you don't realize it. It was something that hit me about twenty-four hours later flying into France to catch our connecting flight. I started to think back to what had happened and there was just a sick feeling when I realized how much pressure there had been. It's like having the whole country's hopes riding on you. When Luc scored the goal that put us ahead and their guy was getting ready to skate in on me I stood there realizing that, well, here it is. It's down to this and you've got to make the save. Fortunately I did.

I am tempted to subtitle the second part of this chapter "Kid on a Roller Coaster." The 1989 NHL All-Star Game was played in Edmonton. The game had been awarded to the Alberta capital more than a year ahead of time and, as luck would have it, between then and game time Wayne Gretzky had been traded from the Oilers to the L.A. Kings. Obviously Number 99 was the centre of attention. I was there working on the Hockey Night in Canada *broadcast and Gretzky rose to the occasion as he usually does. The Great One scored a goal and two assists for the Campbell Conference and was named the game's MVP following his team's 9–5 victory.*

The post-All-Star-Game party was the most unusual ever.

The league rented the West Edmonton Mall, and while the stores in that mammoth shopping plaza were closed, the eating establishments were definitely open. So were the rides in the amusement area where the roller coaster is one of the prime attractions. Sean Burke, then a twenty-two-year-old goalie for the New Jersey Devils, shared the Wales Conference goaltending chores in the game with Réjean Lemelin of the Boston Bruins. Afterwards at the mall Burke was the roller coaster's best customer. I get dizzy on a merry-go-round so I could barely stand to watch the roller coaster, never mind ride on it, much to the amusement of my daughter Nancy Anne who was my date at the party. But Burke had a ball. I don't know how many times he went up, down, and around, but every time I looked there he was, strapped into his seat going up, down, and around, again and again. Whenever I ran into him after that I would ask him, "Been on any roller coasters lately?"

Sean Burke has developed into one of hockey's premier goaltenders and seems to have settled in with the Hartford Whalers. But there have been times when his career has seemed like a roller-coaster ride. Just when Burke appeared on his way to stardom as a New Jersey Devil, after playing for Canada at the 1988 Calgary Olympics, things turned so sour that he went back to the National Team for the 1992 Olympics in France. After Albertville he played a few games for San Diego of the International League. Then the Devils traded him to Hartford in the summer of 1992 and his roller coaster started going up again.

Sean Burke was born in Windsor, Ontario, but grew up in Toronto and played his minor hockey for the Marlies. He was a lean, lanky youngster whose style reminded people of another lean and lanky goalie from Toronto, Ken Dryden. Pro scouts heard about him and began watching him. However, a Minnesota North Stars scout named Gump

Worsley, who was a pretty decent goaltender in his playing days, wasn't too impressed by Sean Burke the first time he saw him play.

SEAN BURKE

I was playing for the Toronto Marlies and I think the team we were playing that night was Kingston. I'm not sure. Anyway, I knew Gump Worsley was there scouting me. When you're a junior and someone like him comes to scout you, it's a big thrill. You want to put on a show. Unfortunately I didn't. They filled the net on me. After the game someone asked Mr. Worsley what he thought of my game and he said, "I could have played better than that at my age right now."

I grew up in Toronto watching the Leafs and I liked Mike Palmateer. And there was Ken Dryden, the guy everybody talked about. They were my two favourites, which is funny because they were opposites in style. You can throw in Bernie Parent too. He was another guy I really liked.

I was drafted by New Jersey in 1985 and I went to their camp and had a pretty good camp. But they realized I wasn't ready to play so they sent me to the Canadian National Team. That was a good move because a lot of teams will rush a kid, especially when they're struggling like New Jersey was.

In 1987 I got to go to the World Championships in Vienna on the Canadian team with a lot of NHL players. The other goalies were Bob Froese and Pat Riggin. We had older guys who were good players like Al Secord and Craig Hartsburg. I was pretty quiet and didn't say much. I wasn't a cocky rookie, which I think served me well. I've got to be honest, I was somewhat intimidated. But I quickly realized if you're gonna be successful in this game you gotta have some confidence and believe in yourself. You get a chance to play with that kind of team in that kind of competition, that's when you can test yourself. You get a good idea if you'll be able to play. I was happy that at twenty I could do a pretty good job on a team of NHL players.

The next year the Winter Olympics were in Calgary. I was young and I didn't really enjoy the Olympics as much as I should have. I was completely focused on hockey, which wasn't a bad thing, but I never really took in the whole atmosphere of the Olympics themselves. I didn't go to see any other events. I was so caught up and wanted to play well that I would just go from practice back to the Olympic Village and keep preparing for the next game. But the hockey was a huge thrill. There were 17,000 or 18,000 at the Saddledome for every game. We were the home team and it was tough.

Three months before the Olympics we played in the Izvestia Tournament in Moscow and we beat the Russians. They were the Big Red Machine with Fetisov, Larionov, all their stars at the time. We won the gold medal. We were the first team to beat the Soviets in Moscow since 1972 when Paul Henderson scored the winning goal. Obviously our win didn't get the same kind of attention in Canada, but for our team and for people in Europe it was a big victory. So we kind of went into the Olympics as a team people thought could beat the Soviets again. But, really, we weren't as talented as they were. We played well and ended up coming in fourth.

The Devils called me up right after the Olympics and I played in my first game against Washington. I played the third period and made my first NHL save off Kevin Hatcher. Then Mike Gartner got a breakaway and he scored. Put it through my legs. I remember making my first save and I remember the first goal. We won the game, 6–1.

The next game was in Boston and I started and played the whole way. We won, 7–6. At the time Jersey was fighting to make the playoffs. The team had never made the playoffs and when I got there people were expecting big things. I had just been in the Olympics, I had been a high draft pick, and they had been waiting for a number-one goaltender. When I got to Jersey there was a lot of talk that I was gonna be the guy to turn things around. So I got my first start and the other team got six goals but we still won the game. I didn't play very well but everybody was ecstatic because it was a big game and we had beaten the Bruins right in Boston. After that game I settled down and had a pretty good run from that point on. With four games to go I got my first shutout. We beat Pittsburgh, 4–0, and then went into Pittsburgh and beat them, 7–2. We were on a great roll then.

The New Jersey franchise started in the NHL in 1974 as the Kansas City Scouts. Two years later the Scouts became the Colorado Rockies. After six years in Denver the team moved again and became the New Jersey Devils. The Scouts and the Rockies never made the playoffs and, for the first five years the team played in New Jersey, the Devils didn't either. Then after thirteen years it finally happened. The Edmonton Oilers won their fourth Stanley Cup that year but the New Jersey Devils' 1988 playoff exploits are likely better remembered, for a lot of wrong reasons.

The Devils made the playoffs on the final night of the season in Chicago. They were trailing, 3–2, in the final minute when John MacLean scored to tie the game. At 2:21 of overtime, MacLean scored again to put New Jersey into the playoffs ahead of the Rangers and the Penguins. The Devils were unbeaten in their last eight games. A great roll indeed, but the fun was just beginning.

The long-frustrated franchise played its first-ever playoff game on the road against the New York Islanders, losing 4–3 on a goal by Brent Sutter, who became the first player since Harvey "Busher" Jackson in 1934 to score an overtime goal in the playoffs while his team was shorthanded. But the Devils recovered. Burke shut out the Islanders in the Devils' first home playoff game and New Jersey won the series in six games. Then they eliminated Washington when John MacLean scored the series-winning goal late in the third period of the seventh game in Washington. That sent the Devils into the Wales Conference final series against the Boston Bruins.

In January of that season Jim Schoenfeld had replaced Doug Carpenter as the Devils' coach. After the Bruins won game three in New Jersey to go ahead in the series, 2–1, Schoenfeld went after referee Don Koharski and, with television cameras and microphones recording every word, accused Koharski of being fat and yelled at him to "Have another doughnut!" To paraphrase Franklin Roosevelt, it was a quote that will live in infamy, in the hockey world, that is. The league suspended Schoenfeld for the next game. Just before the game the Devils got a court injunction which allowed their coach to stay behind the bench. When that happened the referee and linesmen refused to work the game. After a long and embarrassing delay substitute officials from amateur hockey were found to take over. To make matters even more bizarre, nobody could locate NHL President John Ziegler, who should have been sorting out the mess. The Bruins eventually won the series in a seventh game and then lost to Edmonton in the Cup final.

Through all of the above the New Jersey team seemed on its way to fashioning one of those Cinderella stories and their rookie goaltender was front and centre. The Sean Burke story of 1988 was being compared to the Ken Dryden story of 1971. The same ingredients were there: an unknown rookie goalie who arrived late in the season and became a star in the playoffs.

SEAN BURKE

That playoff year was just a blur. It really was. We weren't one of the more talented teams but we got on a roll, we had confidence in Schoenfeld, and the team had a lot of confidence in me. The doughnut thing wasn't upsetting to us. I don't think any of that stuff affected the way we played. But when it was all over you knew that what we had done was done on emotion. We were one win away from beating Boston and going to the Stanley Cup finals. When you're that young you don't sit back and enjoy it. I thought, geez, this is great. This is the way it will be every year. You don't realize that getting to the Stanley Cup finals is a hard thing to do. Unfortunately the next year we didn't even make the playoffs. We had played over our heads and we came back to earth and it was a miserable year.

In his first full season in the NHL, the season the Devils failed to make the playoffs, Sean Burke played in 62 games, and in 52 the year after that. Then, in 1990–91 he appeared in only 35 games. The next year he was back on the roller coaster, out of the NHL and back with Canada's National Team. Everyone thought he left the Devils because of a contract dispute over money. So I asked Sean about the contract dispute. Contract dispute! Wrong again, Dick.

SEAN BURKE

I'm glad you asked me that because to this day everybody who talks about it says I had a contract dispute. I never had a problem with my contract in New Jersey. What happened was, I wasn't playing a lot and I played out my option. Chris Terreri was playing ahead of me and I just wasn't happy in Jersey anymore. It didn't seem that I was gonna be the guy in their long-range plans so I went in and asked to be traded. Because I had played out my option our G.M., Lou Lamoriello, was obligated to offer me a contract and he offered me a great contract. It was a two-year deal for about $450,000 a year, which at that time was well over the league average. It was good money.

But for me it wasn't a question of the money. I simply wasn't happy there. I didn't see them giving me the chance to be successful. There were two young guys on the same team and Chris Terreri was obviously their favourite that year. I thought I was in a situation where I wasn't going to play a lot.

When I left New Jersey I took quite a gamble. It was kind of unsettling. I left the NHL when in this day and age there are so many guys who are talented. If you're out of the league for too long, who knows? People step in and fill all the jobs and there might not be one for you when you try to get back. But I figured I had to play somewhere and get to enjoy hockey again, and the National Team was great. The experience was probably the most fun I ever had in hockey. Eric Lindros stayed at my house in Calgary with me and my wife and I was playing for Dave King again. We had a lot of guys younger than I was this time around. In '88 I was the young guy. This time I was the twenty-six-year-old veteran. I just went out and enjoyed it.

What I remember most of all out of that experience was the evening in France, at the Olympics, when we had the shootout against Germany. I thought I played well at the Olympics but I didn't play well in that game. We tied, 3–3, in regulation and I just didn't have a good night. I was shaky, yet because of the shootout everybody talks about that game. It's hard to tell people that was the one game I was lousy but for a goaltender, it works out that way a lot of times.

In the shootout Eric Lindros got two chances. He missed

the first one but scored on the second and now we have the lead. They shoot next and if they score then we've got to go to another shot. There had been five shots and now it's sudden death. Well, I stopped it. It kind of dribbled behind me and sat on the goal line. If we lose that game we're out of the medal round and we would never have had a chance to win our silver medal. So we won the game and everybody remembers my last stop, the one save at the right time.

My father was in the stands. He was sitting with Dave King's wife and when the shootout started they were so nervous they went out to the parking lot. They couldn't stand being in the arena and they didn't know what happened until the game was over. My mother-in-law was home and she locked herself in a closet because she couldn't stand to watch it on TV.

When I got back after the Olympics the players' strike was looming in the NHL. I hadn't been traded yet and I'm home thinking that if there is a strike the year's over for me. I won't play anywhere. Then I got a call from Fred Comrie, who owns the San Diego team in the International League. I had to decide: do I go to San Diego or do I wait to see if I get traded and hope the strike doesn't happen? He offered me a deal I couldn't refuse so I figured, hey, this is February and I want to play some hockey. So I went there.

It was a tough situation because I felt, no matter how well I played, I couldn't live up to the money he was paying me. San Diego is a beautiful city and I lived right on the beach and it was 80 degrees every day. But as much as I enjoyed that part of it, it was just a different situation. I had never played in the minors before. I thought I played very well although in the playoffs we went out four straight. Coming from Dave King's program where discipline and intensity in practice is so important, it was really a step down. It was another world and made me want to get back to the NHL in a hurry. The next summer, in August, the Devils finally did trade me, and that's how I got to Hartford.

Superstitions? I used to have a million of them. When I played in Jersey I made sure I changed the laces in my skates before every game. I had to drive to the rink the same way, eat my meals at exactly the same time. It was driving me crazy. It got to the point where if something didn't happen the way I wanted it to then my mind was all messed up. So I ditched them, and I don't have superstitions any more. But one thing I do is, I never take the puck out of the net after they score on me. Some guys like to take it out and fire it. But I leave it there. The next time I see it is when the referee drops it at centre ice.

What I like best about goaltending is going out there knowing you have to play well. I look around the league and it's the same everywhere. You can't get by playing average or mediocre. The goaltender has to play well every night. I like that. I like knowing that you have to be at your best to be successful. It's a good feeling.

10

Bad Teams, Lots of Shots

RON TUGNUTT BERNIE WOLFE
CRAIG BILLINGTON

It is pretty certain that, on March 4, 1941, I was the star of the show at 2155 Angus Street, in Regina. That was the date of my ninth birthday, and don't most kids having their ninth birthday have a party after school at their house? I can't remember for sure but there's a pretty good chance I was blowing out nine candles with my buddies from Davin School cheering me on.

A couple of thousand miles away, a few hours later, the Chicago Blackhawks played the Bruins at the Boston Garden. The Bruins were the class of the then-seven-team NHL, finishing in first place and winning the Stanley Cup by sweeping the Detroit Red Wings four straight in the finals. The Blackhawks were one of the league's weak sisters, so they were in tough against Boston. When the game was over, there was no doubt Hawks' goaltender Sam LoPresti had been the star of that show, although unlike the skinny little kid in Regina he didn't exactly have a party. LoPresti faced

83 Bruin shots and stopped 80 of them, both still one-game records. But despite a superhuman effort by their goaltender, the Hawks lost the game, 3–2.

In that same Boston Garden fifty years and seventeen days later, March 21, 1991, the Bruins poured 73 shots at the goaltender for the then-lowly Quebec Nordiques, Ron Tugnutt, and he stopped 70 of them. Both those figures rate the runner-up spot in the category of most shots and most saves in one game. Unlike the Blackhawks fifty years before, the Nordiques took advantage of their goalie's effort and didn't lose the game. It ended in a 3–3 tie. When Tugnutt made a remarkable stop off a Raymond Bourque blast with just eight seconds remaining in sudden-death overtime, the partisan Bruin fans in the Garden gave him a standing ovation. When the final buzzer sounded several Boston players shook his hand.

Off the ice Ron Tugnutt has to rate as one of the best-dressed players in the NHL. If you saw him striding along carrying a briefcase, hair neatly trimmed, wearing mod glasses and a sharp suit out of GQ, you might take him for a young stockbroker. But he's a goaltender and has been since, as a pint-sized five-year-old, he put on a pint-sized pair of goal pads. His pads are bigger these days but he's still pint-sized, at least by NHL standards. In the 1995 season Tugnutt was one of the three lightest players in the NHL along with two other goaltenders, Chris Terreri and Jon Casey. All three weighed in at 155 pounds.

Tugnutt grew up in Scarborough, Ontario, and played minor hockey in the Toronto Hockey League. He was an outstanding junior with the Peterborough Petes and was drafted by the Quebec Nordiques in 1986 when he was eighteen years old. At that time the Nordiques had a good team featuring the likes of the Stastny brothers, Dale Hunter, and Michel Goulet. But by the time Tugnutt played his first game *for Quebec at the age of twenty, that team had been dismantled and the Nordiques were in the process of missing the playoffs in five consecutive years. It was a tough start for a youngster. Bad team, lots of shots.*

RON TUGNUTT

Playing with that team in Quebec I got to the stage where I felt if I played really well we had a good chance to win. I'm usually my worst critic. If we've lost and I feel I let in one bad goal then I say I was probably the one who turned the game in the other team's favour. At one time in Quebec I played 56 games in one season and going into every game I thought for sure we were going to win. It wasn't as bad as it seemed. Sure, at times it was bad but at other times it was also a lot of fun.

When you play on a team like we had in Quebec and you go into games against big teams, the guys can get into a "let's keep it close" kind of thing. I think they looked to me as a leader, as young as I was. They counted on me to more or less keep the games close and save them from embarrassment. I didn't look at it that way. I knew I was gonna go out and play a good game.

Year in, year out, game in and game out, I tried to make things better. Seeing the number of shots I did, I could get into a good groove early in the game. I'd usually face one or two tough shots in the first two or three minutes. If I make those saves it's usually smooth sailing. But with that kind of a team, if I didn't make the saves and we were in a hole early it was usually an uphill battle the rest of the way.

The game everyone remembers is the one in Boston. It just seemed like they kept coming and coming. At times I would look at the ice and say, "Geez, the ice at my end looks pretty rough and at their end it doesn't look so bad." It was a lot of rubber. Over the years Boston has been known as a team that will shoot from anywhere, especially in the Boston Garden with its small ice surface. Out of 73 shots you're going to have a quite a few that are fairly routine but there's also quite a few that are top-notch chances as well.

Guy Lafleur was with the Nordiques that year. Everyone knew he was retiring for good at the end of the season and that night he was playing his last in the Boston Garden. Guy had a great image all over the league. Late in the third period the fans started to get up and there was a standing ovation for Guy. It was a very touching moment. In the overtime I made a save off Ray Bourque with eight seconds to go and it was maybe the best one I made all night. Suddenly I realized there was another standing ovation. I looked around and Guy wasn't on the ice so I said, "Wow, this one's for me." I remember watching the video of that play. I think it was Craig Janney behind the net and he got it back to Bourque and as he wound up to slap it Cam Neely was standing almost in the crease, right in my face. I did the splits and made a glove save and there's Neely shaking his head, and Bourque shaking his head. Those are memories I'll never forget.

Even though I was tired at that time you could say I was energetic, very energetic. The fans were making me that way. I had chills running up my spine. Everyone talked about that save off Bourque. That was the 71st shot. After the face-off in our end with eight seconds to go they had two more. When the game was over and the Bruins started to skate over to shake my hand it was a shock to me. I guess everyone had a great time. When I was playing in Anaheim, Peter Douris, who played for Boston that night, was on the team. I talked to him about that game and Peter said, "We couldn't believe what was going on. The coach kept telling us to keep shooting, keep shooting, that you couldn't keep it up and we had to get one or two more sometime. The guys were laughing on the bench. We kept looking at the shot clock and laughing."

It's funny, but the game that set the record of 83 shots was also played in Boston. That goalie lost, 3–2. We tied, 3–3, so I guess you could say I hold the record for getting the most number of shots without losing.

Late in the 1991–92 season, Tugnutt's fifth with Quebec, he was traded to the Edmonton Oilers. He spent one full season there, playing 26 games as the back-up to Bill Ranford. Tugnutt was then was claimed by the Mighty Ducks of Anaheim in the 1993 expansion draft. He had played 28 games for Anaheim when he was traded to Montreal in exchange for centreman Stephan Lebeau with six weeks remaining in the 1993–94 season. The Canadiens were desperate for a quality goaltender to back-up Patrick Roy. Anaheim's general manager, Jack Ferreira, had worked for the Canadiens between the time he was fired by the San Jose Sharks and hired by the fledgling Anaheim franchise. Perhaps he was returning the favour, after a fashion.

Tugnutt joined the Canadiens in time for an afternoon game in Philadelphia February 21, and for him the timing was lousy. Roy had one of his rare bad games and was yanked by coach Jacques Demers. Tugnutt took over and was beaten for a goal on the first shot he faced. The Flyers eventually won a weird one, 8–7. Again a back-up, Tugnutt appeared in just five more games that season.

The Canadiens met the Boston Bruins in the first round of the 1994 playoffs and Ron Tugnutt found out then, if he hadn't realized it already, how tough it is to play goal for the home team in the Montreal Forum. The teams split the first two games in Boston. Before game three came the shocking news that Patrick Roy had entered hospital for treatment of appendicitis and would not be able to play. So Tugnutt got the call and again the timing was bad because, this time, he was bad. The Bruins beat him for two soft goals early in the game and went on to win, 6–3. Roy came back to play the rest of the series, won by Boston in seven games, but for Tugnutt's image in hockey-mad Montreal the damage had been done. To his credit, when his bad night was over Tugnutt didn't hide from the horde of media types who invaded the Canadiens' dressing room. He hung in, answering every question and making no excuses for a performance that had obviously been one of the lowlights of his career.

RON TUGNUTT

This sounds kind of funny but I would have preferred to have played that game somewhere else. It would have been better for me if the game had been in the Boston Garden. I think Patrick, in all essence, is God in Montreal. He's loved by everybody and so he should be. But he was sick and couldn't play and I had been waiting quite a long time to be in the spotlight at a time like that. As things turned out I was very disappointed in the outcome.

I wasn't myself whatsoever that night. I didn't prepare myself properly for the game. I was much too tense, which is totally uncharacteristic for me, and it showed in the game. But I was more than willing to sit around and talk about it afterward. I took the blame for the two bad goals and said the next game will be better, which I'm positive it would have been. But I didn't get the chance because Patrick came back and played the rest of the series.

I think the job of being a goaltender is the biggest high you could possibly have, with the puck coming at you at about 100 miles per hour and you trying to do something to stop it. You're basically the quarterback of the team. It's just a real high.

It's not lonely in the crease, as a lot of people say it is. I prefer to be back there even though goalies always take a beating. People say the guys who play goal are crazy to do what we do. But I've always had the feeling that I was the smart one because everybody else was chasing the puck and I just stood there and waited for it. That's the way I felt when I was five years old, and I still feel that way.

There have been bad teams for as long as hockey has been played. In the 1930–31 season the Philadelphia Quakers managed only four wins in the 44-game NHL season and then quietly left the scene. Today the benchmark for futility is the record of the Washington Capitals, a team that managed just eight wins in 80 games in their first season, 1974–75, giving up a record 446 goals in the process.

Early in the Caps' second season, when things weren't going any better, Bernie Wolfe arrived. Wolfe had been an outstanding college goaltender while attending Sir George Williams University in Montreal. He remained with the Capitals the next four years before leaving hockey. He is now a successful financial analyst in Washington with several professional athletes on his client list. Analyzing something as volatile as the stock market has probably been easier for Bernie than trying analyze what his teammates were doing in front of him, especially in his rookie season, when the Caps zoomed all the way from eight wins to eleven and their goals against plummeted to a mere 394. In the four years Wolfe played in Washington the Capitals won only 76 of the 320 games they played.

BERNIE WOLFE

I was the first goaltender signed by the Washington Capitals. They signed me as a free agent out of college in June 1974, the summer before they began playing in the NHL. I played my first pro season in the minors. I started with the Richmond Robins but got mononucleosis, and they sent me to Maine when I was ready to play again.

I was back in Richmond to start the next season, but after the Caps' third game Ron Low, who was their regular goaltender, twisted his knee. They brought me up and I joined the team in Los Angeles. I sat on the bench that night and then [coach and G.M.] Milt Schmidt told me I'd start the next game in Kansas City. The franchise had won only one game on the road up to that point and that had been in Oakland in their final road game the previous year. So I played in Kansas City and we won, 6–2, and it was my first NHL game and the second road win in Capitals' history. It was kind of exciting. We picked up a garbage can and put a Stanley Cup label on it. The guys paraded it around the dressing room. That's the closest I've come to a Stanley Cup. [Laughs] All of a sudden I was a star, for a little while anyway. When Ronnie came back they released Michel Belhumeur, the other goalie, and I stayed.

It was tough because I had come from a winning background. We used to win most of our games when I played at Sir George and when I was in the minors we had pretty good teams. Washington was a different story. One night we were in Chicago and they outshot us 55–14. We lost, 3–1. Tommy McVie was coaching us by then and after the game he came up to me and said, "Good game. Now you know how Custer felt." Another time he said, "Most teams put their goalies in an ambulance after the game. Ours come to the game in an ambulance."

Tommy tried to keep our spirits up but it was kind of depressing. We lost so often that sometimes players would get what we used to call the Philadelphia flu and wouldn't show up. That made it even tougher on the goaltenders. [*Players on teams much better than the Capitals would be hit by the Philadelphia flu when they were scheduled to play against the Broad Street Bullies.*]

We always knew it was going to be tough playing against the real good teams. They knew how bad we were and they did things that they would never do against other teams, like send all five people into the corners. We couldn't get the puck out of our zone. Sometimes I would be in my crouch with the play in our zone and I wouldn't have time to catch my breath watching the puck go from corner to corner. We couldn't move the puck past them and they weren't the least bit worried about us getting a breakaway. Both defencemen pinched in, almost right into the corners. They had fun when they played against us, they really did. They were drooling over the chance to fatten up their averages.

For a long time I always started the games against Montreal because I was a kid from there and they thought I would play well against the team from my home town. Those were the days when the Canadiens were winning four straight Stanley Cups with Lafleur, Shutt, Robinson. They had one of the greatest teams in history. At one point my record against them was 0–18. That's right, 0–18. That's when they finally realized maybe they should start someone else.

A couple of nights before we had a Saturday-night game in Montreal the Canadiens had taken over 50 shots against the Philadelphia Flyers, a pretty good hockey team. Tommy McVie told the reporters he wasn't going to put one of his goaltenders through that type of torture so he was going to use two goalies in the game on an alternating basis. He was serious. So he switched goalies, me and Ron Low, about every five or six minutes. We were kind of embarrassed about it. Tommy did a lot of things that were out of the ordinary and that was one of them. But we still lost, 5–2.

I was in goal the night in Washington when the Canadiens beat us in the final game of the '76–77 season for their 60th win. They had clobbered us big-time the night before in Montreal, 11–0. But we came back and gave them a good battle the next night. They beat us, 2–1. There was another game we played against them I remember well. We were beating them, 2–1, late in the third period, and we had never even come close to beating Montreal. Then Lambert scored to tie it. Right after that there was a faceoff in our zone. Pete Mahovlich drew the puck back to Lafleur and he drilled it. I saw the puck but I couldn't move fast enough and they end up beating us, 3–2. We could never win games in that fashion.

One of the other goalies on the team for a while was Gary Inness. He had quite a few idiosyncrasies. In the dressing room before a game he had to have a row of Dixie cups lined up in front of him on a table and there always had to be the same number of cups and they had to be lined up the same way. Gary had to have ice on the right side of the cups and water on the left and a wet towel on the right side and a dry towel on the left. God forbid one of the kids working in the dressing room would mix everything up. He would go completely nuts.

Gary used to throw up before a game if he knew he was playing. One night I got the start and got bombed early so they yanked me. When I was skating to the bench we were passing each other and I apologized to him for not giving him a chance to be sick. But he got sick anyway. He played the rest of the period, went into the dressing room, and got sick.

Sports Illustrated came to Washington to do a story on

goaltenders' superstitions. I guess I was real boring because they asked me if I knew anyone else they could talk to. I gave them quite a list because I played with a lot of them. Like Gary Smith. He used to peel off all his equipment and take a shower between periods. Things like that always made me think I was one of the sanest goaltenders. But my wife doesn't agree with me.

Tommy McVie used to give me hell because I wasn't aggressive enough in the crease. You know, like Billy Smith when he used his stick on guys who stood in front of him. I had enough trouble stopping the puck so I never looked for more trouble that way. Yvon Labre was a defenceman on the team. He's the only Capital whose number has been retired and he's still here in the Washington area. We're good friends. Yvon agreed with Tommy and kept telling me I should be moving guys from the front of our net. I said, okay, I'll try my best. So one night we're playing Minnesota and Dennis Hextall is standing in front and Yvon is trying to push him out of the way. He wasn't having much luck so I figured it was my opportunity to get tough. I take my stick and I two-hand Hextall right across the ankle and he doesn't move. He doesn't budge, he doesn't blink, he doesn't even get mad. Yvon is looking at me, so right away I start explaining that I hit Hextall as hard as I could. Yvon said, "I'm proud of you for trying, but you missed him and you hit me." I almost broke his ankle and he missed two games after that. That was the last time I swung my stick at anybody.

We did things that were just embarrassing because we weren't treated like any other NHL team. McVie would call practice for 5 o'clock in the morning when we were on the road. One time that happened in Vancouver, so the night before one of the players, either Ron Low or Ace Bailey, called the bus company and cancelled the bus. We never had that 5 a.m. practice because we had no way of getting there. They had always given us an itinerary for the trips, so after that day they never wrote down what the bus company was.

I had just one shutout in the NHL and of course I remember it well. [*Wolfe played 120 games in the NHL.*] It was in Detroit, at the old Olympia, and that night there was a big snowstorm and the building was half-empty because a lot of people couldn't get to the game. I don't think anybody felt much like playing hockey so I wasn't exactly overworked. The shots against me were somewhere in the 20s, which in those days was like a walk in the park for a Washington Capitals goaltender. We won, 2–0, and I don't think they really came close to scoring. It wasn't like I was making all kinds of remarkable saves, but at that stage I'd take a shutout any way I could get it.

For the most part, after losing all the time the way we did, it was almost a victory if you kept the goals against to three or under. That's really what you wanted to do. You didn't expect to win but you didn't want to embarrass yourself, and that's a bad way of playing. I was envious of Gary Smith because he was always smiling. He seemed to be having fun. That's something I don't remember, having fun during a game.

I never felt secure a day in my life as a goaltender for the Capitals. They fired two or three coaches in the four years I was there and I figured the next person to go had to be the goaltender. While I was playing I started working in the financial consulting business and I was enjoying it. In the off-season I took some courses in Denver and I worked on a Master's degree at George Washington University here in Washington.

On the first day of training camp for what would have been my fifth year I called our G.M., Max McNab, and told him I was tired of hockey and I wasn't going to the camp. We worked out a settlement of my contract and I retired. I was very lucky that I had become concerned about my future after hockey and had done something about it. I think I'm one of the few to say that I've never missed hockey for as much as a day since I retired.

I never got close to the Stanley Cup, the real one, that is, and I never even got close to the playoffs. One night during the warm-up before a game against Montreal, Ken Dryden said to me, "It must be awful to play in Washington." I said, "Ken, it's still in the NHL, and that's where I always wanted to be." Dryden said, "You're right."

The records in futility established by the Washington Capitals in their first year in the NHL were challenged by the Ottawa Senators in their first season, 1992–93. The "Capitals Watch" was on in Ottawa when it seemed the Senators might not win as many as eight games. But they did, finishing the season with ten victories, nine at home and one on the road, and 397 goals against. There must be something working against new teams that set up shop in capital cities.

Bernie Wolfe arrived in Washington for the Caps' second season, and Craig Billington arrived in Ottawa for the Senators' second season. Wolfe was a raw rookie when he got to Washington. When Billington arrived in Ottawa he had played 111 games for the New Jersey Devils and another 158 with various New Jersey farm teams in the American League. In his first season with the Senators the team struggled up from ten to fourteen wins in the 84-game schedule to finish dead last in the 26-team NHL. Billington played in 63 of those games. A personable young man who played his first NHL game at the age of nineteen after two years with Belleville of the OHL, Craig Billington loves to talk about hockey, and especially about goaltending.

CRAIG BILLINGTON

Don't forget that we belong to the mythical "goaltenders' union." I like to say it's the oldest and, I'm convinced, the strongest anywhere in sports. You can run into a goalie anytime, anywhere, at any level, and sit down and have a conversation that lasts longer than one you would have with your best friend. I get excited, charged up whenever I run into someone who has played goal, regardless of age or if they're still playing or not. Right away you're talking about the latest equipment, or what's going on, or this guy or that guy and what happened to him, the old days, the new days, and what's happening. It's unique.

Another thing we love talking about is the different styles of different goalies. That's one of the great enjoyments. There's a tremendous amount of respect out there. We may not like one guy's style compared to another but we respect what he's doing. If he's doing it successfully, we admire that.

I think most goalies feel for the other goalie during a game. If he's having a bad night, letting in soft goals, we all know how that feels. I don't know if that carries with any other position. I had great support playing for Ottawa, not just from former players but from other goalies in the NHL today who have stopped and talked with me, guys I've never had a chance to talk to before. It's kind of ironic that within the industry you get that kind of support even though we're competing against each other.

I started in the NHL with New Jersey in 1985–86, and I was too young. I was with an organization that was still young. Their goalies were Ron Low and Chico Resch, and they wanted a young guy there too. I was the guy but it wasn't my time. I needed to mature as a player and as a person. I was nineteen and had played only two years as a junior. I really think it hurt me, put me back a few years because I was so inconsistent. I look back on it now and just shake my head and wonder how I even survived one year.

What happened that year was that I was up until Christmas. I had played in just three games and I was 3–0. Then they sent me to play for Canada at the World Junior Championships. The tournament was in Hamilton that year and we won the silver medal. Then I went back to New Jersey and played in 15 more games. The next year I became eligible to play in the minors and I spent the first half in Maine. That was my first experience with Tom McVie. Tommy is legendary, a true character who has spent his entire life in the game of hockey as a player and a coach. He took me aside and worked with me. At the time I probably thought he was a tyrant and he probably couldn't stand me. He was tough but as you get older you learn that the people who are the toughest on you are those who support you the most.

I know a lot of goalies say they never had the benefit of good coaching on their way to the NHL. Tom was different. He had coached players like Pete Peeters, Pelle Lindbergh, Kirk McLean, and Chris Terreri. Maine was co-owned by New Jersey and Philadelphia, and Bernie Parent would show up to work with the goalies. Tom explained to me that he spent a lot of time with Bernie and learned a lot from him. His practices were about 70 per cent geared to the goalies so it was wonderful.

He can be a funny guy. When I first went to Maine I was very light, maybe 145 pounds. One day a bunch of us were in the weight room talking about the New Jersey Devils. Tommy came by and said to me, "You might as well keep talking about them because the closest you're gonna get to the Meadowlands is the racetrack next door, riding the horses, the way you look right now." He always kept you in your place.

The best thing about Tom was that he left you alone. He

wouldn't get on your case. He let you play through tough times and was very supportive. He was usually tougher on you when things were going well than when things were bad. If things were bad he'd put his arm around you, give you a hug, and send you on your way. But if things were really good he'd be ranting and raving. I learned a lot about myself and about life from Tom McVie. He loves what he does for a living. Perhaps the secret in our life is to love what you do. So many people don't.

Another person who was very important to me early in my career was Chico Resch. I lived with Chico and his family my first two seasons in New Jersey. His wife, Diane, who had been with Chico all his years in the league, was very supportive. She could empathize with the situation I was in as a young goalie and it was great for me. At that stage there would have been nothing worse for me than going home after a game to an empty place with no one to talk to about it.

Starting with the 1987–88 season Craig Billington spent three years playing for Utica in the American League. During that time two promising young goalies, Sean Burke and Chris Terreri, staked their claims in the New Jersey goal crease. Burke joined the Devils from the Canadian National Team following the 1988 Calgary Olympics and backstopped them dramatically to within one win of reaching the 1988 Stanley Cup finals. Billington, by then twenty-four years old and obviously frustrated, looked elsewhere and found an opening in Burke's old spot with the National Team.

CRAIG BILLINGTON

Dave King was running the National Team and I was fortunate he was looking for a goalie. I seemed like an insurance policy for the Devils. I talked with the Devils' G.M. Lou

Lamoriello and expressed my concern. Then Dave King came into the picture and things worked out really well.

There are many differences between playing professionally and playing internationally. Number one is that you're playing for your country and everybody is backing you. Secondly, there is no real issue of money, the business end of it. Everything is geared toward developing players and the experience of playing for your country. I felt that the players I was with that year got along better than any bunch of guys I've ever played with and yet none of us was making much money.

They taught us a lot in one year. They taught us about nutrition, visualization, and the psych part of hockey. We had to take a coaching clinic and had classroom discussions. They hammered home a lot of points, but it was an environment where they could do that. I look at it as being a sabbatical year for me. It allowed me to step away from the pro scene, work at my game, become stronger mentally, and then come back to it. As it turned out it was the best thing I ever did.

After my one year there, ironically, Sean Burke and I switched places. He left the Devils because he wasn't happy and he joined the National Team for the 1992 Olympics in Albertville. I went back to the Devils. I had spent the month of August in Germany with the Olympic program and then got a call from the Devils. They were saying, "Hey, Sean's not coming back so we need you here." They had the right to do that. When I got there I knew I was gonna make it. I had that feeling, which I had never had before. On the other hand, it was tough because for the first time in my career I really wanted to play in the Olympics. I had been geared and programmed for a whole year for those '92 Games. So just when all that was in place I went back to New Jersey and the NHL.

Tom McVie was coaching the Devils then. At the start of the season Chris Terreri was playing almost all the games. I only played twice in the first two months so it was similar to my start as a nineteen-year-old. But I played more and more toward the end of the season. I played 42 games the following season and went to the All-Star Game. So my career really took a turn after the time I spent with the national program. It proved to me you have to believe in yourself even when you're in the minors and you're twenty-four years old and people are telling you you're finished.

I had grown up with the New Jersey organization. I had spent eight years with them. I was a baby when I went there so everybody knew my story, knew what I was all about. I felt I was finally contributing. I had just had the best year of my career and played in the All-Star Game. Then just before the expansion draft in 1993, because they could only protect one goalie, they traded me to Ottawa. They decided to go with Chris, and, because I wasn't making very much money, I was attractive to other teams. The Devils didn't want to lose me in the expansion draft and get nothing in return, so they made the deal.

When you get traded to a team that had won just ten games the year before you're always being asked, "How did it feel?" Well, to be honest it was really tough, tougher than I thought it would be. I thought, okay, Craig, you dealt with being with a poor team when you were nineteen but now you're a better goaltender, better-prepared mentally, so it shouldn't be as tough. But it was tougher. The expectation level for my performance was probably higher than it had been in my whole career. I had come off a year when I played in the All-Star Game and they were desperate in Ottawa for a turnaround. It was extremely frustrating, even though I know I played some of the best hockey of my career that year. [*Billington's record was 11 wins, 41 losses, 4 ties.*]

A situation like that becomes one of survival. When you are into the second half of the season you are so beat up, and it's not just in the papers. It's everything, the kids you run into. The people in Ottawa were extremely supportive of me and I love playing in a Canadian city. I've been in the goalie-school business for the past twelve summers so I deal a lot with kids and, let's face it, kids like to attach themselves to winning teams. That part frustrates me.

People don't follow teams that don't win very much, and when you're on a losing team that works on you. And there's obviously the direct impact in the dressing room of not winning. You know that old saying about professional sports, winning is everything. That's what it's all about and when you're not winning it's not a lot of fun.

The mental anguish the players go through is phenomenal. We're not bad guys. We try our best, but the constant losing really grates on you. You have to go out and do your best regardless of the outcome, because if you focus on the outcome all the time and what your stats are – I've got news for you – you won't be going to a game tomorrow. Instead you'll be spending time in a psychiatric ward. That's how crazy it gets. About halfway through the year Brad Shaw came up to me and he goes, "Hey, you're gonna have to relax. This is just the way it is. You're doing everything you can, so relax, because otherwise you're gonna get sick. You're gonna self-destruct." That had a good effect on me and I think I played some of my best games in the last part of the season.

It definitely affected my personal life and I blame a lot of that on myself because I'm such a competitor. You can't be all that upbeat in that environment even though people tell you, "It's just a game." Well, it's my life. I've spent my whole life doing this and I care about it. My wife, Susan, was great, but she got as frustrated as I did. There were nights we'd come home after a game and just sit there looking at each other and it was kind of like, what do you do? People say you should leave it at the rink. Well, c'mon. If you can, God bless you. But I can't just leave it at the rink. The families have to take it too. They're not excluded from this because ultimately the husband and father comes home. And what about the kids at school? They hear it, all about how their dad plays and how his team is no good. It's true.

I remember one time, in Pittsburgh, they were all over us. It had to be 6–1 or 7–1, something like that. It was late in the game – I'm talking the last minute of play – and I freeze the puck at the side of the net and here are Stevens and Jagr poking away at it like crazy. I calmly look up at them and I say, "Do you guys really need any more? Because if you do I'll save you a lot of trouble and put it in myself." They started laughing and the ref started laughing. I just remember their expressions because they were so intense. We just wanted the game to end and they were so determined to score another goal.

It's one thing to play 63 games in a winning environment and it's another to play that many when you're losing almost all the time. I don't think anyone – coaches, general managers, or players – really understands unless they've been in that position. I don't think they understand at all.

The Goalie Shoots, the Goalie Scores!

RON HEXTALL

I have a confession to make. For a long, long time I didn't like Ron Hextall. How could I? Me, a guy from the old school, whose long-time goaltending heroes were Worsley and Plante, Hall and Dryden, goalies who stopped the puck, period. Okay, so Jacques Plante wandered around sometimes but he never swung his goal stick at anybody who tried to bodycheck him. At least not that I can remember. Ken Dryden sat out a whole year, but that was because of a contract dispute, not a season-long misconduct.

Suddenly, in the late 1980s, here's this young guy Hextall, or as fans at Madison Square Garden chant, "Hack-Stall," charging around the ice pell-mell, raising the puck over people's heads, swinging his goal stick at people's ankles, jumping on opponents' backs, and causing all kinds of mayhem. Here's a goaltender, of all people, being hauled onto the carpet at various times and being suspended for six games and eight games and twelve games. But why were we surprised? He had 117 minutes in penalties in one year playing junior hockey. In his first season with the Philadelphia Flyers, "Hexy" won the Vezina Trophy (but not the rookie award), and the Smythe Trophy as the MVP of the playoffs, although his team didn't win the Stanley Cup. Later on he even scored goals. What, in the name of Georges Vezina, was going on?

Now for another confession. During all those years when I didn't like Ron Hextall I had never met Ron Hextall. Then I did, and as soon as that happened my feelings were different. This stodgy old-school type realized right away that there were two Ron Hextalls, The Mr. Hyde who got into all that trouble, and the Dr. Jekyll who is a solid, sensible family man and a great guy to get together with to talk hockey.

Ron Hextall comes from a hockey family. I was at Maple Leaf Gardens the night of April 13, 1940, sitting with my mother about sixty feet away from his grandfather, Bryan Hextall, Sr., when he scored the Stanley Cup-winning overtime goal for the New York Rangers. During the 1970s I broadcast many NHL games involving Ron's father, Bryan Hextall, Jr., and his uncle, Dennis. The first two generations of hockey-playing Hextalls were all forwards, but there was no way the determined little grandson, son, and nephew was going to conform to that part of the family tradition. All he ever wanted to be was a goaltender.

RON HEXTALL

My mom says that when I was two years old I wanted to be a goalie. I remember going to my dad's practices, sitting behind the glass and watching the goalie the whole time. I can't explain it, can't pinpoint it. It wasn't like I watched a certain guy one time and said, "I want to be a goalie like him." It was there from the start.

Sometimes at the end of a practice my brother and I would

go on the ice. But I'd always have a forward stick and we'd just shoot the puck around. I started playing minor hockey in Pittsburgh when I was eight and my dad was playing for the Penguins. Eight is pretty late for a Canadian to start and probably even for an American these days. Then we went to Atlanta for two years. Obviously the minor hockey in Pittsburgh and Atlanta wasn't great, but then we went to Detroit and it was great. My brother and I dominated when we played in the other places. In Detroit we were good but we didn't dominate. My brother is a year older than I am and he was a forward. We were only in Detroit two and a half months and I was really disappointed because we were having so much fun playing there. That was dad's last year in the NHL. He got traded to Minnesota halfway through the season and that was it. We came from Brandon so I was back there growing up from the time I was twelve.

I left home fairly early, when I was sixteen, to play tier-two junior in Melville, Saskatchewan. One time we played the Prince Albert Raiders, in Prince Albert, and I had over a hundred shots. They scored 21. I let in three goals in the first, I let in six in the second, and I let in twelve in the third. In the third period I couldn't even get up. Literally, I would go down on the ice and I was so tired I couldn't get up. They picked me as the first star. Something was wrong there: 21 goals against and you're the first star. [Laughs] I think we had eight skaters. We were the worst team in the league when we had our whole team, so you can imagine what we were like when only eight guys showed up. But it was a good year for me, a good developmental year. What is it they say? If you want to be a good goalie get with a bad team.

I went back to Brandon to play junior A. My first two years there we weren't very good. We missed the playoffs my second year. But we were pretty good my third year. I was drafted by the Flyers in 1982, after my first year with

Brandon. [*Hextall was picked 119th overall and was the sixth goalie chosen. The first two picked, Ken Wregget and Mario Gosselin, played in the NHL. The other three, Dave Meszaros, Shawn Kilroy, and Dave Ross, haven't been heard from since.*]

I didn't have any goalie as a hero and I didn't get a lot of help along the way from anybody in particular. The guy that probably encouraged me the most was Jimmy Rutherford, who played with my dad in Pittsburgh and Detroit. He gave me one of his masks. I was twelve years old and I got my tooth knocked out when I was wearing it so it wasn't a very good mask. But that's what he wore.

My first year pro was '84–85. I played in Kalamazoo for a total of about two and a half months. I was in Hershey for probably the same length of time. They kept moving me back and forth. I was in Philly a couple of times. Pelle Lindbergh and Bob Froese were the goalies. Froese got hurt so they brought me up and I dressed for seven games one time and two another, but I never played. I got engaged to my wife in November of that season. I moved eight times after training camp. It was a tough year. I played some good hockey along the way but it was tough emotionally.

The next year was my first main year as a pro. I played over fifty games for Hershey and we had a good team. We lost out in the finals. There were a lot of older guys there like Dave Farrish, Kevin McCarthy, and Tim Tookey. Guys that showed you how to play, taught you the ropes.

The next year at the Flyers' camp I felt they would give me a shot to make it. I felt I could make it, that I was ready to play in the NHL. Mike Keenan was the coach. He used me the last exhibition game against Washington and I got a shutout. I think at that point they made up their minds to keep me. I was 4–0 in the pre-season with a one-point-something average.

However, I didn't expect to start the season. They had Bob Froese and Chico Resch. Froese had been runner-up for the Vezina Trophy the year before. We were playing Edmonton in the first game, at the Spectrum. The morning of the game Keenan pulled the three of us in and said I was gonna play. I was the most surprised man in the world. I was happy and everything but it was a bit intimidating, I must say. The funny thing was, I went to the airport the night before to pick up my wife. I'm sitting at the gate and the plane is in and suddenly through the door come the Oilers: Gretzky, Messier, Fuhr, Kurri, Coffey, the whole works. They didn't know me from a hole in the ground and I'm saying to myself, "Oh my God! Am I really in a league with these guys now?" Thank God I didn't know then that I was playing against them the next night. I would have been shaking. And then, to top it off, my wife doesn't get off the plane. She was on a later one.

The next night was a great feeling, starting my first game in the NHL. Then Jari Kurri scores on me on the first shot. It wasn't a bad goal but, hey, the first shot. But we settled down and ended up beating them, 2-1. I can't remember any real intimidation factor, although with Gretzky there you know who we were up against. He had a semi-breakaway on me and I chased out and forced him to shoot wide. I think I was the second or third star, and afterwards everybody is saying, "Way to go. You played great." I made some decent saves but I don't think I played that great technically. I was just so high emotionally. I was running out of the net a little more than I should have and I was doing some things I normally wouldn't do. But it turned out good.

In his rookie year Ron Hextall played 66 regular-season games with a 3.00 goals-against average and 26 more in the playoffs where his average was 2.77. He was beaten out for the Calder Trophy as rookie of the year by Luc Robitaille, but was voted winner of the Vezina Trophy as the league's outstanding goaltender. The Flyers played the Edmonton Oilers in the Stanley Cup finals, losing game seven in Edmonton, 3–1. After the game he was named winner of the Conn Smythe Trophy as the MVP of the playoffs, only the fourth member of a losing team to be so honoured. It was a great first season, almost.

Ron Hextall

I'll tell you what. I never had a bigger disappointment than after that seventh game. To this day. It's always disappointing whether you make the playoffs or not, but when you're that close, a goal or two away, it's devastating. It was a good summer, but at the same time it was an awful summer because I just couldn't stop thinking about it.

Mike Keenan yanked me a couple of times. I hate it. It's just an awful feeling. I still want to stay in and work my way through the game. I just feel . . . I don't know . . . I just hate it. I understand why coaches do it because sometimes it does give the guys a spark. I think at certain times it's good for the hockey team, but it's hard to accept. I've never got into a hassle with a coach over it. I've always tried to be a team guy.

After my first three years in Philadelphia [*playing 62 or more games every year*], I ran into an injury problem. I had a big problem with my groin. I don't remember which game it was but all of a sudden I was hurt. It happened three or four times.

After I'd been out for about a month and a half they sent me to New Haven to play one game with Hershey. They had a limo for me so I rode to New Haven. I was supposed to play one game then go back to Philly and start playing there again. In the third period I went down again. That was the bad one.

It was the worst pain I ever had. I didn't sleep the whole night and finally at 5 in the morning I called our doctor. I was on crutches for two weeks after that and couldn't play again for two and a half months.

It was an awful feeling for me to sit out. I remember thinking that there I was, twenty-five years old, and my career might be finished. I always said I wanted to play until I was thirty-five. When I was hurt I revised that down to thirty-two. I'm not a real spiritual guy but I must admit I said a prayer or two just to play until I was thirty-two. At that point I was scared, very scared, that I was finished.

Ron Hextall's career wasn't finished but neither were his injury problems. He came back in 1990–91 but the combination of the recurring groin injury and a knee problem forced him to miss 35 games. He did manage to play in 36 games, an improvement on his total of eight the year before. His stats for '91–92 show 45 games played, nine games missed because of a shoulder injury, and twelve games missed because of a suspension. The beat went on.

The Flyers finished out of the playoffs both seasons. Then, Eric Lindros entered the picture. Not the Eric Lindros who today is the Philadelphia team's captain, but the Eric Lindros who wouldn't play for the Quebec Nordiques after they drafted him number one overall in 1991. From that moment, the battle line was drawn as the Lindros family from English-speaking Ontario took on the Nordiques from French-speaking Quebec. The Lindros team won. At the draft a year later Eric was traded to the Philadelphia Flyers following a series of wild negotiations that saw the Flyers steal him out from under the New York Rangers' bank account. The price the Flyers paid in human flesh was high, not to mention the $15 million (U.S.) that changed hands too. One of the humans they traded to Quebec was Ron Hextall.

The Nordiques had missed the playoffs five straight years. Hextall helped change that, playing in 54 games as Quebec improved by a league-record 54 points from the year before and finished second in their division. Oh yes, he missed 14 games with a thigh injury. But Hextall was in great form when Quebec began play against their hated rival from Montreal in the first round of the playoffs. He was brilliant as Quebec won the first two games on home ice. After that the Nordiques, including Hextall, started to fade. The Canadiens won the next four on their way to an unexpected Stanley Cup. Montreal clinched the series with a 6–2 win on a night when Nordiques' coach Pierre Pagé yanked Hextall and then put him back in again.

That summer the Nordiques decided their future lay with two young goalies from their home province, twenty-two-year-old Stephane Fiset and eighteen-year-old Jocelyn Thibault. Hextall was on the move again, this time to the New York Islanders and, surprise, an injury-free season. He dressed for all but one of the Islanders' 84 games, played in 65 of them, and had five shutouts. Then he and the rest of the team ran into a fired-up Mark Messier and the Cup-bound Rangers, and their playoffs were over quickly, four straight. After training camp '94 came the lockout of '94. By then, Ron Hextall had moved again. The Islanders traded him to Philadelphia for Tommy Soderstrom. He was not displeased. Some players are always associated in fans' minds with one team, no matter how many others they play for. Terry Sawchuk played for several teams but I remember him best in his prime as a Detroit Red Wing. Likewise Jacques Plante as a Montreal Canadien, and Gump Worsley as a New York Ranger. When you talk with Ron Hextall you sense that, no matter where he has gone or may go, he will always be a Philadelphia Flyer.

RON HEXTALL

Quebec was a great experience and the key was that my wife had a good attitude about it. It's easy for the guys. All we do is go in the locker room and speak English to everybody. It's harder on the wives. My oldest daughter was in grade one and we weren't sure how that would work out. As soon as I got traded they had us up there. We looked at the school, which was an English one. I think it was a good experience for our kids. They remember a lot about it.

Until the playoffs we had a great year. We had 104 points. I still don't know what the hell happened in the playoffs. I played good for four games and then the wheels fell off. Funny. Things go sour just as quick as they go good. That last game was a long night. I always say Montreal had a Canadian God looking after them when they won that year. But overall we had a fun year. I wouldn't trade it for anything.

The Islanders experience was different. They had a good bunch of guys and with New York City right there you've got a lot to do. The organization was all right, I guess, but the way I was treated in Philly and in Quebec was a little bit different than the way you get treated on the Island. I had heard rumours about a trade in the summertime. I didn't want to get traded out of the Island but if I was gonna go to Philly then I thought, "Let's do it." That was kind of my attitude. The trade was welcomed by my wife and I. We were thrilled.

Ron Hextall is, in my opinion, the most entertaining goal-tender in hockey. The starting goalie is the first onto the ice for the warm-up and then the game. When it's Hextall he comes barrelling out of the gate with his goal pads pumping furiously and his intensity in full view. He is never still. While the national anthems are being played, his head is swivelling, his shoulders twisting, his arms flapping, and his feet shuffling. During stoppages in play Hextall is constantly skating around. He often goes for a skate when a goal is scored on him. A trait he established early is his habit of slamming his goal stick against the posts, first one and then the other, as the players line up for a faceoff in his zone.

Then there is his skill at handling and shooting the puck, "creating offence," as we say. Jacques Plante started it, Ed Giacomin developed it further, and Hextall has perfected it. If Bill Durnan or Turk Broda could see it they wouldn't believe it. I don't think the thought of scoring a goal ever crossed their minds. But many goalies have tried. Charlie Rayner and Cesare Maniago both, in minor-league play, joined a rush and tried to score. Rayner actually scored twice. He first did it while playing for a Navy team during the Second World War and again when the New York Rangers played an exhibition game against an All-Star team from the Maritime Senior League, March 31, 1951. And Gary Smith took off on his famous rush in Montreal only to be bodychecked out of his dream by J.C. Tremblay.

The first professional goaltender to score when the opposing goalie had been removed for an extra attacker was Michel Plasse. He did it February 21, 1971, playing for Kansas City against Oklahoma in the Central League. There had been a snowstorm that day and only 850 fans were in the building. Plasse always explains, "I wasn't trying to score. I was just clearing the puck out of our zone." The next to do it was Darcy Wakaluk for Rochester against Utica in the American League, December 5, 1987. Wakaluk just made it. The goal went in at 19:59 of the third period.

Which brings us to Billy Smith. (Smith declined to be interviewed for this book, choosing to save his stories for his *own book which he plans to write in the future.) Smith became the first NHL goalie to receive credit for a goal. On November 28, 1979, in a game between the Colorado Rockies and the New York Islanders, the Colorado goaltender Bill McKenzie left his net and skated to the bench for an extra attacker when the referee signalled a delayed penalty against New York's Mike Kaszycki. Rockies' defenceman Rob Ramage picked up his own rebound deep in the New York zone and passed it back to the blue line. One problem. Nobody was at the blue line. The puck rolled all the way down the ice and into the empty Colorado net. Smith was the last Islander to touch the puck so he got credit for the goal.*

It wasn't surprising that Ron Hextall became the first NHL goalie to score a legitimate goal. When people saw how hard and how high he could shoot the puck they started thinking he might get one. On December 8, 1987, the Flyers were leading the Boston Bruins, 4–2, late in the third period in Philadelphia. The Bruins pulled their goalie. Boston shot the puck into the Flyers' zone and Hextall shot it back, but not at the net. Veteran Boston broadcaster Fred Cusick was calling the game and remarked at that point that Hextall had such a good shot he might score a goal someday. On the return rush the Bruins shot it in again and Hextall shot it back out. Cusick was right. That time Hextall scored.

RON HEXTALL

I don't think I really did try to score a goal, but they were pushing me in Philly. The reporters kept asking, "Are you gonna score a goal?" and I'd say, "Yes, I'm gonna score a goal. Get off my back." Know what I mean? Everybody wanted it more than I wanted it. As much as I thought, yeah, it would be great, it would be fun, this and that, I didn't think it was that big a deal when I actually scored the goal. Twenty seconds before I scored they dumped it in but it was to my right and I couldn't turn around to get a good enough shot. I'm a left-hand shot. Then they came back and Gord Kluzak dumped it in to my left side. I just fired it up and over everybody and it went in.

Our whole team came off the bench to congratulate me and it was like we'd won a playoff series. Guys were yelling and screaming. I was happy but, you know what I mean, I didn't feel like we'd just won a huge game or a playoff series. I was just sort of happy. I maintain to this day there were guys on our team who were happier than I was.

When I got my second goal it was in the playoffs [against Washington April 11, 1989]. We were up, 7–5, and there was still about a 1:50 left. Something like that. I was happy because it salted the game away, but I don't know. It was a thrill and when I look back it will still be a thrill. But it won't be in my book of the greatest memories of my career. I doubt if either of my goals will be there.

Coming out of the net and shooting the puck are things I always did. When I was young I used to get bored in the net. I used to skate around in the zone and behind the net. I was just bored. Then I started handling the puck. That's just sort of the way it started. When I was twelve years old I could shoot the puck in the air from the goal crease over the red line. I remember watching Jimmy Rutherford shoot in practice and I thought, wow, he can raise it, even hit the glass. I still enjoy getting out before practice and playing pass with the guys and shooting the puck into the top corner of the net from the slot. I just enjoy it, but it all started out of boredom.

I've always done what I do during the national anthems and a lot of other stuff I do, like banging the posts. I used to bang the posts when I was eight years old. Here I am now, thirty years old, a mature man, and I'm still banging the posts. [Laughs] Sometimes I think, geez, what's this all about. You need to grow up. You're a grown man with three children. Maybe it's time to stop. But I can't bring myself to do it. I never will. It makes me feel good so I figure, what the heck.

Talking about shooting the puck, I'd like to mention that rule that gives a goalie a penalty if he shoots the puck over the glass. Why a goalie? My gloves and my stick are a lot bigger and clumsier than a forward's. Am I right or wrong? Yet, they can shoot it over. To me, it was somebody in the office who probably didn't like me and they said let's try to do something here. I think it's a ridiculous rule. None of the refs like it. I do it and they give me a penalty and I say to the ref, "That's terrible," and they say, "I know, I know, but I have to call it. I've got no choice." That's gonna cost me a Stanley Cup sometime and then they're gonna wake up to the fact that it's not right.

There are inconsistencies from referee to referee but most of them are doing a pretty good job looking after the goalies. I got burned in Quebec the other night when Bob Bassen absolutely ran me right into the net and the referee allowed the goal. He said I initiated the contact. And I'm lying in the net. I talked to another referee who saw it on tape and he said he couldn't believe what a joke that call was. I'm not crying, but I think that I don't get the benefit of the doubt. Maybe I shouldn't, but I don't. That's for darn sure.

Which brings us to the "Mr. Hyde" of Ron Hextall, the one I didn't like, and some of the incidents that became so much a part of his image almost from the beginning of his career. It's what prompts him to say he doesn't get the benefit of the doubt from referees who might think, "Hey, this is Ron Hextall. It must have been his fault."

Hextall told me he is a kinder, gentler guy now. He calls

it maturity. Yet a couple of nights after we chatted he became involved in two separate fights in a game against Washington and ended up being thrown out. I saw replays of the incidents and in my opinion he was more than a little provoked into doing what he did. (See, I told you I changed the way I look at him.) But Ron Hextall's reputation precedes him thanks to a long rap sheet on file at league headquarters. The main indictments read:

• Suspended for the first eight games of the 1987–88 season for slashing Kent Nilsson of the Edmonton Oilers in the fourth game of the Stanley Cup finals.
• Suspended for the first twelve games of the 1989–90 season for attacking Chris Chelios of the Montreal Canadiens in the sixth game of the 1989 Wales Conference final.
• Suspended for the first six games of the 1991–92 season for slashing Detroit's Jim Cummins in a pre-season game.

Gerry Melnyk, a former Flyer and now head of the team's scouting operation, scouted Hextall when he was a junior in Brandon. Melnyk once told hockey writer Jay Greenberg, "This kid wasn't polished by any means, but he stood up. He played for a terrible team but he didn't seem to let it beat him.

"He was a little crazy, too. Teams knew it and ran at him to get him going, And he'd retaliate, almost every time I saw him. He was so damn competitive.

"Really, I liked what most people probably didn't like about him. There were teams that thought he was a little loony. That's probably why he lasted until the sixth round."

A little loony? Maybe. Competitive? Definitely.

RON HEXTALL

It's always been there. I remember being a kid and bawling my eyes out because we lost a game. There's always been something in me that's driven me to want to win. I think part of it is passed on. My dad was a pretty determined athlete and they tell me my grandfather was too. I would want to win at everything. My brother and I used to brawl over street-hockey games because I beat him or he beat me. I don't know. It's just something that's born in me, I guess.

It shows on the day of a game. I talk to my wife but I get quiet when I go to the rink. When I get there around 5 o'clock or 5:30 I'll start to get quiet. I'll talk a bit about the game and stuff if somebody comes up to me. But that's when I start putting my focus toward the game.

People say to me I have to change my game. You get suspended, this and that. Not so much now but back then. I've always played aggressive. It's part of my nature. When I get on the ice or if I play racquetball, I'm gonna be off the wall. That's my nature. I'm an aggressive athlete and I've been successful so there's no reason to change.

I'm not gonna say there weren't incidents that happened that maybe shouldn't have happened. There are things that I wish I wouldn't have done like the Kent Nilsson one. We played Montreal that year and they were absolutely brutal to me. Little stuff, pulling my foot out, spearing me, this and that. Then we got to Edmonton and they were doing the exact same thing, spearing me behind the legs, pulling my arm when a guy's ready to shoot, doing this and that. Finally I just had enough. Ten or twelve games, whatever it had been against those two teams, and I'd had enough. The refs weren't protecting me so I was gonna protect myself. And that's what I did. It was something I regret doing but I look back and I know why I did it. It wasn't like just one thing happened and

I snapped. It was a matter of probably fifty or sixty things over a period of 10 or 12 games that were unfair. We were down and I was frustrated. It was my boiling point, I guess.

I've played a lot of hockey and I've got two years left on my contract. That's what I'm aiming for right now. I'll turn thirty-three that summer, so if that's the time to go I'll know it. I'll go and I'll have no regrets. I'll have given it everything I had and I'll be happy with the career I've had as long as we win the Stanley Cup in the next couple of years. I look at guys who play just four or five years and I feel fortunate being able to play as long as I have. The end of this contract will give me thirteen years' pro. That's a long time.

I'm a little more mature than I was. I think I waste less energy now when it comes to my preparations for the game. As you get older you've got to. I wouldn't say I take short cuts but I don't want to waste my legs in the warm-ups or the pre-game skate. But as for my competitiveness, I think the day when there's not much difference for me between winning and losing is the day I'll probably say goodbye to the game.

12

Saint Patrick

PATRICK ROY

In the first week of March 1985, the Montreal Canadiens
made a road trip to play games in Calgary, Minnesota, and
Winnipeg. One of the team's regular goalies, Steve Penney,
was injured, so a nineteen-year-old from the Granby junior
team in the Quebec League was taken along to back up
Doug Soetaert. I was on the trip doing radio broadcasts back
to Montreal. When the team arrived home and everyone
was filing off the plane, Mario Tremblay, a veteran, said to
the nineteen-year-old rookie, "Now you can go back with
the rest of the animals." Tremblay referred to "animals"
because Granby has a large zoo. Veterans don't have much
sympathy for rookies, at times. For some reason Tremblay
spoke in English to the youngster who spoke only French. I
understood what he said but I don't think the kid did. A
little over fourteen months later the kid Tremblay had so
little sympathy for was winning the Smythe Trophy as the

MVP of the Stanley Cup playoffs and on his way to becoming one of the best-known hockey players in the world. Kid named Patrick Roy.

Patrick Roy didn't see game action on that trip, but two weeks earlier he had played one period for the Canadiens, his first in the NHL, facing just two shots and getting credit for a win over the Winnipeg Jets. That was a small step toward what has become a very large and lucrative career. In recent years most observers have referred to Roy as "the best," a title he assumed from Grant Fuhr after Fuhr's glory days with the Edmonton Oilers. He is also one of the game's most popular players. There are autograph-seekers waiting for teams to arrive at airports and hotels in every NHL city at all hours of the day and night. Most could be called professionals. You see the same faces year after year with their same hockey-card albums. They chase after all the players, veterans and rookies alike, and when the Montreal Canadiens arrive in town their number-one target is Patrick. They are not alone in this. Often, when a hockey fan says to me, "I hate to bother you but can you get me . . . ," I finish the sentence for them by saying, "Patrick Roy's autograph." I'm usually right.

Early in 1995, just after the NHL resumed play after the lockout I met Patrick Roy's grandfather, Ed Miller. Mr. Miller worked as a telegraph operator and sent many a hockey-game story over the wires in years gone by from both Montreal and Quebec City. He told me that while Patrick's mother (his daughter) hoped her son would be a swimmer, it was obvious his grandson wanted to be a goaltender. Mr. Miller told me, "Patrick was competitive right from the start. It didn't matter what he played, hockey or ping-pong, he always wanted to win."

PATRICK ROY

My mother wanted me and my brother to do lots of sports. They made us play tennis, we played baseball. She was the coach of the swimming team but swimming was too cold. We didn't like it at all. It was the last thing we wanted to do. It's hard to say why. The rink was beside the swimming pool. We didn't work hard at swimming. We wanted to be next door playing hockey.

The first time I really wanted to be a goalie was when I was watching *La Soirée du Hockey* on Saturday nights. I was really attracted by the goalie pads. We would go in the hall upstairs at home and I would take two pillows, tie them around my legs with a belt, and those were my pads. When I was really young my mom gave my name to an outdoor league and I played forward. One game the goalie got hurt and the coach said, "Who wants to be the goalie?" I raised my hand and he said, "You're too small to be a goalie." Another kid played. The next year my mom gave my name again for a novice league and I asked her if I can be the goalie. When she gave my name she told the group I wanted to be a goaltender and that was it. I remember my first game. We played across the ice, boards to boards. There were three games going on at the same time, one inside each blue line and one at centre ice. I had a shutout. We won, 2–0. That was the first time I played goal.

My first year of midget was a big story. It could have been my career right there. I was about fifteen. In my area there was no more midget double-A so I went to the training camp for midget triple-A in Ste-Foy. I had a bad training camp and didn't deserve to make the team. So they scratched me and I went to try out for the double-C team in my little town, Cap Rouge. They scratched me in the first practice. They told me I was going to have to go into B. I said I wasn't going to go into B. I was so mad I said, "I'm gonna quit." They called me a couple of times and told me I had to go there because they needed me as the goalie. I said I wasn't going there, that's for sure. At that moment I was finished playing hockey.

Then a team in the same league from a place called Cartier Laurentien called my mom and told her they had no goalie. A lady my mom knew was in charge of the team and when my mom told her I had just got trashed from the team in Cap Rouge the lady said, "What? I want him. We need him." They had a rule in those days that a kid had to play in his home town at that level. The lady asked Cap Rouge if I could get my release to play for her team for one season and they said no because I had to play B in their league. Then they went in front of the league, and all that, and finally they made a ruling that I could go to the lady's team for one year. If they had not made that ruling I would be finished as a hockey player.

So I went there and we won everything. They had a really good team. We played in a midget tournament in Beauport and we won the championship. I finished with a goals-against average of 0.40. We were first in our league, maybe lost one or two games all year. We got to the provincial finals and lost against Vanier. It was a close game but they had a really good team.

I went to play junior in Granby and that's where I was when the Canadiens drafted me in '84. We were a young team with no experience. After the first six games they fired the coach. In the three years I was there they were always rebuilding the team. They changed coaches too many times and every coach had a different system. In my second year we had a good team but didn't go anywhere because they couldn't mix all the players properly. Then in my third year we had a bad team and didn't make the playoffs.

There was one game in my third year, in Hull, when

they had 86 shots against us. The other goalie started the game and he let in three goals the first four shots. So I went in and had 82 shots the rest of the game. In the second period we played three against five for most of the time and they had 30 shots on me. I can't remember how many goals they scored but near the end of the game a guy had a break-away and I made the save. I threw the puck back at him and said, "Take another shot," and he did. I can't remember the guy's name but he went back to the bench and said to Pat Burns, who was coaching their team, "That goalie's crazy! He just threw the puck at me and told me to take another shot." Burnsie told me the story when he came to coach in Montreal.

In my last year of junior (1984–85) I dressed for some games at the start of the season with Montreal but I never played. Steve Penney got hurt. He got hit by the puck in prac-tice in a spot that is a very important part of your life so they called me up. Doug Soetaert was the other goalie. Then in February they called me up for a game against Winnipeg. [*February 23, 1985, to be exact.*] Penney was hurt again. Soetaert was in goal and after two periods it was 4–4 and he had only 11 shots. Jacques Lemaire was the coach, and after the second period he came in the dressing room and said to me, "You're in for the third period." I was like, wow! I was so nervous but I think the guys were more nervous than me. They didn't know what to expect. But I just faced two shots, two inoffensive shots, and we won, 6–4.

I stayed for another couple of weeks but didn't play again. We took a trip west and I was always practising with the team. I wasn't even a rookie. I was just replacing Steve Penney, but I was trying very hard to stop every shot. I was on the ice on this side, on the ice on that side. Lemaire sent his assistant, Jean Perron, to talk to me and he said, "Lemaire asked if you want a bed." I didn't understand, but what he meant was I was on the ice too much, lying down too much. It was his way of saying, get a bed or a pillow if you're going to lie down so much in the crease.

That was a tough trip. We went to Calgary and then there was a big snowstorm in Minnesota and we had to land in Salt Lake City and spend the night there. We finally got to Minnesota about 7:30 the next night, but they played the game anyway and we lost. The guys were kind of nervous. After the game Lemaire came in the room and started to put a rating for every player against his name on the blackboard. This guy, 1, this guy, 2. He gave a rating for everybody and then, *boom*, he left the room. It was kind of impressive for me because I had never seen things like that.

In Granby we were out of the playoffs with seven or eight games left in the season. Montreal asked me to go to their American League team in Sherbrooke. I could not play because the season was not over in Granby. I practised with the team and that was the first time I worked with François Allaire, the Canadiens' goalie coach. He helped me lose a lot of bad habits I had from junior. I played one game, against New Haven, in the regular season, and then played thirteen games in the playoffs and we won the Calder Cup. [*Roy, then nineteen years old, had a 2.89 average in the AHL playoffs and won ten games.*]

The next year I had a great training camp in Montreal. I was confident because I had a good end of the season in Sherbrooke. I thought it was a pretty big step from junior to the American Hockey League, but it was not as big a step from the American League to the National League. The shots were almost as hard when I played in Sherbrooke. Jacques Lemaire had quit as coach and Jean Perron had taken over. Just before the first game he came to me and said, "Okay, Patrick. You're gonna start." I was kind of laughing, but at the same time I was nervous. It was my twentieth birthday.

We played the game in Pittsburgh and I gave up a goal early in the game. Larry Robinson came to me and said, "Okay, relax. Things are gonna get better. I'm gonna put one in." Gilles Meloche was the other goalie and I remember seeing Larry grab the puck and he let it go from the blueline. He blasted one and, *boom*, it's in. It's a 1–1 game and I said, wow, this guy is for real. I started to feel more comfortable, more confident. We won the game, 5–3.

That first season was tough. [*Patrick played in 47 games with a 3.35 average.*] I was giving up a bad goal per game. One day late in the season I was in the sauna and Larry came in. He said, "Hey, Pat, there's one thing you've got to do. You've got to cut down that bad goal per game and we'll be okay." I just said, "Yeah," but I thought about it. I was definitely the question mark on our team when the playoffs started. Everybody thought the weakness in Montreal was the goaltending. At the same time I tried to use the Calder Cup experience to give me confidence. I said, "You've got to believe." I told my dad, "I think we ought to win the Cup." He kind of laughed and I said, "I really believe we're gonna win the Cup." We opened at home against Boston and I had 10 shots at the start of the game. Really quick, bing–bing–bing. I made a few good saves, and that was it.

That was it, indeed. In 1986 the Montreal Canadiens won a Stanley Cup nobody expected them to win and their previously unknown rookie goaltender was the big story. The Canadiens eliminated the Bruins three straight. An exciting series against Hartford wasn't decided until overtime of the seventh game. The Canadiens then eliminated the New York Rangers in five games and the Calgary Flames in five to win the Cup. Roy played every minute of the 20 games, posting a remarkable 1.92 GAA. That average wasn't quite as low as the 0.40 he had in the midget tournament five years before, but it wasn't bad. To top it off, he was named the MVP of the playoffs.

If you were to ask Montreal fans to vote on their best memory of the 1986 playoffs I think it would be unanimous: Patrick Roy's performance in the third game of the Wales Conference final against the Rangers, in New York. The Canadiens won the first two games in Montreal and were tied, 3–3, after regulation time in game three. In the first nine minutes of overtime Roy made 13 saves, most of them in the "miraculous" category. At 9:41 Claude Lemieux scored the game-winning goal on only the Canadiens' second shot of OT. Long-time superstar Jean Béliveau was at the game and called Roy's performance "the best nine minutes of playoff goaltending I've ever seen."

PATRICK ROY

That game in New York was definitely my best memory. That was probably one of my best games in my life. It was probably my first one as important as that. Winning or losing that game was a big difference. We lose and it's a 2–1 series and they would get momentum. It was funny. I was so bad in English and after the games in New York all these guys are coming to interview me. Gaetan Lefebvre [the Canadiens' athletic trainer] was always beside me and helped with the questions I didn't understand. I didn't want to say any stupid things. So he was there translating for me and they asked me, "Why did you turn around and stare at your net after the national anthem?" I said, "I was talking to my goal posts." They made a big thing out of that and it was so funny, especially in New York where they like things like that.

It's not really talking to my goal posts, you know. I just turn around and look at the net. I like the vision of seeing the net getting smaller. It gives me confidence, makes me feel bigger. For goaltenders everything is playing between your ears. If you can believe it, you can do it. If you're not confident when you start, it makes a difference. A little pass might hit your pads and hit the post and go wide. Or it might hit your pad and then the post and then it goes in. But it's not a big thing. It started in Hartford where we have to turn around and face the flags. I turned around and I started to look at the net and say, hey. I started to feel good in that first period. I made some good saves and we tied. We went to Boston the next night and I tried the same thing. We tied again. I got a good call from the ref, Paul Stewart, on a shot from Ray Bourque that I think went in. They didn't count it. After that I kept doing it.

I agree with Patrick when he talks about his first playoff game against Boston and says, "That was it." That was the night Patrick Roy the rookie started to become Patrick Roy the All-Star. He made everyone sit up and take notice and he kept building his reputation from that point. The NHL Official Guide *tells how well he built it in the section "Individual Trophies." In 1987, '88, and '89 he shared three straight Jennings trophies with Brian Hayward for being the goalies (minimum 25 games played) on the team with the fewest goals against. Roy played in 46, 45, and 48 games those three seasons. In 1992 he played 65 games and won it by himself. The general managers in the NHL vote on the Vezina Trophy which goes to the outstanding goalie. Roy won that in 1989, 1990, and 1992. In 1993 he won his second Stanley Cup and second Smythe Trophy as the playoff MVP.*

Late in the 1995 season a rookie with the Ottawa Senators, Steve Larouche, scored three goals on Roy. Afterwards he explained that he was extra happy because, "I scored three goals on the best goalie in the world." John Davidson talked about Roy while we chatted for this book.

J.D. doesn't throw accolades around too freely, especially when it comes to goalies. But he said about Roy, "Name me one who has been any better the past twenty years." Montreal sportswriter Red Fisher refers to the Canadiens' Number 33 as "Saint Patrick."

In 1989 the Calgary Flames defeated the Montreal Canadiens in the Stanley Cup final. I couldn't get much out of Patrick on that one. All he would say was, "It was a tough loss for us. Maybe Calgary was more hungry than we were." The next season Roy signed a new contract. In its final season, 1992–93, he was paid a million dollars. That was the good news. The bad news was the way it affected his play, for a while anyway.

PATRICK ROY

That was tough, that one. The first time you make over a million per year you feel like everybody should be satisfied the way you're playing. You want everybody to be happy. You have to do this, you have to do that. I think that's the worst thing I did. I put lots of pressure on myself and I just couldn't take it.

It was probably the toughest year I had in my career. I was watching everything that was happening around me and I wasn't watching myself. If people were mad at me, I was pissed off. If there was something bad written about me, I was mad. I was really affected by everything around. They made a survey in Montreal and the survey said, let's trade Patrick Roy. Seventy per cent of the people were in favour of trading me.

That was the year the All-Star Game was in Montreal and things didn't go very good in the skills competition. The people booed me. In the game the next afternoon I played the first period. I gave up no goals on 10 shots and I felt better. I

start to say, "Just be yourself." Pierre Lacroix was my agent
and we did lots of talking. He was really important to me that
year. I tried not to put extra pressure on myself because I was
making that kind of money. When I stopped doing that I
enjoyed the game more. I started to play better. I'm the type
of guy that loves to go to the rink. If I don't like to go to the
rink because of the critics, I'll have a problem. So I started to
enjoy myself and I finished the season pretty well.

*Patrick Roy finished the 1992–93 season "pretty well," and
two months later he finished the playoffs by screaming into
a TV camera, "I'm going to DisneyWorld!" That opportunity,
and the money that went with it, was his moments after the
Canadiens defeated the Los Angeles Kings at the Montreal
Forum to win the Stanley Cup.*

*Between his rookie-year Cup win in 1986 and the play-
offs in 1993, Patrick Roy was among the dominant goaltenders in the NHL. But as brilliant as he was, most of the
time there were critics who insisted he wasn't so hot in the
playoffs, in the big games. Roy felt a lot of heat that way after
Boston eliminated Montreal four straight in 1992. The heat
was still on the next season when the pollsters found that a
majority of Canadiens' fans thought their team should trade
him. But that would change in 1993. Roy has fond memories of that year's playoffs. For starters, the Canadiens played
20 games and 11 went into overtime. They lost the first,
then won the next 10. Ten consecutive OT wins in one year
had never happened before in Stanley Cup competition, and
it's a safe bet it will never happen again. In those ten games
Roy blanked the Nordiques, Sabres, Islanders, and Kings
through 77 minutes and five seconds of playoff overtime
pressure. Against the Islanders he stopped both Benoit
Hogue and Pierre Turgeon in successive games on overtime
breakaways.*

Between the first and second games of the finals Patrick's wife, Michele, gave birth to their third child, Jana. A few nights later, in Los Angeles, the TV cameras caught Roy making a save and then winking at Tomas Sandstrom, the player he had just stopped. Non-Montreal fans across the country were no doubt complaining about "those cocky Canadiens" and their cocky goaltender.

I've always felt the turning point for the eventual 1993 champions came in the fifth game of their first series against the Quebec Nordiques. Quebec had won the first two games on home ice and the Canadiens had won the next two in Montreal. In the second period of the fifth game Roy suffered a shoulder injury and had to leave the ice. It looked serious, but he was back in his crease to start the third period. Had he not been able to return his team would have had to make do with back-up André "Red Light" Racicot for the rest of the night. That would have meant goodbye to that game and, very likely, to the series and the Cup for Montreal.

PATRICK ROY

At the start of the second period Mike Hough took a shot that hit me on the shoulder and I couldn't move my arm. I went to the dressing room and the doctor froze the back of my shoulder. It didn't work. I still couldn't move my arm. Then the same doctor came back and said, "I think I've got it," and he froze me right where I got hit. Right on the puck. You could tell where it was because there was already swelling there. In two seconds it was like nothing had happened. I went to see Jacques Demers and Serge Savard was with him, downstairs by our dressing room. That was something I had never seen in the past, Serge so close to the rink. I asked Jacques, "Can I go in again?" and he said, "If you want to go, go." We were losing, 4-3. Gilbert Dionne scored to tie the game and we went into overtime. [*Roy made two or three game-saving stops between the tying goal and the end of the period, as did Ron Hextall at the other end. It was a great battle between the two.*] When the overtime started I could feel my shoulder hurting me again. I was standing there hoping someone would score soon. Kirk Muller did it, on a perfect pass from Vincent Damphousse.

In those overtime games we were definitely in what you call a zone. I guess when you win one game, then two, then three, you almost say, "Hey, let's go in overtime. We're gonna win it there." Going into overtime was not something that we were scared of. We were happy to be there. At the end, like in those two games in L.A., everybody was like, okay, that's perfect. We're tied at the end of three and now we're in overtime. That's the way it was when we won both those games out there. Just lose one and the series would be tied, 2-2, and then you go back and forth again and there's all the travelling. I'm not too sure the travelling would have been an advantage for us. I think the Kings were more used to that than we were. It was good to win those two games out there in overtime.

I didn't know the cameras were on me when I did that wink. I was surprised the day after when I heard about that. They made a big thing out of it. I was just in the zone at that moment. I felt really solid and confident. I knew Sandstrom was a guy who could score goals for that team. When I made that save I saw him turn around and come back in front of me. I couldn't resist showing him how confident I was. Maybe I was cocky but you get kind of cocky when you feel that confident. I wanted to show him it was gonna be tough for him to score on me.

When our baby was born in the finals, that was a good one. We lost that first game and then I went to the Lakeshore

Hospital with Michele. We didn't want the baby born when we were in L.A. for the games there so we asked the doctor to induce labour and he agreed. I slept at the hospital all night. Around 6 in the morning Michele started to feel the contractions and, *boom*, about two hours later Jana was born. Then I went to the hotel where we were staying during the playoffs to sleep for a couple of hours and then went to a team meeting.

A couple of weeks later the Roy family went to DisneyWorld. A couple of weeks before the start of the following season Patrick signed a new contract. That one made him a 4-million-dollar man, per season.

Goaltenders are creatures of habit and Patrick Roy is no exception. Here are a few of his on game day:

Morning practice: *Works with François Allaire, who might have noticed recent problems. Feels practice, good or bad, is never an indication of how he will play that night.*
1 p.m.: *Lunch. It used to be spaghetti. Now it's a steak. No more food until after the game.*
1:30 p.m.: *Takes a nap. Never has any trouble going to sleep.*
3:30 p.m.: *Kids charge into bedroom and wake him up. (On the road it's an alarm clock.)*
4:30 p.m.: *Leaves for the Forum.*
5:00 p.m.: *Arrives at the Forum.*
5:10 p.m.: *Puts on hockey underwear. Prepares equipment using same routine every time. Starts preparing sticks (always two).*
6:00 p.m.: *Team meeting with coaching staff. Goes over videos of opponents.*
6:30 p.m.: *Completes dressing for game. Always puts on equipment in same order, left skate, right skate, left pad, right pad. Just like almost every other goalie in captivity.*

6:50 p.m. *On ice for warm-up. Never pays attention to other team. Has the same player take first shots at specific targets, always in the same rotation. (Gloves, pads, corners). For years, Mats Naslund did it. Recently, Kirk Muller and Vincent Damphousse. Skates to blueline and briefly stands beside same player every night. Then back into net.*

7:10 p.m.: *Back in dressing room. Takes off gloves, sweater, and mask and plays with a puck. Uses the same one all season. Bounces it on floor several times, then places it beside him on floor, always to his right. Seven minutes before game time puts sweater and gloves and mask back on.*

7:33 p.m.: *Before national anthem, all players on team get in position around net and perform a head-butting, pad-patting ritual at goal crease. Every player has the same role to play every game.*

7:35 p.m.: *After anthem, turn and look at net.*

During official time-outs: *Goes to bench. Never lets skates touch blueline or red line.*

First and third periods: *Often winks at wife, Michele, who sits behind Roy and to his left.*

Between periods: *Takes off helmet, gloves, sweater, wristbands, and neck protector. Equipment man dries his gloves. Gets dry wristbands and neck protector and puts everything back on seven minutes before start of period.*

After the game: *Tries to be accommodating to the media, win or lose. Takes off equipment, showers, and changes into civvies very slowly, usually too slowly to suit Michele. Sometimes takes an hour. The Roys often stop and eat on the way home. Patrick drives. They don't talk hockey.*

Obviously Patrick Roy does not have time to listen to how most English-language hockey broadcasters mispronounce his last name. The most common mispronunciations are

"RAW," "WAH," and "Roo-HAW." His former coach, Pat Burns, who is fluently bilingual, often refers to Patrick as "Paddy Roy," as in "Rob Roy." The correct way? It's tough to say and tough to write. The trick is to roll the R like . . . "R-r-r-Wah." It took me a while but my French-speaking friends tell me I've finally got it right and they insist, correctly, I keep it that way despite what the boys beside me in the booth are calling him.

In 1993 Michele Roy went to the hospital during the play-offs. In 1994 it was her husband's turn. The Canadiens met the Boston Bruins in the first round. The teams split the first two games in Boston. Then, back in Montreal, the fate of the Montreal Canadiens suddenly depended on Patrick Roy's appendix.

PATRICK ROY

It was bad luck. I went to the Forum the day after we got back from Boston and I told Gaetan Lefebvre I had a pain in my right side. It was really bothering me. He sent me to the Montreal General to see our doctor, Dr. Kinnear. When I got there I sat down and he started to press my right side. He said, "Is it painful?" I said, "It hurts." He didn't say a word. He left, then he came back with three more doctors. He told them to press me. It hurt me every time. He gave me a prescription, told me not to eat anything, and said we would see what's gonna happen. I stayed in the hospital.

Nothing happened. I woke up in the morning with as much pain as before. He gave me some ultrasound to see how big it was and he said it was almost double in size. Then he said, "You can't play tonight." I wanted to play but he said it was too dangerous. They were confident I could play in the fourth game. I went to the Forum and talked with the guys.

I said, "Let's win that game, guys." [*They didn't.*] Then I went back to the hospital.

The day after, it was not much better. I still had lots of pain in my right side. The doctor said, wait, it takes 48 hours. That night I had my first real dinner in a few days. The next morning they came in around 8 o'clock. And you know what? I had no more pain. I couldn't believe it. I said, "Wow, I'm ready to go." They sent me downstairs for another ultrasound to make sure I wasn't lying. They found out it was almost normal. They told me to practise and if I felt good then I could play in the game. I was free and I was happy. But to tell you the truth I was tired. Really tired. But when I heard the crowd that night I had goosebumps. That really got me in the game and we won.

Game five in Boston went into overtime. Montreal won on a goal by Kirk Muller at 17:18. But the big story was Roy, who made 60 saves. It was one of the best games I ever saw him play.

PATRICK ROY

In Boston the number of shots doesn't mean anything. It's a small rink and they shoot from everywhere. That was a good game for me but I think that was the end for me because I was so tired. When we came back to Montreal and lost the next game, that was the killer. I needed that win because I was already very tired and that would have given us a few days off before we played New Jersey. But we didn't win it and back in Boston they beat us in the seventh game. After the playoffs they took out my appendix.

After what happened with my first big contract I learned to put money on the side and concentrate on my real goal which is to play hockey and win the Stanley Cup. For me, money is business but hockey is my game. I love the game. Every time I'm going on the ice all I think about is winning. There's not a big difference for me before the games now. I'm always nervous but I feel better when the puck is dropped. You always have the fear of losing, especially in Montreal. It makes me play better, I guess.

Of course what I make is lots of money. It's something I never thought I would make in my life. I was making one hundred [thousand], one fifty, one seventy-five when I started, and I was just as happy as I am today. It's just that the game changed and the money is big if you compare it with what it was before. Not big. I should say huge. But it's there and there's no reason why we should not go for it. But after that it's more important for me to win games than make money.

I think it's important at a certain point in your career to prepare for your retirement. I'm kind of scared for the end. I guess everybody's like that. I love the game and I know I'm gonna miss it. I don't want to see it come to an end but I want to be prepared. Right now hockey is finished for most of us between thirty and thirty-five. There's not too many guys over thirty-five years old. It's important you've got something in front of you.

Sometimes when we lose a game I want to retire. When we win a game I want to play ten more years. My contract has two more years. I'll be thirty-two. When I signed it I said when it was over I would look seriously at what I'm going to do. I still think that way. I'll see how good I think I can still be. I don't know if I could take it not to be as good as I am now. I'm tough on myself. I want to play well year after year. That's my objective. But if I find I'm slowing down, if I can't get my objective, I don't know if I can handle that. I'll see if I have the same desire to keep going. Like I said, I'm really scared of the end.

13

Some Current Voices

MIKE RICHTER   TIM CHEVELDAE

JEFF HACKETT   CURTIS JOSEPH

FELIX POTVIN   MARTIN BRODEUR

MIKE VERNON

As I looked at the relaxed young man sitting across from me
dressed in his hockey underwear, a cup of coffee in his hand
and a smile on his cherubic face, I thought to myself, "This
guy's got it made." The guy was Mike Richter of the New
York Rangers and we were in the Hockey Night in Canada
production office at the Montreal Forum the morning of a
Canadiens–Rangers game midway through the shortened
1995 NHL season.

Mike Richter was still basking in the glow of 1993–94.
After a few seasons sharing the Rangers' goaltending duties
with John Vanbiesbrouck, the job had become his alone
when "The Beezer" moved to the expansion Florida
Panthers. Richter played in 68 regular-season games and set
a franchise record with 42 victories. He became the first
New York goalie in twenty-five years to lead the NHL in
games won. He went through a 20-game unbeaten streak,
another team record. In the 1994 All-Star Game in New

York, Richter played the second period for the Eastern Conference and stopped *19 of 21* shots to earn a new car as player of the game.

When the season was over the Rangers had finished first overall. Two months later, after Richter made a couple of dramatic saves in the dying minutes of the third period of the seventh game of the Stanley Cup finals against the Vancouver Canucks to preserve a *3–2* victory, the Stanley Cup was back in Madison Square Garden for the first time in fifty-four years. In the fourth game of the finals Richter stopped the NHL's leading goal scorer, Pavel Bure, on a penalty shot. Emotions were running so high in New York one of the newspapers in the Big Apple headlined that one as *"THE GREATEST SAVE IN HOCKEY HISTORY."* I guess after fifty-four years you couldn't blame them for getting a little carried away.

The day after the Cup was won, Mike Richter along with teammates Mark Messier and Brian Leetch, plus the Stanley Cup, appeared on the *"Late Show with David Letterman."* Five days before we had our chat he had signed a new four-year contract worth *$13* million. Mike had become RICH-ter. The guy had it made.

MIKE RICHTER

From the first time I saw a hockey game I wanted to play in the pros. I grew up in the Philadelphia area and in the '70s hockey was a pretty big thing because the Flyers were winning the Stanley Cup. That's when they were the Broad Street Bullies. Like most of the kids I played a lot of street hockey. My two older brothers played ice hockey ahead of me. Joe, the one closest to me who is three years older than I am, was a goalie. He bought a set of used equipment and really enjoyed playing goal so it was just a matter of time before I followed in his footsteps. My brothers and I practised all the time together, taking turns in the net and shooting at each other. I mean, it was an everyday thing all winter long and all summer long.

You had your pro heros you tried to imitate. I always pretended I was Bernie Parent. Then in 1980 the Olympics were in Lake Placid and the Americans won the gold medal. We went in to watch the gold-medal game and when we went back out to play in the street I was Jim Craig. It captured the spirit of so many kids, not only in America but everywhere.

I had wanted to go away as early as possible to Canada to play junior or in any league that would enable me to make it to the pros. I always felt I was at a bit of a disadvantage playing in Philadelphia where the programs weren't as serious as in Canada. But because of that my brother and I ended up working harder in the summer and going to hockey camps and doing whatever we could do to get extra ice time. We played in high school at a place called Northwood and they had a fantastic program. We played some games right in the Olympic Arena in Lake Placid and it was a great stepping stone for me before I went to the University of Wisconsin.

After two years at Wisconsin I spent a year with the U.S. National Team and played at the Calgary Olympics. We had a talented team with people like Kevin Stevens, Brian Leetch, and Craig Janney. But we really didn't have a lot of experience. The potential was there but we never seemed to realize it. It turned out to be a disappointing Olympics and we finished seventh. We lost to teams we were supposed to beat and beat teams we were supposed to lose to. Given a little more experience we could have gone a long way in that tournament. I think we were just a little young.

I had been drafted by New York in 1985. Right after the Olympics I turned pro and they sent me to Denver. I spent the rest of that season there and all of the next one. In '89, just as the NHL playoffs were starting and we were heading into our playoffs, they called me up. That's how I came to play my first game in the NHL in the playoffs. That's pretty rare. People say, geez, that must have been a tough way to break in. I never really thought of it that way because I hadn't known any other way.

Phil Esposito was the G.M. and they were playing Pittsburgh. New York had gone through a lot of turmoil that year. Coach Bergeron had been fired just before the end of the season and Phil took over behind the bench. We went to Pittsburgh and lost the first two games. Nothing seemed to be working for them. They were going to dress me as back-up for one of those games but they didn't. In the second game John Vanbiesbrouck came in to relieve Bob Froese and played well. But he got beaten pretty soundly in the next game in New York. They thought they would try something to give the team a lift so they started me the next game.

It was really a fantastic experience. We were down three games going into the fourth on home ice. The fans were pretty restless. I can remember, right off the opening faceoff, Mario Lemieux and Paul Coffey came down on a two-on-nothing break. That was really something. It was like one moment I was watching Mario on TV, and the next I was playing against him and he's coming in on a two-man break with Coffey. But they didn't score because they never got a shot off. I still don't understand how that happened and I was shaking my head after the play stopped. I think each of them was fighting for the puck to see who could get the goal on the new guy in the net. [Laughs] They did score early on me but I settled in and I ended up playing okay. We lost, 4–3, and the series was over. But I felt I had taken a pretty important step heading into the next year. I didn't have to worry again about playing my first game. Certainly I didn't have to worry about playing my first playoff game because that was behind me. It was an experience that helped me come into the next year with confidence.

Mike Richter started the 1989–90 season with the team and got his first NHL win October 19 against the Hartford Whalers. But shortly after that he was sent to Flint, of the International League, where he stayed until called back to play against the Soviet Wings in an exhibition game on New Year's Eve. He stayed in New York after that. The goaltending job was being shared by Vanbiesbrouck and Bob Froese. But Froese was bothered by an injured shoulder which eventually forced him to retire and for most of that season and the next three it was the "John and Mike Show" in the crease at Madison Square Garden.

Roger Neilson was coaching the Rangers in those days and didn't give either goalie the feeling that he was number one. In 1990–91 the two men alternated without interruption through the first 76 games of the season. (That's an obscure NHL record.) Then Richter played the final four games of the regular season and all six games in the playoffs when the Rangers were eliminated by the Washington Capitals in the first round.

MIKE RICHTER

It was incredible. The year before that we had just gone with whoever Rog thought was playing well. We had success in the regular season but came up short in the playoffs. But whether it was John playing two games and me one, or vice versa, it had worked and that was the biggest thing. Then that one year it started right from the beginning. I'd play a game and John would play a game and since we were both playing fairly well and the team was having success he kept the rotation going. He stayed with it through the first 76 games. Then I guess he thought I was a bit warmer than John. It was quite an experience. John and I got along very well and Rog stayed with it.

In 1993 the NHL added two more teams, the Florida Panthers and the Mighty Ducks of Anaheim, to its constantly expanding family. This time the lords of the game finally took some pity on the newcomers and decided to give them a better break for the $50 million they paid just to get in the door. They ruled that existing teams could protect only one goaltender before the expansion draft. With two good ones on their roster the Rangers had a tough decision to make. Rather than having one drafted and getting nothing in return they traded John Vanbiesbrouck to the Vancouver Canucks for defenceman Doug Lidster. The Canucks protected Kirk McLean and the Beezer was claimed by Florida, who had hired Roger Neilson as their first coach. Neilson had been fired by New York after the Rangers failed to make the playoffs in 1993. Mike Keenan took over from Neilson in New York and the stage was set for Richter and the Rangers to have their championship year.

The ghost of 1940 had haunted the New York team in its half-century quest for another Stanley Cup and Mike Richter had a playoff ghost of his own hanging around. In 1992 New York had played the defending-champion Pittsburgh Penguins in the second round. New York won the third game in Pittsburgh, in overtime, to take a 2–1 series lead. In the fourth game the Rangers were leading, 4–2, when the Penguins' Ron Francis took a shot from outside the Rangers' blueline. Richter missed it. The Penguins had been struggling but the long-shot goal gave them a big lift. Pittsburgh came back to win that game, 6–5, and went on to eliminate New York in six games. From then until the playoffs of '94, thanks to a lot of media types and a lot of fans in New York, Mike Richter was haunted by the "Ron Francis goal."

MIKE RICHTER

A lot of weight has been placed on that goal. It was a pivotal game and we were playing Pittsburgh in Pittsburgh. In the third period Francis came across the red line and right around our blueline, almost on the faceoff spot, he took a slap shot. I got a piece of it but it went in. It was a long enough shot where you could pick it up but I didn't until it was a little bit late. I misjudged it and he scored. But we were still ahead, 4–3, at the time. However, it was Pittsburgh we were playing and they have fire power and you can't give them an inch. Well, that was the inch I gave them. They tied the game with about ten minutes to go on a more-or-less good-work goal that I think bounced off one of our defencemen. But they got it and tied the game and Rog pulled me. We ended up losing in overtime and the difference was they had got so much momentum from that goal.

Many people pointed to that goal as being the pivotal change in the whole series and in some ways it probably was. In other ways, you know the game is comprised of 60 minutes and there were many saves I made in that game that I felt other goalies couldn't have made. In some ways I felt it was unfair that so much weight had been placed on that one particular shot, that one particular goal, because you're in there the whole time. After that one goal people said I'm not a pressure performer. I read somewhere that what happened in '94 meant I had finally put to rest the idea that I wasn't a playoff goaltender. After we won the Stanley Cup people actually came up to me and said, "Now you can finally put to rest the Ron Francis goal." I don't know how many goals I finally put to rest. To be honest, I'd like to have them all back.

The New York Rangers' trail to the Stanley Cup in 1994 was a smooth one through the first two rounds as they eliminated the New York Islanders in four straight games and the Washington Capitals in five. Then the theatrics began as they faced the New Jersey Devils in the Eastern Conference final. It was a great series that went the full seven games. Three games went into double overtime, including the last one, which ended on a goal by the Rangers' Stephane Matteau.

The Rangers dominated the first game against the Vancouver Canucks in the Stanley Cup final but didn't win because of a great goaltending performance by Vancouver's Kirk McLean. McLean stopped 51 shots, 14 of them in the first ten minutes of overtime, enabling his team to win, 3–2, on a goal by Greg Adams. Had McLean not been as good as he was that night the series would have been over in straight games because the Rangers won the next three, 3–1, 5–1, 4–2. On the day of the fifth game the New York Post headlined "TONIGHT'S THE NIGHT." It wasn't. The Canucks scored three goals in the third period to win, 6–3. Two nights later in Vancouver it was 4–1, Canucks. The travel-weary teams headed back to New York for the dramatic seventh game, the first in a Cup final since 1987. Final score: New York 3, Vancouver 2. Nobody said it would be easy.

MIKE RICHTER

I can't necessarily put my hand on one defining moment in the playoffs in 1994. We played 23 games and what I can do is admit to a feeling of complete satisfaction when it was over. It wasn't just winning the last game, because there were other games I felt were equal to it in intensity. The Devils tied the score in the seventh game with seven seconds to go.

We had to overcome the shock of that happening right in our building when we were thinking of going to the finals. Suddenly we were saying, "Geez, our season could be over."

Like Kevin Lowe said, if it was easier it wouldn't be as much fun. The feeling that you get from having your back against the wall and then coming through was a real growing experience. I know I'm definitely a better athlete for having gone through it.

In the last few seconds of the last game, well, there was a special interest in them because of what had happened in the Jersey series when we had been scored on from a faceoff in our zone. Vancouver had hit posts, it was 3-2, and the clock's winding down. We go into the last ten-second countdown and the puck is shot out of our zone. It looks to me like it's gonna just wrap around the corner and I think we've won. The place was just electric and you couldn't hear the whistles or anything. Brian Leetch and I are hugging each other. The gloves are starting to come off but nobody's coming off our bench. The whistle had gone because there was an icing and there was still 1.6 seconds on the clock. We look around and put our tail between our legs, quickly, and put our gloves back on.

You know, as I sit here in this chair 1.6 seconds doesn't seem like an awful lot of time. But it's long enough for a shot, maybe even a rebound. We had been stunned late in games in the playoffs and I was thinking to myself, other teams have scored like this but the odds are, the puck's gonna hit me. I was anticipating getting at least one shot. I kind of hoped for it. But Craig MacTavish did exactly what Neil Smith brought him in to do. He won the faceoff, put it in the corner, and Steve Larmer was there fighting for the puck. It was over.

It was such a sense of relief. Every player had been saying, "I'm not a part of 1940. I wasn't around then." But you are. It's part of your organization. You're working for this team and you want to bring pride to the people you're working for. It had been a long climb, an emotional up-and-down time. There were all kinds of things swirling around by the time the finals were going on. There was all the talk about Mike Keenan maybe leaving and about him benching certain guys. There was a lot of controversy.

When it ended there was almost a sense of loss because I was disappointed it was over. You're so involved. You're playing the best you can and for a period of about two months we'd been playing a game almost every other night. It was the most professional, disciplined team I'd ever been around. It was so much fun to go out there and work hard every day. In a sense I didn't want the summer to come.

I look around and see so many goaltenders who have played a lot of years in the NHL and never won a Stanley Cup. I have to remember that I was on a great team. I met Gump Worsley in the summer and there's a guy who won, how many Cups here in Montreal? You look at guys who have been on dynasties. Messier and Lowe getting their sixth rings. It's just an amazing thing. I've experienced it once and it certainly makes you hungry to do it again.

While things couldn't have been much better for Mike Richter in 1993–94, they couldn't have been much worse for Tim Cheveldae. When the season began Cheveldae was starting his fifth season as the number-one goaltender for the Detroit Red Wings. By the time it ended the fans in Detroit had booed him out of town and all the way to Winnipeg.

Cheveldae had been a workhorse in Detroit. In the previous three seasons he had played 65, 72 (a league high), and 67 games. While the reasons he left the Joe Louis Arena weren't pleasant, the way he arrived there was quite bizarre.

TIM CHEVELDAE

I was playing for Adirondack in the American League and the Red Wings phoned me at 1 o'clock in the afternoon. Greg Stefan was hurt and they needed a back-up for Glen Hanlon. I was all excited. A lot of different emotions were running through my mind. The Adirondack team was based in Glens Falls, which was an hour from Albany, where I had to go to catch a 2 o'clock flight to Detroit. I got there just as the plane was taxiing down the runway. The next plane to Detroit wasn't until 6 o'clock. It's an hour-and-a-half flight and of course the game is starting at 7:30.

When I arrived in Detroit it was already 7:30 and they had cops waiting at the airport to rush me to Joe Louis Arena. The police chief was at the hockey game and he gave orders for them to fly me downtown in a police helicopter. So we drove to a little airport beside the Metro Airport and, sure enough, they flew me in a helicopter. We landed on the roof of Cobo Hall, which is next to the Joe Louis. By the time I got into the dressing room the first period was over. If something had happened to Glen Hanlon in the first period the back-up would have been the team psychiatrist who hadn't played hockey in about twenty years.

I didn't play that time, but they brought me up later and I played my first game in Calgary. That was the year they won the Stanley Cup. The game was on TSN and I knew it was going back to my home town [Melville, Saskatchewan]. I remember standing there during the national anthem. At a time like that you say to yourself, "Geez, what am I doing out here with these players?" We lost, 3–2, in overtime. I stopped something like 46 shots.

A person who had a lot of influence on me was Dave Dryden, our goalie coach my first year in Adirondack. Your first year as a pro is a very difficult one for a goalie. It's such a big change from junior. Dave worked with me a lot, taught me little things. I found him to be very intelligent about goaltending. He didn't bring a lot of different things to the table right away. But he slowly got to know you and understand how you work. I really liked that about him.

When I got to Detroit to stay I played a lot. I played in over 60 games three years in a row. I played 66 games my last year junior in Saskatoon so I was used to it. At that time several teams had one goalie playing the majority of games. It can be fun, especially when you're on a winning team. You get into a routine where you never think about not playing. It's a mindset. You wake up in the morning, it's game day, and you say, "I'm playing tonight. We're practising tomorrow and I'm gonna play the game after that." You never worry about ice time.

The hardest part is when you're losing. You get down and start second-guessing yourself. It's not the physical part so much. The coach might give you a few days off or you don't practise as hard. It's the mental part. You find yourself drained when you come to the rink the day after a loss. You're not on the emotional high like you are when you're winning.

We went to a seventh game in the playoffs every year when I was playing all those games in Detroit. We lost to St. Louis, beat Minnesota, and then lost to Toronto in overtime in '93. We had been down to Minnesota, 3–1, so that was a positive feeling. The one against Toronto was, without a doubt, the most emotional experience I've gone through. It's really tough to take when you lose a seventh game in overtime on your home ice. I remember having trouble sleeping every night for two weeks after the series. My wife wasn't really enjoying living with me a whole lot.

The next season, after that Toronto loss, I started with a three-game winning streak at home. Then right after that I remember letting in a goal against New York that came from the blueline and right away they were all over me. They were just waiting in the weeds for something negative to happen. They kept booing me. I was in a bad situation and started to wonder how I was going to get out of it. If I won ten games in a row and had one bad game I knew they'd be all over me for that one bad game.

If the home crowd is booing its goalie it's a negative influence on the whole team. You know how they announce the starting line-up just as the players are coming on the ice? Well, in Detroit they changed that around. They did it before we came on the ice so I wouldn't get booed and the other players wouldn't hear it.

I kept wondering how I was going to get out of the situation I was in without being traded. I got to love playing on the road where I was winning more games than at home. But I knew a trade was going to happen. It was just a matter of time and you try to prepare yourself. But that was hard because it had never happened to me. When I was traded to Winnipeg [March 8, 1994] I was glad it was over with. There was a little disappointment going from a first-place team to a team that was basically out of the playoffs. That was probably the hardest thing to get used to. But the people in Winnipeg were great and the organization treated me real well.

After it was over in Detroit I had a bad taste about certain things. I still go back in the summer and do hockey schools and the people I meet in the street are great to me. But there were a few people in management there I didn't like a whole heck of a lot. My last year there Scotty Bowman was the coach and he treated me well. I'm sure he wanted another goalie and he wanted the trade but he was one of the few people in Detroit who tried to take the pressure off me. I had no complaints about him.

A couple of weeks after the trade Detroit played in Winnipeg. We won, 4–2, and that was quite a night for me. You obviously want to perform well against the guys you played with. Probably the thing I enjoyed most was the last 30 seconds when the fans were on their feet cheering. I enjoyed those 30 seconds the most of any game I can remember for a long time. The atmosphere was great. At the end of the game Steve Yzerman came up to me and said, "You played great." Barry Smith, the assistant coach, shook my hand. I probably enjoyed that part of it the most.

I like all sports. I love playing tennis and I've become a collector. I collect autographs, eight-by-tens, autographed baseballs, and autographed footballs. I've got a Bo Jackson game jersey from when he was with the L.A. Raiders and a Dan Marino game jersey from when he was with the Miami Dolphins. They'd be the most valuable things I've collected so far.

Obviously every goaltender would love to win the Stanley Cup, be the goalie that carried the team, that sort of thing. Like Patrick Roy the year he won ten straight overtime games. That was amazing. I don't know if that will ever happen but one thing I do know is that someday I'd like to coach. I've had a passion in me the last three years to see how I would do. You have five, six, seven, or eight coaches during your career and you pick up what you like and what you don't like and think about what type of coach you want to be. That's what I'd like to do in the future.

The strangest events surrounding any hockey game I have broadcast occurred January 4, 1992, in San Francisco, California. The Montreal Canadiens played the San Jose Sharks in the Cow Palace, where the Sharks were playing home games while their new arena was under construction in San Jose. Why were these events strange? Let me count the ways:

1. Just as the teams were coming onto the ice to start the game, and I was starting my broadcast for CJAD Radio in Montreal, it was discovered the Zamboni had picked up one of the pegs that support the goal posts and dragged it around a few times. The driver hadn't noticed and there were big gouges in the ice surface. The teams were sent back while the damage was repaired. That took forty-five minutes. For me, it was "fill time," as we say in the radio business. Luckily I was able to interview some old friends who were at the game, including former Montreal players Terry Harper and Gerry Heffernan. Hockey writer Red Fisher, my long-time travel buddy, knew I was in trouble and came by to help bail me out.

2. At the end of the first period there was a wedding – that's right, an honest-to-goodness wedding. As soon as the period was over the happy couple and a preacher skated out and the ceremony was performed at centre ice. When it was over, the newlyweds were pelted with popcorn instead of confetti.

3. During the second intermission the Zamboni driver did it again. This time he missed the gate as he was leaving the ice and crashed into the boards. Fortunately that repair job took only five minutes, not forty-five.

4. During the third period a violent rainstorm hit the Bay area and the Cow Palace roof started to leak. Water was streaming down about three feet in front of Patrick Roy's goal crease.

5. To top things off, during the regulation three periods nobody scored a goal. Considering all the weird things that had been happening I thought 0–0 would be a fitting final score and hoped it would stay that way. But Guy

Carbonneau spoiled that wish with a goal in overtime and the Canadiens won, 1–0.

The goalie for the Sharks that night was Jeff Hackett. A good-looking young man from London, Ontario, Hackett started his pro career in the New York Islanders' organization in 1988, then was selected by San Jose in the expansion draft in 1991. After two seasons with the Sharks, Hackett was traded to the Chicago Blackhawks.

I have to confess I don't remember anything about Jeff Hackett's performance against Montreal on that bizarre night at the Cow Palace. I guess I got too carried away by the lovely wedding ceremony. But I definitely remember seeing him in action two years later when I attended a Blues–Blackhawks game in St. Louis. Brett Hull was flying that night for the Blues. In the second period Hull had five shots, every one a bullet, and Hackett made great stops on all five. If you wanted an example of what a goalie goes through facing pucks travelling at 100 miles per hour, and then some, in today's NHL, that was it.

JEFF HACKETT

I guess I started out as a goalie like a lot of guys have. My older brother was a forward and he needed somebody to shoot at and that somebody was me. I got interested in the position and started to follow the career of Tony Esposito. That's who I pretended to be when I was playing goal as a kid. I played two years of junior in Oshawa and we got to the Memorial Cup finals.

In my first year pro I played half the season with the Islanders and half with Springfield. The next year I stayed in Springfield and we won the Calder Cup. Jimmy Roberts was the coach and he was a great influence on my career. He was tough, sort of from the old school. But everybody liked and respected him. He was the real leader when we won the championship.

The first time I played in the NHL was in St. Louis. I started out that night backing up Billy Smith. After the first period the score was 3–0 or 4–0 for them. In the dressing room after the period Billy comes over to me and says, "You know, I never played good in this building. You'd better be ready, kid." In the second period they got a couple more so Billy came out and I went in. We ended up losing, 8–0, so it wasn't a very memorable debut.

That was Billy Smith's last year, but I was around enough to see what a great competitor he was. I was a young guy and very impressionable at training camp. I was watching Smith all the time. He hated to lose. Al Arbour had retired for the first time and Terry Simpson was the coach. At camp they had a competition called "The Arbour Cup." They formed teams, everybody put in twenty bucks, and the winning team split the money. Billy wouldn't pay until he lost. He just hated to lose, even in scrimmage. He wasn't even going to think about losing, so why pay?

I've had over 50 shots in a game a couple of times in the NHL. The first was with New York when I had 55 in a game against Chicago and we won. Los Angeles had 59 against me one night when I was with the Sharks and we won, 7–2. When you're in games like that you're just in a zone. Everything seems to be clicking and you're excited to have a shot because everything's going so well. You don't mind the shots. In fact, you want shots, you want the puck because you feel so comfortable and confident. You know you're going to make the save.

When you play teams with big stars, especially when you're first in the league, you're on pins and needles. For me it was when I played against Wayne Gretzky. When I was a kid everybody idolized him. Then you're playing against him and at first you can't believe you're actually on the ice with the guy. After you play against him a few times you're not quite as intimidated and you start feeling better about yourself, about being in the league, about everything.

The first year in San Jose wasn't all that bad. We did better than people thought we would and ended up with 39 points. But the second year was a disaster. We only had 24 points, the same as Ottawa, and they were a new team. I played in 36 games that year and we lost 30 of them. It was easy to lose your confidence. It was tough on everybody, the players and the coaching staff.

Every once in a while, maybe in practice, I stop and wonder why in heck I'm making my living as a goaltender. Like, why am I here? But then you get involved in the thrill and excitement of a game and you don't think that way anymore. There's nothing like it when you have made a great save or played a great game. The greatest feeling a goalie can have is to have played well and know you've really contributed to the cause when your team has won the game.

During a 1993 playoff series between the St. Louis Blues and the Toronto Maple Leafs, the Blues' Curtis Joseph put on one of the most brilliant goaltending displays ever seen. In the first three games Toronto blasted 159 shots at the St. Louis net. Joseph stopped 154 of them and the Blues were ahead two games to one. The Maple Leafs won the next two games. In the sixth game Joseph made 40 more saves and his team won, 2–1. St. Louis lost the seventh game but Joseph had demonstrated again that with a good goalie you'll often win when you deserve to lose.

The coast-to-coast audience watching the series on Hockey Night in Canada *was treated to a great battle*

*between two young goalies, Joseph and Felix Potvin. They
even had nicknames: "Cujo" and "Felix the Cat," just like
goalies in the old days.*

*Dealing with all those shots in the playoffs wasn't exactly
a new experience for Joseph. During the regular season that
year he played 68 games and faced an NHL record of 2,202
shots. He stopped 2,006, also a record. The following season
he appeared in 71 games and, whether he wanted to or not,
broke his own records by facing 2,382 shots and saving
2,169. There aren't many quiet nights in the crease for Cujo.*

*Curtis Joseph was a late bloomer, as Canadian goalies go.
When he became available in the draft, nobody picked him.
But he persevered, thanks in part to a year spent roughing it
as an easterner playing goal for the Hounds at Notre Dame
College in Wilcox, Saskatchewan, the famed school founded
by the legendary Father Athol Murray.*

CURTIS JOSEPH

The reason I started late was because my mom was always
afraid I'd get hurt playing hockey. I always had a love for the
game. I finally started to play when I was ten or eleven, and
because I couldn't skate I became a goalie. I'd fall down all
the time and stop all the shots because nobody could raise
the puck. All the parents would say, "Oh, you were great out
there." I believed them and just kept on playing goal.

I didn't get drafted. I couldn't even get a scholarship and
that's all I'd been dreaming about. I played three years of tier-
two junior in Richmond Hill, Ontario, and then I went out
west. The son of friends of ours had gone to Notre Dame to
play football and they put me on to Martin Kenney [son of
the famed orchestra leader Mart Kenney], who was the president of the school. He said, "Son, you come out here and
you'll get a scholarship, guaranteed." It was worth a try

because I was twenty years old and was an over-age junior. I thought it would be my last chance. That was the first year Notre Dame had a junior hockey team.

So I went west and, sure enough, after our first exhibition game I got offered a scholarship to North Dakota. I was just amazed. Three-quarters of the players on the team were still midget age and the colleges were lined up outside the dressing room with scholarships. Rod Brind'Amour was on the team. I think we ended up with seventeen Division 1 scholarships that year.

Things weren't very sophisticated at Notre Dame. Six of us lived in the same trailer. There was no guarantee there would be hot water every time you went to take a shower. I had never been out west and at twenty I was like an old man in the middle of a bunch of kids. I worked on maintenance, building fences for some of the teachers and cleaning up the yards. Stuff like that. Only one or two guys had cars. If you wanted to go in to Regina you had to make sure that there was gas in the car because the gas station closed at 5 o'clock. At times I would say to myself, "Geez, I'm twenty years old. What am I doing out here?"

But you know what? I learned a lot at Notre Dame. Barry McKenzie, probably one of the best coaches I'll ever have, taught us so much in his speeches. They didn't pertain just to hockey, they pertained to life. Everybody was treated equally and I learned what a team was all about. I wouldn't have traded that experience for the world.

I decided on Wisconsin when it came to getting a scholarship. Mike Richter had been there but he was wasn't coming back. He was turning pro and I thought that was the best opportunity, the best school with the best program. I was there for one year because I was a free agent so that speeded things up for my career.

I hadn't really been noticed before I went to Notre Dame

and Wisconsin. I never had a goalie coach and nobody ever told me what to do. I played on a last-place team in a small town and always had a ton of shots. It was the same thing when I played junior. But that's one way you learn. Playing on bad teams was good for me in the long run.

After my year at Wisconsin I signed as a free agent with St. Louis. A few teams were bidding on me so I had some choices. St. Louis seemed to be the best opportunity. I went to their camp and Greg Millen, Vincent Riendeau, and Pat Jablonski were there. On the third day I hurt my knee and couldn't play for a month. I started in Peoria. Just before Christmas they traded Millen to Quebec. I came up January 1. Probably the proudest moment in my life was my first practice when I got there.

They broke me in slowly that year and the next one too. [*Joseph played in 15 and 30 games those seasons.*] Then I started to get the call most of the time. [*In the next three seasons he played 60, 68, and 71 games.*] I feel like I get up for every game. I'm excited about being in the NHL so that helps. You try to motivate yourself every night. Maybe 71 is a bit too many. Sixty might be a good number for a guy who wants to play a lot. You might not be as sharp as you think you are every night if you play more than that.

The playoffs in 1993 were probably the highlight of my career so far. First we had a good series against Chicago and shut them out twice. Then the Toronto series that went seven games. The playoffs are so intense, especially when you've given up so many shots. The whole atmosphere was new to me. I got a lot of notoriety in the Toronto series. You try to stay focused and not get wrapped up in all the media attention. You try to downplay it because in this game you can get humbled pretty quick.

I watch and appreciate what other goalies do. I guess you'd say we have a strong union. If the other goalie is hot and keeping his team in the game you're telling yourself you've got to do the same thing. I like to look at things objectively after a game and I give all the credit in the world to a guy who has stood on his head against us.

I never really thought I was gonna make it, even when I was in college. I was surprised the NHL scouts were looking at me because I had never been looked at before. Then, when I first got to the Blues I was the happiest kid in the world. I was excited, that's for sure. I'm still excited. This is the best job in the world.

A few weeks after Cujo and Felix the Cat put on their great show in the 1993 playoffs I happened to be on the same plane as Felix Potvin travelling from Toronto to Montreal. At that time the big hockey story in Toronto was an ongoing contract dispute between the Maple Leafs and Potvin's agent, former NHL defenceman Gilles Lupien, who was seeking, and eventually got, a couple of million dollars per year for his twenty-two-year-old client. As I chatted with Potvin when we were boarding the plane the thought suddenly struck me, "My God, this kid is going to be a millionaire pretty soon and he's still got zits!!"

As Potvin becomes one of hockey's front-line goaltenders there must be some hockey moguls who have questioned their wisdom, or lack of it, at the 1989 draft in Minnesota. The Cat was not only available that year, he was right there in the building waiting for his name to be called. It never was.

FELIX POTVIN

It was after my first year of junior and everybody said I was going to be drafted, even though I was only eighteen. So I went to Minnesota and I sat there and I didn't get drafted. I didn't have to sit all day because my name was up only for the first three rounds but they were pretty long rounds. At least it seemed that way for me by the time they ended. That was a terrible feeling, the worst feeling. After that I said I didn't care who picks me next time just as long as I get picked. When I was drafted by Toronto the next year [second round, thirty-first overall] I was happy because it's a great hockey town.

Before, in that same year, I was on the Canadian team at the World Juniors in Saskatoon. That was another tough experience for me because I only played in one game. Just one period. But it's always good when you win the gold and it's always a good experience when you play against teams like the Russians. I mean, for me, those games were fun to watch. Pavel Bure was with Russia that year.

The next year in junior was much better for me, a great team experience. We had a big year in Chicoutimi, pretty much the best year I had in minor hockey. We finished first overall, won the playoffs in Quebec, and then went to the Memorial Cup in Quebec City. That went pretty good. The best thing was that I was really a part of it. [*Potvin was voted major junior goaltender of the year for 1991.*]

I grew up in Montreal but the Canadiens weren't my team. My favourite team was the New York Islanders and Billy Smith was my favourite goalie. I don't know why. I guess it was because they were winning all those Stanley Cups when I was a kid. I saw Billy Smith once but I didn't talk to him. That's why it wasn't really a big deal like people said it was when I started playing against the Montreal Canadiens. They talked about how big it was for a French-Canadian kid from Montreal to play against the Canadiens and Patrick Roy and things like that. It's always fun playing Montreal but I always liked the Nordiques a lot better than I liked the Canadiens.

Of course the first or second game you play against Montreal there is a lot of excitement because it's your home-town team. But after that I guess it just becomes a game like any other. I can tell you that right now I like playing in our division a lot more. It's much more exciting.

That series against St. Louis was a big highlight for me. Coming off beating Detroit in seven games, which was my first NHL playoff series, was good, and we were confident we could beat St. Louis. But Curtis played so well and every game was tight until the last one. I wasn't as busy as he was and in some ways that makes it tough. It was a fun series.

The next year in the playoffs I had three shutouts in the series against Chicago. They were all 1–0. Maybe that's the best I've played but that was another series when I wasn't as busy as the other goalie, Ed Belfour. You know a guy like Belfour isn't going to give up too many goals. I find it easier to get a shutout when the game is close. I mean when it's 1–0 or 2–0 instead of when you have a 5–0 or 6–0 lead. That's probably what happened there.

The playoffs are so different. There's so much more enthusiasm, especially in Toronto. The second year was different than the first year for me. People expected a lot from us. After we beat Chicago there were big hopes for us against San Jose. People thought it was a fluke they beat out Detroit but they had a good team. In the seventh game they could have beaten us, and they came one post away from doing it. Garpenlov hit the post.

Everybody with the Maple Leafs has been good to me. I spent my first year pro in St. John's and I needed that. I got experience playing and it helped me learn a lot more English because I didn't speak too much when I went there. Of course you don't have as many French media people in the American League. I had time to learn. I'm still working on it.

What I like best about being a goaltender is the good challenge. You're on your own back there. You work for your team and you try to give them a chance to win and you put a lot of pressure on yourself. I always enjoy having the pressure.

The province of Quebec has produced some pretty good goaltenders. Quebec natives Gump Worsley, Jacques Plante, and Bernie Parent followed Georges Vezina into the Hall of Fame. Today the beat goes on. Patrick Roy is now a veteran with several younger Quebec players snapping at his heels. There's the Cat in Toronto, and the tandem in Denver of Stephane Fiset and Jocelyn Thibault.

In 1994 the NHL's rookie of the year was another young goalie from Quebec, Martin Brodeur of the New Jersey Devils. Brodeur comes by his goalkeeping talents honestly. His father, Denis Brodeur, has been one of Canada's best sports photographers for many years. Before he started taking pictures for a living, Denis was a goaltender in senior hockey and also played for Canada in World Championship and Olympic tournaments. He was the goalie for Canada's bronze-medal-winning team at the 1956 Winter Olympics.

Martin Brodeur

When I was very young I didn't know my dad had been a goalie. I started playing forward and was one of the best players on my team. It just happened that I decided to be a goalie. It was never a case of, well, my dad was a goalie so I want to be a goalie. Once I started playing goal I kept doing it because I loved it.

My dad helped coach me when I was starting. He had good comments but he was never pushy. Sometimes parents want their kid to do well and they push, push all the time. My dad didn't do that. He kept telling me to just have some fun. I'm still having fun.

After my first year of junior I was drafted by New Jersey [first round, twentieth overall]. That's when I figured I might have a chance to play in the NHL. I just went for it. It takes a lot of sacrifice but it wasn't too hard for me to do because I was brought up in a family that was involved in sports. My brother Claude played pro baseball. He was a pitcher in the Expos' organization for five years. My dad knew a lot of the NHL players and I had chances to meet and be around those people.

In my third year of junior they called me up. Both goalies were hurt, so they called up me and a guy from the American League. I was playing against St-Jean on Monday night and on Thursday I was playing against the Boston Bruins. The game was in New Jersey and it was unbelievable. My family came down and it was just a great feeling. I had a shutout with about ten minutes left in the third period. Everything happens so quick at a time like that. You make a couple of good saves and you just get into the rhythm. We won, 4–2.

I stayed with the team and played in two more games, but then the NHL players went on strike. So I had to go back to junior. We got kicked out of the playoffs and then the strike was resolved. I went back to New Jersey and played a half-game at the end of the season and another half game in the playoffs.

The next year I played in Utica. I started late because of a knee injury. Robbie Ftorek was the coach and he didn't believe in putting me in every game. We didn't have a really good team. He told me just to play well and learn how to deal with professional hockey. He did the right thing. It was a learning process and he taught me well.

When the 1993–94 season began Brodeur was with the Devils. Long-time Montreal Canadien star Jacques Lemaire had taken over as head coach and brought with him another Montreal legend, Larry Robinson, as his assistant. The Devils finally had to learn to play defence, a welcome change for the team's goalies. Lemaire told me that Brodeur made the team because of the way he played at training camp. Brodeur alternated with Chris Terreri, played in 47 games, and set a team record with 27 wins. Then came the playoffs, and the fun really began.

New Jersey played the Buffalo Sabres in the first round. Game six of the series, in Buffalo, lasted into the fourth overtime period before Dave Hannan backhanded the puck past Brodeur to even the series, 3–3. The teams had played 65:43 of overtime in the sixth-longest game in NHL history.

New Jersey won the seventh game, then eliminated the Boston Bruins in six games in the division final. That set up a Devils–New York Rangers "Tunnel Series," with the winner getting to the Stanley Cup finals. I worked it for Hockey Night in Canada *and it was a dandy. Three games went into double overtime, including the seventh, which the Rangers won. The Devils' rookie goalie played in 17 of his team's 20 playoff games, including all the long ones. He turned twenty-two during the series against Boston. By the time his 1,203 minutes of pressure-packed playoff hockey were over he likely felt like sixty-two.*

MARTIN BRODEUR

The long game? I'm still tired. [Laughs]

Bernie Nicholls kept telling me in the playoffs, "If you shut them out, kid, we'll win the game." Well, that night I did two shutouts and we never won the game. The toughest part of the experience wasn't physical, it was mental. You go into the second overtime, the third, the fourth, and the teams have chances but, really, not too many good shots on the net. The ice is brutal, everyone's tired. They just want to get a shot and go for a line change. They tell you to stay calm, to stay focused. But that night we jumped on the ice for the warm-up at quarter to seven and we left the building at 2 o'clock in the morning. That's a long time to stay focused.

When the goal went in, well, I didn't have what some people call an emotional letdown. It was kind of a relief. Okay, you got scored on, but this one's over and we've got to go back and play them again. And Hasek was unbelievable for them. He had 70 shots. You wish the goal is gonna be for your side. But it wasn't and then we had to think about starting again the next day.

The series against the Rangers was a great experience. The long game in Buffalo helped me there because we played them three times in double overtime. When you lose a seventh game in double overtime it's hard to describe. We scored with 7.7 seconds to go in the third and then missed a couple of open nets in overtime. You had to go through a lot of emotional things to play in that series.

I talked to some of the other goalies a little bit in my first year. I talked to Sean Burke. I used to have his picture in my room at home and pictures of Kirk McLean and Ron Hextall. I always liked big goalies. I'm a big guy, too, you know, and I just loved the size and style of those guys. I didn't talk to Kirk McLean but Ron Hextall almost fought with me one night. There was a big mix-up, kind of five on five, and he started to jump on one of our guys so I had to go in. I had to grab him but I'm thinking "No, not me. Don't do anything to me." With Ron Hextall you never know what he's gonna do. But nothing happened.

I want to play as long as possible. Right now [during the 1994–95 lockout] we can't play hockey and I'm pretty miserable about it. I think I'm gonna be like that all my career. I'd like to be as successful as Patrick Roy. I want to be consistent. That's why Patrick is so good. You never see him really down or really up. That's one thing I want to accomplish. I've had a good start. Now I want to keep on going.

I interviewed Martin Brodeur during the lockout which delayed the start of the 1994–95 season. Once the season began, Brodeur, despite his Calder Trophy win the previous year, was still the lowest-paid player in the NHL, with an annual salary of $140,000. When the 1995 playoffs ended on June 24, he was helping his New Jersey Devils' teammates carry the Stanley Cup around the ice after they swept the Detroit Red Wings in the final series.

Brodeur played in all but eight minutes of his team's 20 playoff games in 1995 and recorded a goals-against average of 1.67. (In 1993, Patrick Roy's Cup-winning playoff average was 2.13 in 20 games. In 1994, Mike Richter's was 2.07 in 23 games.) Brodeur's ranking as the NHL's lowest-paid player was obviously about to become a thing of the past.

A few NHL goalies have been born in NHL cities but not too many have ended up playing in their home town. Not Felix Potvin or Martin Brodeur or Bernie Parent, who were all born in Montreal. Bill Durnan was born in Toronto but never played for the Maple Leafs. Gump Worsley came from Montreal and played for the Canadiens, but it took him a long time find his way to the Forum on a regular basis.

Mike Vernon is an exception. Mike was born in Calgary in 1963, played his minor hockey there, was drafted by the Calgary Flames in 1981, and played 510 league and playoff NHL games wearing a Calgary uniform. But that home-town association ceased when the Flames traded Vernon to the Detroit Red Wings on June 29, 1994.

There have been some strange stories about how goaltenders got to suit up for the first time in the NHL. In Mike Vernon's case, the story began when a little girl knocked on his door.

MIKE VERNON

The year after I was drafted I was still playing junior in Calgary. I just finished dinner one night when there was a knock on the door. I opened it, and there was a little girl standing there. She said, "They're looking for you at the Corral." Then she ran away. I'm wondering what that was all about and then the phone rings. It was Al Coates, the Flames' assistant G.M., calling to tell me they needed me as back-up because one of their goalies had gone down in the warm-up. The Flames were playing at the Corral in those days and the game was on TV. When the show started [broadcaster] Ed Whalen had put out a call for me to go to the Corral but I didn't have the TV on.

It happened again that season. I think the second time it was on *Hockey Night in Canada*. I was watching and they came on and said, "Mike Vernon, if you're watching please call the Flames' office." So I did and it was the same story, they needed me to back-up. I didn't play in either of those games but they were short a goalie later in the season and I took a trip to Detroit and started my first game. They got six goals on me and they pulled me after the second period. We lost, 7–1.

My second game was that same year at the Corral against Montreal. I wasn't supposed to play, but after the warm-up they found out Tim Bernhardt had pulled his groin. Bob Johnson came to me and said, "Kid, you're playing." I went,

"Huh? Montreal Canadiens? Come on." I was stunned. I couldn't believe it. We lost, 5-4.

I turned pro the next year [1983] and they sent me to Denver in the Central League. I went up to the Flames for one game and that was another interesting experience, to put it mildly. They were playing in Edmonton and Don Edwards started the game. He let in three or four goals so they threw me in and Edmonton was already on a power play. That's when I got a taste of Gretzky at a very young age. They faceoff the puck in our end and he goes behind the net, flips a nice saucer pass over my stick onto Messier's stick for a one-timer, top corner, before I could even move. I'm thinking, "Wow! The NHL. This is pretty quick." They left me in for about ten minutes and they got three more on me and I was gone after that. That was my only game that year so I didn't have what you would call an impressive goals-against average after four goals in ten minutes. [Laughs]

The Oilers won that game, 9–6. The NHL record on Mike Vernon for 1983–84 after that one brief appearance shows 11 minutes played, four goals against, no wins, one loss, and a GAA of 22.22. Definitely not impressive. It gets better after that.

Vernon spent most of the next two seasons with the Flames' American League farm team in Moncton. They called him up in 1985–86 and he was in the NHL to stay. He played nine years for his home-town team and experienced more than his share of highs and lows. With Vernon in goal the Flames lost to Montreal in the 1986 Stanley Cup finals, beat Montreal in the 1989 finals, and were eliminated from the playoffs twice by an overtime goal in a seventh game. There were a lot of frustrating years for Flames' fans but it was rarely dull.

MIKE VERNON

In '86 it was like winning the Stanley Cup when we beat out Edmonton in the second round. They had all their big shooters and had won the Cup the previous two years. The Battle of Alberta was at its peak then and just beating Edmonton was a feat in itself. We went on to play St. Louis and made a mistake in the sixth game when we blew a 5–1 lead and they came back to win in overtime. So we had to play another game. Montreal was sitting at home resting and waiting. We beat the Blues and won the first game against Montreal in Calgary. They might have been a little rusty because they beat us the next four games.

Then in '89 we had the experience of going all the way. We won the Cup at the Montreal Forum. The Canadiens had never lost a Stanley Cup-clinching game in their home building. At the end we came into the dressing room all jubilant and celebrating. I sat down and grabbed myself a pop and just sat there and looked at everybody and took it all in. I was totally drained. I had no more energy. The whole series went that way, the whole playoffs had gone that way. You had to spend every ounce of energy and I was at the end of my rope. I had nothing left.

That was the year we beat Vancouver in the first round in overtime in the seventh game. What everybody remembers about me in that series is stopping Stan Smyl on a breakaway in overtime in the last game. On that one, well, for starters I couldn't believe a guy could get a breakaway in overtime but there he was, coming right at me. I managed to get a glove on it and make the stop. But there was another save that sticks out in my mind in that same OT and it was one I made off Petri Skriko. I can't remember the other player, but they had a two-man break and the player passed it over to Petri and he had the whole net to shoot at. He shot it at the middle of the net and I managed to get a toe on it and the puck went into the corner. I think that was a bigger save than the one I made on Smyl. Maybe it didn't look as pretty.

In '91 we lost in the seventh game against Edmonton when Tikkanen scored in overtime. That one kind of redirected off Frank Musil's stick and went into the top corner. It was the kind of a goal you can't do anything about. A lot of people claim that was one of the greatest series ever played. That was the heartbreaker of them all.

In '94 Pavel Bure scored. We had done such a great job on him all season and in that series. Then in OT in the last game he split the defence. It was the first time he'd been able to do that in the whole series. I remember him accelerating when he took the pass at our blueline. I came out, then tried to get back as quick as possible but by then he was pretty much by me and the puck was in the net. What made that one even worse was the fact that we'd been up on them, 3–1. The last three games all went into overtime. All we needed was one goal in any of them and we didn't get it. Another heartbreak.

I had some good coaching right from the start. I always wanted to be a goalie. I strapped them on when I was probably in a diaper league when I was about four years old. When I was about eight I went to a goalie clinic run by a fellow named Ron Leopold and Gary Bauman, who played in the NHL with Montreal and Minnesota. My father or my coach at that time would come on the ice with me and instruct me in the basics, like dropping to one knee to make the skate save to coming right back up in the butterfly. All that fun stuff.

When I was with the Flames Glenn Hall was my coach. Mr. Goalie. Probably one of the best guys I've ever met. He loves the game. He helped me out tremendously. There's more to goaltending than just stopping the puck. There's the mental part and Glenn is great at settling you down and giving you confidence. He would write three or four pages about what I was doing during a game, the good things and the bad things. He was very helpful over the years, and also a great friend.

Tell you who also helped me out. Wayne Gretzky. That might sound strange but because of Wayne and the things he can do the game is more skilful now. You used to see Guy Lafleur come down the wing and Gerry Cheevers come flying out at him to cut down the angle and Lafleur would blast one at the far corner. Gretzky has changed things with his tic-tac-toe passes. You have to stay back in your net more. He made me learn at a very young age that if you're gonna move out of your net he'll just pass it around you. That's why he's been the greatest player in the league. I can honestly say it's a pleasure being on the same ice with him and watching him play.

There was a lot of pressure playing in Calgary and at times it wasn't good for me. But it forced me to be a better goaltender. I have no regrets. I had a lot of great moments there. It's a great city, a great organization, and the guys I played with were outstanding. I won a Stanley Cup there and they can't take that away from me. I think I can go back to Calgary and still have a lot of pride.

So I'm not really disappointed that I won't be finishing my career in Calgary. I wanted the experience of getting away and playing somewhere else. Now, in Detroit, I'm playing for a team very much like the Flames. Scotty Bowman is the coach and he is emphasizing good defence, so we'll see what happens.

14

The Back-up Brigade

BRIAN HAYWARD   GLENN HEALY

JEFF REESE   BOBBY TAYLOR

On February 6, 1960, the Chicago Blackhawks were playing the Rangers at the old Madison Square Garden on 8th Avenue, in New York. Thirty-three seconds into the second period Bobby Hull swooped in from left wing on Ranger goaltender Gump Worsley. Worsley sprawled on the ice to block the shot and, while he was down, Hull's momentum carried him into the goal crease. One of Hull's skates cut through the glove on Worsley's stick hand, cutting two tendons. Worsley was taken to St. Clare's Hospital and, for the balance of the game, the New York goaltender was Joe Schaefer. And where did Joe Schaefer come from? From the press gallery where he had been keeping statistics as one of the NHL's office officials.

Joe Schaefer was thirty-four years old and worked for a company that manufactured business forms and stationery. His hobby was goaltending and he had played amateur hockey for various teams in the New York area.

In addition to his statistical duties at Rangers' home games, Schaefer was also the "house goalie" at Madison Square Garden, the man on standby to fill in for either team should their goaltender have to leave the game. Amazingly, that's the way it was in hockey's big league from its inception in 1917 until the 1965–66 season when reason prevailed and teams had to put two goalies on their payroll, and in uniform for every game.

It would be nice to report that Joe Schaefer came out of his seat in the press gallery to spark the Rangers to a dramatic victory over the mighty Hull and the Blackhawks to make his lifelong dream come true, but it didn't work out that way. The Rangers were leading, 1–0, when he took over, but Chicago won the game, 5–1. Schaefer got another chance the following season, March 8, 1961, again against Chicago. That time, 14 minutes into the first period, Worsley tore a hamstring making another save off Bobby Hull. Again Schaefer was summoned from the press gallery. The Blackhawks were leading, 1–0, when he took over, and they won the game, 4–3. But Schaefer acquitted himself much better and made 27 saves. For his two brief moments in the hockey sun Joe Schaefer earned $200. His deal was $10 per game to stand by, and $100 if he played.

During the late 1950s the standby goaltender at the Montreal Forum was Bob MacLellan, who had been the star goaltender for the McGill Redmen at the same time I was their star bench-warmer. Bob quit playing to concentrate on his dental-school studies for his last couple of years at McGill. At the same time, although he wasn't even practising with the Redmen or anybody else, he was hired by the Canadiens to be the standby goaltender on game nights at the Forum.

I was the official scorer at the Forum in those days. Before each game I would get the visiting team's starting line-up first and then get the Canadiens' starters from Toe Blake.

One night when the Rangers were in town I got their line-up from the coach and then headed for the other side of the building. There I found Standby Bob in his usual spot, relaxing and chatting it up in a small medical room next to the Canadiens' dressing room. I decided my ex-teammate was ripe for some picking. Knowing that on the other side of the wall Maurice Richard, Jean Béliveau, Boom-Boom Geoffrion, Dickie Moore, and Doug Harvey were all set for the game, I said to Bob, "I was just in the Rangers' room and Gump is pretty sick. It looks like you're going to have to play tonight." The Forum's standby goaltender didn't exactly race to the Rangers' room to don the pads. In fact he didn't move a muscle. His eyes glazed over and for the next several seconds I watched the colour drain from his face. However, I couldn't keep a straight face for very long and when I started laughing the jig was up.

"I had the standard deal," Bob told me. "Ten dollars per game, a hundred if I played, and a free seat along the boards. I had never worn a mask and Jacques Plante suggested I wear one if I ever had to play. I told him I couldn't see properly if I wore a mask. Plante said, 'What do you care if they score ten or twelve on you? You'll still get the hundred dollars.' From what I knew about Plante and his miserly ways, I think he was serious. I never did have to go in."

With only one goaltender at practice, teams would hang a board in one of the nets. The Toronto Maple Leafs had one with five holes drilled in it for target practice. They called it "Woody." The team's trainer would sometimes suit up, all of this prompting Johnny Bower to remark, "I wasn't worried about losing my job to Woody or the trainer."

One trainer who did get to play goal in the NHL was Ross "Lefty" Wilson, who worked for the Detroit Red Wings for many years. Wilson practised on a regular basis with the team and he was the standby for games at the Detroit

Olympia. In 1954 he played one period for the Red Wings and didn't give up a goal. In 1956 he played thirteen minutes for the Toronto Maple Leafs against the Red Wings and didn't allow a goal. His big game was on December 29, 1957, when Boston goalie Don Simmons suffered a dislocated shoulder in the first period. Wilson took over and played almost an entire game against the team that was paying his salary. Detroit was ahead, 1–0, when Simmons was injured. The game ended in a 2–2 tie. You may be prompted to think Lefty Wilson might "accidentally" step aside once in a while and let his team pot a couple. Not Lefty. He once told me, "There was no way I wanted those guys to score on me. It would have been terrible to go to work in the dressing room the next day and have them give me the needle about how many they scored. I wanted to be the one giving the needle." As it turned out, he was.

There are many bizarre stories about standby goalies taking over, and some who weren't officially standbys. The most famous is the Lester Patrick story. On April 7, 1928, during a Stanley Cup-final game in Montreal between the Montreal Maroons and the New York Rangers, the New York goalie, Lorne Chabot, was struck above the eye by a puck backhanded by Nels Stewart and had to leave the game. Patrick, the forty-four-year-old coach of the Rangers, took over. His team ended up winning, 2–1, in overtime and one of hockey's greatest legends was born. The Rangers went on to win the Stanley Cup.

On the day the 1938 Stanley Cup finals were about to begin in Toronto between the Maple Leafs and the Chicago Blackhawks it was discovered that Chicago goalie Mike Karakas had a broken toe and would be unable to play. To show how loose the system was, the Hawks tried to get permission to use Dave Kerr, the New York Rangers' goalie and one of the best in the business, who happened to be in

Toronto at the time. The Leafs protested, leading to a shouting and shoving match in a corridor at the Gardens between
Chicago coach Bill Stewart and the Maple Leafs' tempestu-
ous owner Conn Smythe. Finally, the Hawks tracked down
Alfie Moore, an itinerant pro goalie who had spent that
season in the minors. Moore was found in a watering hole
near the Gardens and it was difficult to tell if the bar was
holding him up, or vice versa. Instead of the bartender
pouring Moore another drink he was hustled to the Gardens
where Hawks poured him into a uniform. Gordie Drillon of
the Leafs promptly scored on the game's first shot. But Moore
shook away the cobwebs, blanked the Leafs from then on,
and Chicago won the game, 3–1. To finish the story, Moore
was ruled ineligible for the next game and Toronto won, 5–1,
with minor-leaguer Paul Goodman in goal for Chicago. (That
was the first NHL game I attended. I was six years old.) The
best-of-five series then switched to Chicago. Karakas came
back, limited Toronto to two goals in two games, and the
Chicago Blackhawks won the Stanley Cup, something
they've managed to do only once since.

In those days, if a goalie was hurt late in a period a forward
or a defenceman would take over, minus goaltending equipment save for the stick and maybe the gloves. In 1933
Toronto's King Clancy did it once for one minute without
being scored on. Clancy's teammate Charlie Conacher, one
of the greatest goal scorers of his day, played goal in three different games for a total of nine minutes and didn't allow a
goal. On February 22, 1940, Montreal goalie Wilf Cude was
injured with five minutes to play in the second period of a
game in Chicago. Charlie Sands, a forward, put on the pads
for the first time in his life and played the last 25 minutes of
the game in the Canadiens' goal. The score was 5–1 for
Chicago when Cude was hurt. The final score was 10–1 for
Chicago.

A last-minute fill-in goalie who did live the impossible dream was Claude "Suitcase" Pronovost. On January 14, 1956, when the Boston Bruins arrived in Montreal to play the Canadiens, their goalie, "Long John" Henderson, had a problem. He was in Montreal but his equipment had been left behind in Boston. The Bruins contacted Pronovost, then a twenty-year-old goaltender for Shawinigan in the Quebec Senior League. He arrived at the Forum just in time to suit up for his first NHL game against the powerful Canadiens. I was at the game and like everybody else in the Forum sat there marvelling at the acrobatics of the young, unknown fill-in who stopped the likes of Béliveau, Moore, Geoffrion, and the Richard brothers all night. Final score: 2–0, Boston. Claude Pronovost, whose brothers Marcel and Jean had long careers, didn't surface again in the big leagues until three seasons later when he played two games for Montreal, giving up seven goals. He never played again in the NHL.

Pronovost's career lasted a bit longer than some of the legitimate back-ups who played once the two-goalie era came into vogue. The record for fewest minutes played by a goaltender in the NHL is held by Robbie Irons. One of the back-ups used by the St. Louis Blues when Glenn Hall and Jacques Plante were sharing the regular duties, Irons got into one game for two minutes and 59 seconds, November 13, 1968, against the New York Rangers. That was the extent of his NHL career.

During the 1988–89 season the Montreal Canadiens dressed Randy Exelby for a few games as the back-up to Patrick Roy. The year before Exelby had been a "rent-a-goalie" in Toronto, playing for anybody looking for a goalie who phoned a magic number. Exelby saw the ice in the NHL for the first time on January 27, 1989, in Buffalo, when Roy suddenly left the ice and headed for the dressing room. As Exelby took over I was in the broadcast booth excitedly promising my radio listeners I would let them know what injurious calamity had befallen the Canadiens' star goalie as soon as the information became available. Shortly thereafter Roy returned looking none the worse for wear. Exelby, who had held the fort for the Canadiens for two minutes and 55 seconds and made one save, was back on the bench and his career with Montreal was over.

Now, at long last, I can reveal what really happened that fateful night in Buffalo. Randy Exelby got his long-awaited chance to play in the National Hockey League because Patrick Roy had to go to the bathroom. That was one time a goalie couldn't hold it until the end of the period, as I'm sure many have done over the years. Now you know the rest of the story. Exelby held the record for least time played by four seconds over Robbie Irons for about a year until he made his only other NHL appearance, playing one game for the Edmonton Oilers.

Taking nothing away from the goaltenders of today, you have to marvel at the toughness of those who played the position in bygone years. You know they were playing hurt, as the saying goes, many, many times. In the 1940s Buzzy Bavasi, who was to become one of major-league baseball's top executives, was running the Brooklyn Dodgers' farm team, the Royals, in Montreal. On the eve of the opening of the Little World Series between his team and St. Paul, Bavasi and several of his players attended a Canadiens–New York Rangers game. Montreal goaltender Bill Durnan was hit in the face by the puck and the game was delayed for twenty minutes while Durnan was being patched up. Bavasi was sitting with his star first baseman (and future "Rifleman" on TV), Chuck Connors, who had been complaining about a sore thumb that might prevent him from playing the next day. As Bavasi recounted in his autobiography, when Durnan returned to the ice with blood still oozing from the cut on his stitched-up and bandaged face he quietly asked Connors, "How's your thumb?" Connors played the next day.

I remember seeing Toronto goaltender Harry Lumley take a puck on the side of his head during a pre-game warm-up in Montreal in the early 1950s. The start of the game was delayed for several minutes while Lumley received fourteen stitches to close the wound. Naturally, he came back and played the game.

In 1937–38 there were eight teams in the NHL and the season was 48 games. Only ten different goalies saw action. In 1942–43, during the Second World War, when there were six teams and good help was hard to find, five teams used only one goaltender for the entire 50-game season. The last time as many as four goaltenders played in every game was in the 70-game 1951-52season. The 1957–58 season was the last in which as many as three appeared in every game. The last goalie to start every game for his team during a season was Roger Crozier of the Detroit Red Wings, in 1964–65. But Crozier was twice replaced during a game for a total of 33 minutes.

The last goalie to play an entire season without being replaced was Ed Johnston. In 1963–64, the season Glenn Hall's consecutive game streak ended at 502, Johnston played every minute of every game for the Boston Bruins. The Bruins finished last, winning only 18 times in the 70-game schedule and finishing 23 points out of the playoffs. Obviously management didn't blame E.J., who is now the coach of the Pittsburgh Penguins.

ED JOHNSTON

Let's see now, I was making about $300,000 a year at the time. [Laughs] It was really about $8,500. I finished that year with a 3.01 average, which was third-best in the league, I had six shutouts, and the lowest goals-against for a last-place club in NHL history. I remember one stretch in that particular year when out of the last four games we had won, three were shutouts. After the season I went in to see the manager, Lynn Patrick, and told him I thought I had a thousand dollars coming to me because they would give me a bonus if I had an average of 3.00. He said, "Did you read the fine print? You had 3.01." But he gave it to me.

I was playing at the same time as some of the greatest goalkeepers that ever played. You had Bower, Plante, Sawchuk, Hall, Gump, and myself. Playing with people like that was just great.

With the kind of equipment we had we were black-and-blue right from training camp through the whole year. All we wore on our arms was just a little padding and our underwear. I had no protection at all on my skates. My toes were always hurt. I'd walk around the whole year with swollen toes. That year I played every game I broke my nose three times and had the lobe of my ear sliced off. But with only one goalkeeper you were afraid to come out of the net. Somebody would step in and you might be gone. That's the way it worked for everybody.

Today, I don't think a guy could play 84 games, for a lot of reasons. Travel is probably the biggest. Sometimes in the course of a week you play in two or three different time zones. But the equipment is so much better now. It's great with the helmets, the arm pads, the way they're protected everywhere. They've got the thing underneath their chin. The biggest advantage they have today is the equipment. It really is.

Everybody involved isn't totally happy with the two-goalie system. Either you have a young goalie backing up who becomes impatient to play, or more often a veteran who has had his life style in the crease changed from playing a lot to playing very little. Grant Fuhr, for instance. Fuhr, arguably one of the best goaltenders ever to play the game, found himself in a back up role with the Buffalo Sabres when Dominik Hasek became "Dominant" Hasek. When Buffalo traded Fuhr to the Los Angeles Kings during the shortened 1995 season he said, "It's always tough to be a back-up. It's not something I adjusted to very well, and I admit I didn't play very well in that role."

Brian Hayward found himself in a somewhat similar situation after being traded in the summer of 1986 from the Winnipeg Jets to the Montreal Canadiens. Hayward had been a workhorse in Winnipeg and had played in 113 games over the two seasons before the trade. In 1984–85 he set a Winnipeg franchise record with 33 victories. When he arrived in Montreal the Canadiens had just won the Stanley Cup and their rookie goalie, Patrick Roy, had just won the Smythe Trophy as the MVP of the playoffs. Ironically, Hayward was playing for Winnipeg in Montreal the night Roy saw his first NHL action when he played one period against the Jets while he was still a junior.

Hayward was with Montreal the next four seasons and in three of them shared the Jennings Trophy with Roy. But those were the years Roy was becoming the NHL's top goaltender and the Montreal team's number-one personality, on the ice and in the marketplace. Hayward went from being number one with the Jets to being Roy's back-up in Montreal, a situation that finally ended his stay with the Canadiens.

Brian Hayward, a native of Toronto, is currently the goaltending consultant and television analyst for the Mighty Ducks of Anaheim. After he left Montreal he played for the Minnesota North Stars and San Jose Sharks. He was with

Minnesota in the 1991 Stanley Cup finals when he stopped
Mario Lemieux on a breakaway with one of the greatest
saves I have ever seen. Brian earned a degree in business
management from Cornell University in 1982. He was an
NCAA All-American goaltender at the Ivy League school
that was put on the hockey map by another goaltender who
once played there, Ken Dryden.

BRIAN HAYWARD

Ken was pretty much forgotten by the time I got to Cornell,
although the numbers he put up there no one could even
approach. I got a big kick out of the fact that I finally established a Cornell goaltending record. I couldn't approach Ken's
numbers on wins or goals against, but I got mine for minutes
played. That was my claim to fame there. The reason Ken
didn't own that record too was because when he first went
to Cornell freshmen weren't eligible to play on the team. I
got to play four years while he got to play only three.

I needed those years at Cornell. I see some kids today
being broken in at age nineteen. When I was nineteen I don't
think I was remotely close to being able to play at a professional level. I encourage a lot of young goaltenders to consider the college route. I think it's important to get a couple
of extra years at that level before you get rushed into a pro
situation.

I went to the Jets' camp in 1982 and started the year in
Sherbrooke. Then I joined the big club in January. My first
game was against Philadelphia. Darryl Sittler was with the
Flyers then and right off the bat he got a breakaway on me. I
grew up in Toronto and he was my idol as a kid. All I could
think was, 'Geez, this is Darryl Sittler coming on a breakaway.' I can't even remember if I moved. But I know he
scored.

My time with Winnipeg was up and down, inconsistent. I had great stretches. I had one that I was on all year long, the year I played 61 games. The problem was, I was burned out by the time I got to the playoffs. I had played with muscle pulls, things like that. Physically, I just wasn't able to handle a 60-game season and playoffs.

We had a young team in Winnipeg and I enjoyed playing there. At one point we had fourteen guys who were single and we were all very close. It was a nice way to make a transition from a college environment to a pro environment. Guys like Dale Hawerchuk, Scott Arniel, Jim Kite, and Dave Ellett were there and they were pretty much the same age. They had all come straight from junior so I was a bit older. Everybody says Winnipeg is so cold but when you're hanging out with a bunch of guys, you create your own fun. I don't think we had too much fun, but we had a lot of it.

John Ferguson was the general manager and he kept things pretty exciting. He was tough on me in the papers where he'd blame everything on the goaltender. Then he'd call me into his office and say, "You're not really the whole problem here but I know you can handle the criticism. I'd say, "Gee, thanks a lot, Fergie. I really appreciate that. But you're not making my job any easier because the fans are starting to believe goaltending is the only problem here." And he goes, "Well, I certainly don't feel that way."

Rick Bowness was working for the Jets' organization then, and in the summer of '86 he called me at my summer home and told me that the last year was history, that they knew I had a tough time but they were counting on me for the future. I was gonna be the number-one guy and they were looking at me for 50 or 60 games again, we're real excited, etc., etc. That same afternoon I was traded to Montreal. He called me back and he was all apologies. Turns out Fergie went with one of his hunches. The scouts and everybody else had told him not to trade Hayward but Fergie had a hunch so he traded me for Steve Penney.

After the deal Fergie was great. He said to me, "Look, Brian, I just felt this was best for your career. Possibly it was my fault for putting so much pressure on you in the media and it got to a point where you need a change of scenery. I think you'll be in the league for many years to come. If I can help you in any way to make the transition easier you have *carte blanche.*" A lot of managers would have said, "You're with Montreal now. Call Serge Savard." Fergie didn't do that, so it was a nice way to leave. I'll never forget that.

But it had been really tough on me at the end in Winnipeg. When I'd be introduced as the starting goaltender the fans would boo. If we lost there'd be the articles in the newspapers. It made it tough to play. I felt all along it wasn't my fault. Those were the days when the Oilers and the Flames were pretty potent teams and when you're giving up all kinds of two-on-ones and three-on-ones in a game you're going to get scored on. In my last season there we were fighting with Vancouver and Los Angeles for the last playoff spot and I played most of the games. I think I played seven of the last eight games and played very well. We made it and then when the playoffs started against Calgary Fergie went with another of his hunches and started Daniel Bouchard. They beat us three straight. But as it worked out maybe Fergie was right. Maybe the trade was the best thing for my career.

The first thing I did with the team in Montreal was attend their golf tournament just before training camp. I got an invitation to go to a club called Elm Ridge and I thought the players would just play golf, have a few beers, and go home. All I had with me were my golf clothes, shoes, and clubs. I get there and the clubhouse is gorgeous, everyone has brought a change of clothes for dinner, and there's a buffet table for brunch that is unbelievable. The course is beautiful with thirty-six holes and every one of them has two four-somes on it at tee-off time. Players, executives, sponsors, old-timers like Maurice Richard, Jean Béliveau, and Yvan Cournoyer, the whole works. After golf the men change into suits and ties, the wives show up dressed to the nines, and there's a formal dinner with an orchestra for dancing. I'm sitting there all night in a golf shirt. It was quite an initia-tion, a different perspective altogether. That was true of playing in that city. You always realized how important it was. The Canadiens are more than just a professional sports team. They matter to everybody.

Right from the start I was the back-up to Patrick. I've always thought you have to approach a situation like that with the idea that you're going to outplay the number-one goalie in practice, every day. Somewhere along the line you hope you make an impression and someone will say, "Hey, let's give this guy a real good shot." That was the way I approached it the whole time I was there. It was a direct com-petition with Pat. Every skating drill, every shooting drill was a competition, especially when I first got there. I settled into a comfort zone later on. They'd have drills where they took shots at both ends and I'd keep track of the score, how many goals I let in versus how many Pat let in. We did break-aways and if they scored more on me than on Pat I'd be frus-trated and upset with myself. I think that's the way a back-up goaltender has to approach it.

Do I feel I got a fair shake in Montreal? No. I always felt I deserved to play more games there. I feel that there were a couple of years I outplayed Pat, based on a whole season. I was extremely disappointed my last year there. I had a great camp and Pat had been struggling. Pat had just signed a million-dollar contract. I went to Serge Savard and said, "Am

I ever gonna play here again? I don't want to be here and play just 15 or 20 games." He told me right then and there not to worry about the million-dollar contract, that I was gonna get a fair shake.

I played great every pre-season game and Pat was going through a tough time. Pat Burns was the coach. We started the season in Buffalo and came home two nights later for the home opener in Montreal. When he told me Pat would start in Buffalo I said, "Okay, when am I gonna play?" Then he told me Pat would be playing the home opener and after that we had Hartford, and Pat would play against them too. I said, "Wait a minute, when am I gonna play?" He said there was a road trip coming, back-to-back against the Rangers and Hartford, and I'd probably get one of those games. Now it was one of the first five games I'd be playing and I said that wasn't what I had been told. Pat said, "Patrick is kind of struggling and we've got to get him going." That's when it hit me. I was never gonna play more than 15 games there. If the other guy's not playing well enough to deserve a start and he's getting all the starts because they want to improve his level of play, I knew I'd play 15 road games and that would be it. That wasn't what Serge and I had talked about. I asked to be traded, and I was. I went to Minnesota. I never played a game that season for the Montreal Canadiens.

I have some good memories of my time in Montreal. In '87 we played Quebec in the playoffs. Patrick had played the first two games at home and we lost both. I played the rest of that series. We went into Quebec down 2–0 and ended up beating them in seven. I think that was the high point of my career.

Probably the most enjoyable games I played in were against Edmonton when I was in Winnipeg. They were in their prime and they were an awesome team to watch, probably the most entertaining team I've ever seen. Before the league changed the four-on-four rule they'd send Semenko into the corner to face-wash a guy whenever the score was close. The guy would retaliate and they'd end up with a four-on-four situation. They'd throw out Gretzky and he'd be flipping passes to everybody, Kurri would be firing at you, Messier would be in full flight, and Coffey would be backing them up. We had a very offensive-minded team in Winnipeg so the Oilers games were wide open and fun, even though they would light it up against you.

There is still a fear factor in goaltending. The head is still a vulnerable area, but I don't think they worry about any part of their body now other than their head and their throat. And with the new kind of mask that has been developed it's not nearly as dangerous any more. I remember one night against Calgary my helmet got knocked off. The puck went floating out to the top of the circle and here comes Al MacInnis. He hammers it as hard as he can and it zips right past my ear, hits the glass, and goes out of play. I was shaking for two minutes afterwards. I could hardly put my helmet back on.

I had an interesting conversation about that once with Eddie Giacomin. I told him I didn't know how they did it in his day, not wearing masks. He said they had a whole different approach to the game. He said, "We would first position our body, then we'd worry about our head. If I knew I had the angle cut off I'd start looking for my defenceman's rear end. I'd tuck my head in behind it and wait for the puck to hit me. With the equipment you guys have now you don't have to worry so much about protecting yourself." And I went, "Geez, I never thought of that before."

Eddie also told me how different practice is now. He said, "They're a lot more dangerous for a modern-era goalie than they ever were for me. Nobody would ever raise the puck in our practices. I can't believe the lack of respect the shooters have for goalkeepers now."

He's right. I watch our practices here in Anaheim and I just cringe.

When the 1988–89 NHL season began the most eagerly awaited opening game was to be played at the Great Western Forum in Inglewood, California, between the Los Angeles Kings and the Detroit Red Wings. October 6, 1988, was billed as the biggest night in the history of the Kings' franchise because Wayne Gretzky would be playing his first game for his new team. The shock of the Gretzky trade had reverberated for two months. Now reality was about to set in.

When the big night began the Kings received their customary player-by-player introduction, standard fare for home openers. Nineteen players skated out as the 16,005 paying customers waited patiently for the twentieth. Then came the announcement, "Number 99, Wayne Gretzky!" Sure enough, there he was skating out in a Los Angeles Kings uniform. Yes, Virginia, the Edmonton Oilers really had traded away hockey's greatest player. A thunderous ovation began and went on, and on, and on. As the television cameras shot Gretzky standing at the blueline looking properly embarrassed, the Kings' starting goaltender, Glenn Healy, was standing beside him. With a shy, what am I doing here? kind of grin on his face, Healy looked more nervous than Wayne. Today he remembers it as, "My Andy Warhol fifteen minutes of fame. That was it. After that everyone knew where I played. Up to then they weren't sure where I was, the minors, L.A., wherever."

Glenn Healy was the number-one goaltender in L.A. at the time but lost that job when the Kings' obtained Kelly Hrudey from the New York Islanders late in the season. The following summer the Islanders signed Healy as a free agent and he was with that team the next four seasons.

A native of Pickering, Ontario, who played collegiate hockey at Western Michigan, Healy had more than Andy's fifteen minutes of fame in the 1993 playoffs. The Islanders eliminated the defending-champion Pittsburgh Penguins in a dramatic seven-game series sparked by the goaltending of Healy, who was brilliant against Mario Lemieux and the rest of the NHL's most potent scoring machine. He continued his fine play against Montreal, even though the Islanders were eliminated by the eventual Stanley Cup winners. Throughout those playoffs Healy became the Islanders' team leader, a rare role for a goaltender. He's the type who never met a camera or a microphone he didn't like, and the media took full advantage of his wit, insights, and availability when he was hot in '93.

Ten days after the 1993 playoffs ended the Islanders obtained Ron Hextall from the Quebec Nordiques which surprised a lot of people, considering how well Healy had played for them. So where was he headed this time? Here's what happened to him as outlined in the NHL Official Guide: *"Claimed by Anaheim from NY Islanders in Expansion Draft, June 24, 1993. Claimed by Tampa Bay from Anaheim in Phase II of Expansion Draft, June 25, 1993. Traded to NY Rangers by Tampa Bay for Tampa Bay's third round choice (previously acquired by NY Rangers – Tampa Bay selected Allan Egeland) in 1993 Entry Draft, June 25, 1993." That sort of stuff could make a guy feel unwanted. But the Rangers did want him, and slightly less than a year later Glenn Healy was on a Stanley Cup-winning team.*

After appearing in 47 regular-season games for the Islanders the year before, Healy played in only 29 for the Rangers in 1993–94. He played in all 18 playoff games for the Islanders in '93. In the Rangers' 23-game run to the Stanley Cup in '94 he played in one complete game and eight minutes of another. He spent the rest of the time on the bench watching Mike Richter tend the Rangers' goal for Mike Keenan. Another number one had been traded into a number two. Typically, Healy can find humour in his frustrating new role.

GLENN HEALY

We were playing in Dallas and losing, 3–2, with about three minutes to go. Mike Keenan was pacing back and forth behind the bench questioning whether guys wanted to play or had the desire to play. We were shorthanded and he said to the team he was going to put someone on the ice who wanted to play. I'm thinking to myself, "I wonder who that could be?" and then he says, "Healy, get out there." I'm surprised but that sort of thing had happened before with Keenan. So I jump on the ice as quick as I can, forgetting that I've still got my skateguards on. I'm trying to stand up but I keep falling down. The crowd sees this and they're into it and I'm still trying to stand up with my skateguards on. Finally, after I'm on my knees for the third time, I chucked them off and said to Mike, "Okay, I'm ready to play." By then he's probably wondering why he told me to go in in the first place.

After the Islanders experience in '93 and then going to the Rangers my mindset was strictly to win the Cup. Very few people get that chance. Playing on the Island I saw the potential of the Rangers. I believed that with the right mix, and some luck, we really had a shot at it. This may be my only chance, but I also knew that if we didn't win the Cup I was gone. Absolutely.

Where you have a dilemma as a back-up is that as a player you want to play but from a team standpoint you have to have all the pieces in the puzzle fit together. I obviously had to sacrifice but a lot of players had to sacrifice. Craig

MacTavish came here late in the season. He was used to playing fourteen minutes a game, but with us he was getting only thirty seconds in some games, maybe just a couple of key faceoffs. When you win it's in large part because players adapt to certain roles and don't complain.

Mike was smart. He did his homework on me. I'm not a player who has a lot of talent. In fact I likely have very little talent. Most of what I've achieved has come from hard work. I've always worked hard in practice, so that part of the game didn't change for me. There was a time when goalies who played a lot took days off from practice. You really can't do that nowadays. Coaches don't want that sort of thing any more.

Can a goalie play 60 or 65 games these days? In many ways it's easier to play a lot than not very much. When you play less I think it's a matter of survival a lot of nights. You haven't played in a month, or you haven't played in two weeks. Generally they don't give you the most glorious of starts. Like it's on the road, fourth game in six nights, the team's exhausted and wants to get home and that's your game. When you do get a start you know it might be your last one in a month so you want to seize the opportunity. There's no question it's survival. You don't get in the groove, you don't get focused. Take playoff runs. You do get in a groove, you do get focused. You don't even notice the crowd. Well maybe you see the people in the first few rows. When you're in a groove, you see the puck well. When you're the back-up there's not a whole lot you're seeing well except the backs of the other teams' sweaters. [Laughs]

I started out on defence. I was four years old in a league that went up to nine years old. That first year when I was four I went the whole year without touching the puck once. Not once. Every time I'd get to the puck either the buzzer went to signal a change of shift, or someone would shoot it away from me. My brother was the goaltender and he was nine. So the next year he jumped up and we didn't have a goalie. They said, "We'll put Glenn in. He can't skate so we'll let the puck come to him. He won't have to chase it." So here I was, five years old, and now I'm a goaltender. I had such a hard time playing defence and goaltending seemed to come a bit easier. I didn't have to chase guys around and never catch them. Everything seemed so simple. They just came to me.

I found out early that you can make an impact on the game, either positively or negatively, and sometimes quickly. The game can be seven seconds old and you're making an impact. You make a big save and the bench jumps up, "Awright. Way to go." Let one in from centre and you can't even see the guys' heads. They're looking for the water, looking for the back-up. "Get him in there."

There isn't as much respect for goaltenders as there was in the old days. When Billy Smith was in his last years with the Islanders his warm-ups were like slo-pitch, the pucks were coming in so slow. Check the practices now and the way the guys shoot. For them goals equal money, so what better way to sharpen up than in practice? They might want to respect the goaltenders' rights but they also know they can't turn what they do on and off like a switch. So for us practices are often more challenging than games. Games are easy. Twenty shots, thirty shots. You get at least 300 at you in practice.

Guys in the past did a lot of things differently. Tony Esposito used to put that hot stuff on himself. It was like a jelly. Doug Crossman told me about it. His first year in Chicago he sat beside Tony in the room and before every game Tony used to put that hot stuff all over his body. Crossman didn't know what it was. You never touched Tony Esposito's stuff but one day Tony wasn't there so Crossman opens the jar and puts his finger into it and right away his finger was on fire. He had to rush and put water on it. He couldn't believe how hot the stuff was and especially he couldn't believe how a guy could put it all over his body. He put it on so the pucks wouldn't hurt him so much when he got hit.

Speaking of fingers, I'm practising with the Islanders and Steve Thomas skates over me and severs part of a finger. The end of the finger is in the glove. The trainer rushes me to the hospital and they sew it back on. All the guys on the team think my finger fell off because I had been digging in my garden in Pickering, where the nuclear plant is. After that they kept waiting for my limbs to fall off because I live in Pickering.

While Glenn Healy and Brian Hayward had a taste of being top dog in the goal crease of an NHL team Jeff Reese has never enjoyed that experience. Reese hails from Brantford, Ontario, where Wayne Gretzky first laced on skates and where he and Wayne's brother Keith were minor-hockey teammates. Reese played junior for the London Knights and was drafted by the Toronto Maple Leafs in 1984. From the time he turned pro in 1987 until he was traded to Calgary in the big ten-player swap in 1992 Reese burned a lot of rubber commuting between the Maple Leafs and their American League farm team in nearby Newmarket. He spent almost two years with the Flames and then was traded to the Hartford Whalers in November 1993.

Jeff Reese

When I became interested in goaltending Ken Dryden was the first guy I really liked watching. I liked that old mask he wore, the one that had hardly any protection. Then my favourite was Bernie Parent. No question. He was just poetry to watch. He was so great in the finals. His career was cut short by an eye injury and I was disappointed when that happened.

I only went to one hockey school. I don't understand why parents want to send kids to hockey schools all summer long. Give the kid a break. Let him be a kid and have fun in the summer. He doesn't have to play hockey all through the year.

Toronto is a great place to play when things are going well. Probably similar to Montreal. When I was there things basically weren't going well. We struggled and it was a tough time to be a goalie in that city. We took a lot of heat but, looking back on it, if I could play there I could play anywhere. The best year we had in Toronto was '89–90 when we had 80 points in 80 games then lost in the first round against St. Louis. It was fun. We had guys like Vinny Damphousse, Daniel Marois, and Ed Olczyk, and we were scoring five and six goals a game.

When things weren't going well in Toronto I learned that I had to stop reading the newspapers. It was tough because you'd walk into the dressing room and there'd be papers lying around and they'd always be flipped open to the sports section. I remember one article when they had three goalies, Mark LaForest, Alan Bester, and myself. It called us Larry, Curly, and Moe, the Three Stooges. That was the headline. Stuff like that was very tough to take.

I left the Maple Leafs as part of the big ten-player trade with Calgary. That was a shocker for me. I remember we were at practice and Bill Watters, the assistant G.M., came down to the bench and started looking at guys. He kept looking at me and I was thinking, oh no. I had driven in with Gary Leeman that morning. He wasn't playing and he knew something was up. He said, "I think something's going to happen today." I figured Gary would be gone but I didn't think it would happen to me. The funny thing was, we all got called into the office. The guys just kept coming in, one after the other, until there were five of us standing there. It was such a huge trade. It was the first time I had been traded and it was easier when you went with four other guys you knew.

My second trade was from Calgary to Hartford and I didn't have a tough time with that one at all. Calgary wanted to go with their young guys so it was time for me to move on.

I had both Johnny Bower and Glenn Hall as goalie coaches and that was something else. They were both great to talk to, especially Glenn because Johnny wasn't around all that much. They were phasing him out in Toronto when I was there. But when I got to Calgary, Glenn had started coming out on the ice with the goalies. He was jumping around in there, back and forth. He was amazing. He'd say, "I couldn't practise. I could play games right now but I couldn't practise." The guy was sixty years old but I think he meant it.

I've been the back-up pretty much my whole career. I'm not the kind of guy that's gonna bitch about not playing. I don't think that does anybody any good. Certainly you like to play as much as you can but I've made a good living at what I do now. That's not to say I wouldn't like to play every night. I've played behind some great goaltenders – Fuhr, Vernon, and Burke – and I understand the situation. I'm gonna keep working hard and try to come up with a big game when I do get put in.

Out of all those who are members of our "Back-up Brigade" perhaps Bobby Taylor should be named captain for representing the true meaning of the position. While most back-ups play in 20 or 30 games a year, Taylor almost never played during the years he was with the Philadelphia Flyers. In his second season with the Flyers, 1972–73, he played in 23 games. At the same time Bernie Parent was also in Philadelphia, but then he was playing for that city's WHA franchise. The following year Parent jumped back to the Flyers and Bobby Taylor became a back-up goalie, and then some. His "Games Played" stats the next two seasons read 8 and 3. The Flyers played 34 playoff games in those two years and won the Stanley Cup both times. While Parent was winning two Conn Smythe trophies Taylor didn't play a minute. Through it all he was always upbeat, always ready, and, being a member in good standing of the Broad Street Bullies, sometimes in trouble with the law even though he was just backing up Bernie.

BOBBY TAYLOR

The practice was my game. When I went to practice I forced myself to be mentally prepared, just as though I was going to a game. It served two purposes. Number one, it helped the guys at practice because they knew they had to work hard against you, that you just weren't out there going through the motions. Secondly, it helped me keep sharp. You had to picture yourself in a game, what would happen if the red light went on and 18,000 idiots were yelling at you. I know you don't have that in practice, but that is what I feel a back-up goalie has to do because you only play in a real game once in a while. In my case once every four weeks, if I was lucky. [Laughs]

I'll tell you one thing. Whenever I saw Bernie go down suddenly my heart was in my throat. I'd think, "Oh my God, now I've got to go in with no warm-up." Another thing, you knew if you didn't play well when you did get the chance then you'd sit again for a long time. That added a lot of pressure.

I always had a good relationship with Bernie. He used to laugh and say, "We're going be doing this for ten years." The back-up can be a support for the starter. Nobody really knows what a goalie goes through other than another goalie. If you're there with him, patting him on the back, it makes for a much easier relationship. It creates a better atmosphere in the room. The players treat you better and have more respect for you because they see what you're going through and they understand it to a degree. If you have bad rapport, if you're a jealous guy and pout and complain, everybody leaves you alone. For the number-one guy it can be like Alcoholics Anonymous. When you're A.A. and you're struggling you make a phone call and somebody comes over to talk to you. Well, if you're struggling in goal you can go over to the back-up and talk to him and that helps.

I guess I gained whatever notoriety I have for the incident in Vancouver when I ended up in jail. Our team used to get so pumped up because Fred Shero did such a great job of convincing us it was us against the world. In his view it was almost us against management. Freddie and his players against everybody. That night in Vancouver a fan came down out of the stands when there was a fight between Don Saleski and Greg Boddy. The fight was up against the glass maybe eight or ten seats down from where I was sitting. The fan grabbed Saleski by the hair and was pulling him over the glass. It was really dumb. I just reacted to it. I jumped over the railing beside our bench to go after him and keep him off our player. There I was lumbering through all the people with the big pads and everything and it took me so long to get there the guy could have left the building and been on a plane to L.A. Then the cops came after me and Cowboy

Flett and now a bunch of our players are coming up into the seats. During the melee a policeman got hit, but not by me. I know that.

The fight ended and we all got penalties and nothing else happened until a couple of weeks later when the Crown pressed charges against us. We had to go to trial, but they waited until after the season. We went there when the draft was being held in Montreal. There were seven of us and we called ourselves the "Vancouver Seven." You know, like the "Chicago Seven." At the trial we were all fined and then they held me over because the policeman testified that after he got hit all he saw were goal pads.

That was on a Friday and they held me over until Monday. That's when the judge charged me with assault. I think he gave me a sixty-day sentence or something and they threw me in jail. That's what really hurt. They took my belt and tie and all that stuff. I was in jail for about twenty minutes and then the Flyers bailed me out and filed an appeal. They had a lawyer there at the time. The judge who sentenced me was running for office up there and he was really gonna get his name in the paper. He accused me of being the reason demonstrations and riots were going on in Vancouver.

They had another judge for the appeal and what he said was right. He said, "You have a responsibility to the youth of this nation. They look up to you whether you think they do or not." He dismissed the sentence but the $500 fine stood.

Fred Shero had a great line when it was all over. He said, "I wish they'd kept Taylor in jail until September. Then he would have been in the best shape of his life when he reported to training camp."

The Last Save

As I leaf through team photos from hockey's earliest days I sometimes wonder: Who was the first player to smile when his picture was being taken? Almost without exception they were a serious-looking bunch. Goaltenders then, as now, were usually in the front row which gives us a good idea of how their equipment changed over the years.

Captain James T. Sutherland, a Hall of Fame Builder in hockey's earliest era, once wrote: "The very first goaltenders wore no pads at all. That was because nobody had learned to shoot a puck into the air. All shots virtually skidded along the ice. It wasn't long, however, before players got the knack of the backhand-lift type of shot. Then the harassed goalies went to local cricket teams and borrowed the wicket-keeper's leg pads."

A picture of the 1896 Victoria Hockey Club of Winnipeg shows the goalie wearing those cricket-like pads, which were about the same width as the shin pads worn by today's forwards and defencemen. A picture of the 1917 Seattle Millionaires shows the goalie wearing pads much more like today's models, although somewhat narrower. But while the pads changed early, it would seem the goalie's gloves didn't change much until the 1930s. Until then most goalies wore gloves no different than those worn by the rest of the team, proving they couldn't have been shooting the puck very hard way back then.

Emile "The Cat" Francis was the goaltender who introduced the big "trapper" mitt goalies now wear on their catching hand. Francis was a top-rated goalie and ball player in his native Saskatchewan and started wearing a first-baseman's mitt in goal. When he got to the NHL with the Chicago Blackhawks the legality of the glove came into question but the Cat, a talkative and persuasive type, convinced them to let him wear it and it wasn't long before all goalies were wearing a similar type of catching glove.

Donnie Marshall was a solid, role-playing forward in the NHL during the 1950s and '60s, and became one of the first former players to work as an analyst on *Hockey Night in Canada*. We were in the broadcast booth at the Montreal Forum watching a pre-game warm-up and I noticed Donnie slowly shaking his head. When I asked him why, he replied, "I can't believe the way they can shoot the puck now. When I played, a team was lucky to have two players who could shoot hard. Now, they all can."

That was some time in the 1970s. Today Brett Hull, Al MacInnis, Al Iafrate, and dozens of others can shoot harder than any of the players Donnie Marshall and I were watching some twenty years ago. Iafrate twice won the shooting contest at the All-Star Game with shots clocked at over 100 miles per hour. That's why goaltending equipment today has to provide better protection for the brave young men who wear it. Gump Worsley and Terry Sawchuk each wore the same chest protector for over twenty years. They'd likely change to a modern model after twenty games today. Maybe after twenty minutes.

With all due respect to the players of the past, the players today do skate faster and shoot harder. During the 1994–95 NHL labour lockout, the CBC programmed some "Classic Games" from the past. One was a 1959 Stanley Cup final between the Toronto Maple Leafs and the Montreal Canadiens. Two greats, Johnny Bower and Jacques Plante, were the goaltenders, and there were several other future Hall of Famers in the game. Watching the black-and-white pictures – with no replays – you could see how much longer the shifts were for the forwards than they are today. Penalty killers worked the entire two minutes of a minor penalty. Both teams used only four defencemen most of the game. Today coaches regularly change lines two or three times in less than a minute and use two or three sets of penalty killers in less than two minutes. They try to make the pace of the game so much quicker and the goaltenders have had to adjust accordingly. Goals have always been scored on screen shots and deflections, but not with the frequency we see in today's game. And oh yes, all the players in that 1959 game had straight sticks. Nobody was cranking his stick above his head to fire a slap shot with a curved stick.

Things have changed as well for parents of aspiring young goaltenders of the future. A newspaper clipping from the 1930s on display at the Hockey Hall of Fame includes an advertisement for "Top of the Line" goal pads for $35.95 a pair. Today the price tags at your local sporting-goods store show goal pads ranging from $400 to $1,500. The best goal gloves are $1,000, skates $400, while the combined chest-shoulder pad regalia goes for as much as $1,500. And then there's the mask, which can run as high as $500. There are likely a lot of double takes when Junior tells Dad, "I think I'd like to be a goalie. Can you buy me some good equipment?"

Until recently goal pads were made of leather and horse hair and gloves from leather. In the early 1980s, John Garrett weighed his equipment and it tipped the scales at 45 pounds. The goal pads weighed 25 pounds when they were dry, and more when they got wet during a game. Garrett told me, "with all the games and practices, it seemed your equipment was wet from the start of the season to the end."

Today's goalies wear equipment manufactured from a variety of synthetic materials. Goal pads weigh about 5 pounds instead of 25, and they don't absorb moisture. When a slap shot scores a direct hit the sound is more like a boom than a dull thud and the rebounds bounce out much farther. Today's gloves are bigger but lighter, one reason why we refer to so many goaltenders having "quick hands."

There are not as many characters in the crease these days, and the mask is one reason. In the days before goalies' faces were covered it was great to watch the fierce concentration of Terry Sawchuk and his painful look when a goal would get past him. We could see the cold, calculating, "I'm in control" look of Jacques Plante. Gump Worsley's expressions of disgust and frustration were priceless. Today, who are the guys behind those multi-coloured masks? In many cases the artwork on a mask is more recognizable than the goalie wearing it: Ed Belfour's eagle, Stéphane Fiset's ice cubes, Felix Potvin's cat-eyes, John Vanbiesbrouck's panther.

Somehow I feel there won't be as many "goalie stories" in the future as there are now about the goalies from the past. Today's young men in the crease are a more serious, business-like group, which is not really surprising considering the money they make. There won't be many stories like the one they tell about Hank Bassen when he was playing for the Detroit Red Wings in the 1960s. One night in Boston, Bassen was felled when hit in the head by a shot. At times like that the trainer will ask the injured player some basic questions to make sure he's all there. The Detroit trainer said to Bassen, "What team do you play for? What team are we playing? And who's the President of the United States?" Bassen replied, "I play for the Detroit Red Wings, we're playing the Boston Bruins, and how the hell should I know? I'm a Canadian."

Then there was Al Smith, a much-travelled and colourful goalie who at one time was the back-up for the Buffalo Sabres. When the Sabres' regular goalie was injured, Smith became upset when the team brought in a minor-leaguer to start the next game in Buffalo. Smith took the warm-up and stood at attention during the national anthem. Then he skated out from the bench and looked up to where the team's owners, Seymour and Northrop Knox, were sitting. Smith waved at them and hollered, "So long Seymour! So long, Nordie!" Then he skated off the ice, disappeared into the Sabres' dressing room, and was never seen again in Buffalo.

But there is always hope that a few characters will come along in the future. At the 1995 Quebec International Pee Wee Hockey Tournament one of the stars was an energetic twelve-year-old goalie with the nickname "Mad Dog." Painted on his mask was the face of an animal with sharp fangs and blazing eyes. The animal looked like, well, a mad dog.

Sounds to me like the kid can't miss.

Index

Acknowledgements

I wish to thank the men whose thoughts and memories make up the majority of this book. It could not have been written without their co-operation. In addition to sharing his personal recollections, John Garrett was particularly supportive in offering advice and encouragement.

Mac McDiarmid, Denis Brodeur, and Diane Sobolewski were helpful in supplying photographs, as were the publicity departments of several National Hockey League teams. Carole Robertson transcribed the many hours of recorded interviews.

McClelland & Stewart assigned a very skilful editor, Jonathan Webb, to take charge of the literary goal crease, which he did in fine style. Jonathan was aided by Peter Buck, who made sure I didn't give up any factual or statistical rebounds. I thank them both for their help and, especially, their patience.

Finally, love to Wilma, Nancy Anne, and Doug, who, as always, were part of this from the first shot on goal to the last.